# Quality Across the Curriculum

## Integrating Quality Tools and PDSA with Standards

Also available from ASQ Quality Press:

*Tools and Techniques to Inspire Classroom Learning*
Barbara A. Cleary, PhD and Sally J. Duncan

*Thinking Tools for Kids: An Activity Book for Classroom Learning*
Barbara A. Cleary, PhD and Sally J. Duncan

*Continuous Improvement in the Science Classroom*
Jeffrey Burgard

*Continuous Improvement in the Primary Classroom: Language Arts K–3*
Karen Fauss

*Continuous Improvement in the Mathematics Classroom*
Carolyn Ayres

*Continuous Improvement in the History and Social Sciences Classroom*
Shelly Carson

*Successful Applications of Quality Systems in K–12 Schools*
The ASQ Quality Education Division

*Orchestrating Learning with Quality*
David P. Langford and Barbara A. Cleary, PhD

*Improving Student Learning: Applying Deming's Quality Principles in Classrooms,* Second Edition
Lee Jenkins

*Charting Your Course: Lessons Learned During the Journey toward Performance Excellence*
John G. Conyers and Robert Ewy

To request a complimentary catalog of ASQ Quality Press publications, call 800-248-1946, or visit our Web site at http://qualitypress.asq.org.

# Quality Across the Curriculum

## Integrating Quality Tools and PDSA with Standards K-5

**JAY MARINO** and **ANN HAGGERTY RAINES, Editors**
with Lesson Plans created by teachers from Rock Island School District, Rock Island, Illinois

ASQ Quality Press
Milwaukee, Wisconsin

American Society for Quality, Quality Press, Milwaukee 53203
© 2004 by ASQ
All rights reserved. Published 2004
Printed in the United States of America

12  11  10  09  08  07  06  05  04      5  4  3  2  1

**Library of Congress Cataloging-in-Publication Data**

Quality across the curriculum : integrating quality tools and PDSA with standards,
K–5 / Jay Marino and Ann Haggerty Raines, editors ; with lesson plans created by teachers
from Rock Island School District, Rock Island, Illinois.
      p. cm.
   Includes bibliographical references.
   ISBN 0-87389-599-1 (softcover, perfect bind : alk. paper)
   1. Education, Elementary—Curricula—United States.  2. Education, Elementary—
Standards—United States.  3. Curriculum evaluation—United States.  I. Marino, Jay, 1969–
II. Raines, Ann Haggerty.
   LB1570.Q36 2004
   372.19—dc22                                                        2004004420

ISBN 0-87389-599-1

Publisher: William A. Tony
Acquisitions Editor: Annemieke Hytinen
Project Editor: Paul O'Mara
Production Administrator: Randall Benson
Special Marketing Representative: David Luth

ASQ Mission: The American Society for Quality advances individual, organizational, and community
excellence worldwide through learning, quality improvement, and knowledge exchange.

Attention Bookstores, Wholesalers, Schools, and Corporations: ASQ Quality Press books, videotapes,
audiotapes, and software are available at quantity discounts with bulk purchases for business,
educational, or instructional use. For information, please contact ASQ Quality Press at 800-248-1946,
or write to ASQ Quality Press, P.O. Box 3005, Milwaukee, WI 53201-3005.

To place orders or to request a free copy of the ASQ Quality Press Publications Catalog,
including ASQ membership information, call 800-248-1946. Visit our Web site at www.asq.org
or http://qualitypress.asq.org.

 Printed on acid-free paper

Quality Press
600 N. Plankinton Avenue
Milwaukee, Wisconsin 53203
Call toll free 800-248-1946
Fax 414-272-1734
www.asq.org
http://qualitypress.asq.org
http://standardsgroup.asq.org
E-mail: authors@asq.org

# Dedication

For my brothers and sister who have encouraged me. For Jessica and Joey who are my motivation. For my mother and father who taught me to never give up.

—J. M.

To my parents, Jean and Ray Haggerty, who made anything a possibility for me; and Pete, Gillian, and Evan Raines who make everything a joy!

—A. H. R.

# Table of Contents

Foreword. . . . . . . . . . . . . . . . . . . . . . . . . . . . . . . . . . . xiii

Acknowledgments . . . . . . . . . . . . . . . . . . . . . . . . . . . . . xv

About the Authors . . . . . . . . . . . . . . . . . . . . . . . . . . . . xvi

Contributing Authors . . . . . . . . . . . . . . . . . . . . . . . . . xvii

How to Use This Book . . . . . . . . . . . . . . . . . . . . . . . xviii

Lesson Plan Format. . . . . . . . . . . . . . . . . . . . . . . . . . . xix

Tool Icon Key . . . . . . . . . . . . . . . . . . . . . . . . . . . . . . . . xx

## Math

**6 +5**

### K–1

| Lesson 1 | Time | 3 |
| Lesson 2 | Measurement | 5 |
| Lesson 3 | Patterns | 9 |
| Lesson 4 | Number Sense | 11 |
| Lesson 5 | Addition | 15 |
| Lesson 6 | Subtraction | 17 |
| Lesson 7 | Probability | 19 |
| Lesson 8 | Sort and Classify | 21 |
| Lesson 9 | Geometric Figures | 23 |

### 2–3

| Lesson 1 | Counting Money | 27 |
| Lesson 2 | Division | 29 |
| Lesson 3 | Story Problems | 31 |
| Lesson 4 | Geometry/Angles | 35 |
| Lesson 5 | Problem Solving | 39 |
| Lesson 6 | Telling Time | 41 |
| Lesson 7 | Regrouping | 43 |
| Lesson 8 | Fact Families | 45 |
| Lesson 9 | Geometry/Solid Figures | 49 |

### 4–5

| Lesson 1 | Multiplication PDSA: Part A | 53 |
| Lesson 2 | Multiplication PDSA: Part B | 57 |
| Lesson 3 | Multiplication PDSA: Part C | 59 |
| Lesson 4 | Multiplication PDSA: Part D | 61 |
| Lesson 5 | Multiplication PDSA: Part E | 63 |
| Lesson 6 | Collecting Data | 65 |
| Lesson 7 | Division | 67 |
| Lesson 8 | Organizing Data | 71 |
| Lesson 9 | Multiplication—Single Lesson | 73 |

x **Table of Contents**

## Science

**K–1**

Lesson 1    Insects . . . . . . . . . . . . . . . . . . . . . . . . . 79

Lesson 2    Living/Nonliving Things . . . . . . . . . . . . . . 83

Lesson 3    Weather. . . . . . . . . . . . . . . . . . . . . . . . . 87

Lesson 4    Tree Identification . . . . . . . . . . . . . . . . . 91

Lesson 5    Five Senses. . . . . . . . . . . . . . . . . . . . . . 95

Lesson 6    Physical and Chemical Changes . . . . . . . . . . 99

Lesson 7    Rocks . . . . . . . . . . . . . . . . . . . . . . . . 103

Lesson 8    Dinosaurs. . . . . . . . . . . . . . . . . . . . . . 105

Lesson 9    Simple Machines . . . . . . . . . . . . . . . . . 109

**2–3**

Lesson 1    Endangered Species . . . . . . . . . . . . . . . 113

Lesson 2    Weather Prediction. . . . . . . . . . . . . . . . 115

Lesson 3    Measurement. . . . . . . . . . . . . . . . . . . . 119

Lesson 4    Rain Forest Animals . . . . . . . . . . . . . . . 123

Lesson 5    Space/Solar System . . . . . . . . . . . . . . . 127

Lesson 6    Dinosaurs and Fossils . . . . . . . . . . . . . . 131

Lesson 7    Forms of Energy. . . . . . . . . . . . . . . . . . 133

Lesson 8    Safety During Experimentation . . . . . . . . . 137

Lesson 9    Renewable and Nonrenewable Resources. . . . 139

**4–5**

Lesson 1    Simple Machines . . . . . . . . . . . . . . . . . 143

Lesson 2    Human Body. . . . . . . . . . . . . . . . . . . . 145

Lesson 3    Ground Water . . . . . . . . . . . . . . . . . . . 147

Lesson 4    Energy. . . . . . . . . . . . . . . . . . . . . . . . 151

Lesson 5    Plants . . . . . . . . . . . . . . . . . . . . . . . . 155

Lesson 6    Magnetism . . . . . . . . . . . . . . . . . . . . . 157

Lesson 7    Physical Properties of Matter . . . . . . . . . . 159

Lesson 8    Rocks and Minerals . . . . . . . . . . . . . . . 163

Lesson 9    Moon's Surface . . . . . . . . . . . . . . . . . . 167

**Social Studies**

**K–1**    Lesson 1    Native American Tribes . . . . . . . . . . . . . . . . 173

Lesson 2    Abraham Lincoln . . . . . . . . . . . . . . . . . 177

Lesson 3    Careers. . . . . . . . . . . . . . . . . . . . . . . . 179

Lesson 4    Map Skills. . . . . . . . . . . . . . . . . . . . 181

Lesson 5    School Rules . . . . . . . . . . . . . . . . . . 185

Lesson 6    Field Trip to the Fire Station . . . . . . . . . . . 189

Lesson 7    Traditions. . . . . . . . . . . . . . . . . . . 193

Lesson 8    Political Systems/Government . . . . . . . . . . 195

Lesson 9    Families . . . . . . . . . . . . . . . . . . . . 199

**2–3**    Lesson 1    Medieval Feast. . . . . . . . . . . . . . . . . . 203

Lesson 2    Waste Awareness . . . . . . . . . . . . . . . . . 207

Lesson 3    Landforms . . . . . . . . . . . . . . . . . . . 211

Lesson 4    Washington D.C. . . . . . . . . . . . . . . . . 215

Lesson 5    Our City PDSA: Part A . . . . . . . . . . . . . . 219

Lesson 6    Our City PDSA: Part B . . . . . . . . . . . . . . 223

Lesson 7    Our City PDSA: Part C . . . . . . . . . . . . . . 227

Lesson 8    Our City PDSA: Part D . . . . . . . . . . . . . . 231

Lesson 9    Our City PDSA: Part E . . . . . . . . . . . . . . 235

**4–5**    Lesson 1    Economics . . . . . . . . . . . . . . . . . . . 241

Lesson 2    State Project. . . . . . . . . . . . . . . . . . . 243

Lesson 3    Regions . . . . . . . . . . . . . . . . . . . . 247

Lesson 4    Comparing Geographic Locations . . . . . . . . 249

Lesson 5    Branches of Government . . . . . . . . . . . . . 251

Lesson 6    Interest Groups . . . . . . . . . . . . . . . . . 255

Lesson 7    Ancient Civilizations . . . . . . . . . . . . . . . 259

Lesson 8    Civil War . . . . . . . . . . . . . . . . . . . . 263

Lesson 9    Holocaust. . . . . . . . . . . . . . . . . . . . 267

**Language Arts**

**K–1**

| | | |
|---|---|---|
| Lesson 1 | Story Sequence | 273 |
| Lesson 2 | Homographs | 275 |
| Lesson 3 | Fairy Tale Elements | 277 |
| Lesson 4 | Prewriting Strategy | 281 |
| Lesson 5 | Writing PDSA: Part A | 285 |
| Lesson 6 | Writing PDSA: Part B | 289 |
| Lesson 7 | Writing PDSA: Part C | 293 |
| Lesson 8 | Writing PDSA: Part D | 297 |
| Lesson 9 | Writing PDSA: Part E | 301 |

**2–3**

| | | |
|---|---|---|
| Lesson 1 | Making Connections | 307 |
| Lesson 2 | Word Choice | 309 |
| Lesson 3 | Fiction/Nonfiction | 313 |
| Lesson 4 | Summarizing Nonfiction | 315 |
| Lesson 5 | Writing Improvement | 317 |
| Lesson 6 | Prediction | 321 |
| Lesson 7 | Following Directions | 323 |
| Lesson 8 | Context Clues | 325 |
| Lesson 9 | Commonly Misspelled Words | 327 |

**4–5**

| | | |
|---|---|---|
| Lesson 1 | Fact and Opinion | 333 |
| Lesson 2 | Sequencing | 335 |
| Lesson 3 | Cause and Effect | 337 |
| Lesson 4 | Homophones | 339 |
| Lesson 5 | Vocabulary Development | 341 |
| Lesson 6 | Fluency Rate | 345 |
| Lesson 7 | Character Analysis | 349 |
| Lesson 8 | Questioning Strategy | 353 |
| Lesson 9 | Responding to Fiction | 357 |

**Appendix (Tools)** . . . . . . . . . . . . . . . . . . . . . . . . . . . **359**
**Worksheets #1–248** . . . . . . . . . . . . . . . . . . . . . . **CD-ROM**

# Foreword

Since the end of World War II, a quality movement has emerged to better meet changing customer needs, reduce costs by reducing errors, identify the best way to accomplish any process or task, and keep our environments safe and productive. At the heart of nearly every quality effort (whether called total quality management or continuous improvement, as these have been labeled over the years) is the plan–do–study–act (PDSA) process. While most of the quality professionals have come from manufacturing, the early 1990s saw the quality movement spring up in education, especially in elementary schools. Many schools and school districts have embraced the Malcolm Baldrige National Quality Program. Schools have found the Baldrige Criteria for Performance Excellence, its integrated management system, and core values to be essential in organizing continuous improvement efforts. Educators are learning the tools and process and passing them along to their students for use in everyday learning and to increase student achievement.

The PDSA process is based on the work of Walter Shewhart and W. Edwards Deming, and has been used to transform how work is done and how customers are served throughout all industries. PDSA uses data extensively to measure levels of performance and help determine root cause. Because of its scientific approach to problem solving, the PDSA process tells us to make strategic changes in how we function, based upon our data, and then suggests improvements based upon our causes. The four portions of the PDSA process can be simply defined as follows:

> **Plan**—baseline data are captured, reported, and understood. Root cause(s) is/are identified, and then strategies for improvement are generated.
>
> **Do**—implement our improvement theory/plan as a trial.
>
> **Study**—monitor the performance against prior baseline data to see if we have generated the results we are seeking.
>
> **Act**—determine what to keep, what refinements might be needed, and what to abandon.

But it doesn't end there. While the PDSA process will help us see positive results, our study data now becomes our plan data for the next iteration of the process, thus the name "continuous improvement process."

Continuous improvement thinking tells us that we need to:

- Use data to drive our decision making.
- Get to the root cause in order to solve the problem and have a chance of preventing reoccurrence.
- Understand the effect of our actions and changes, so we always do a pre-post comparison of the critical performance data.
- Involve all stakeholders in the problem-solving process, solution generation, and plan implementation.

This book has been created to provide you, as a classroom teacher, with ready lessons that support both the use of quality/communication tools and the PDSA process for improvement. These lesson plans were created based on learning standards in the key content areas of math, science, social studies, and language arts. In the age of accountability and high-stakes testing, it is imperative that the classroom teacher focus instruction on learning standards in which state testing is based. In addition to standards-aligned instruction, exceptional educational experiences incorporate effective instructional strategies and differentiated learning techniques to help all students achieve at high levels.

The lesson plans in this book incorporate a variety of quality tools. Lessons (and tools) are designed to be used independently and do not need to be taught in any particular order. Teachers can select lessons that contain the content area and learning standard they wish to address as it relates to their curriculum. Lessons are most effective when taught as part of a unit of study. Also included in the book are three sets of lessons that contain complete PDSA cycles and an abundance of tool usage lessons. The PDSA lessons are connected and build on one another. These lessons are designed to simulate an actual PDSA cycle rotation from start to finish. To provide the most effective experience with the PDSA process, these lessons should be taught consecutively. It should be stated that while students will learn the PDSA process best when the tools are used as an integral part of understanding the problem, getting to the root cause and generating an improvement plan, the use of tools as part of a lesson without the PDSA process will reinforce the utility of the quality tools. The tools that are a part of these lessons are intended to make working together to solve problems, either in a classroom or in future employment, easier and more productive.

The tools fit into a few categories of purpose. You will find tools to help collect, organize, understand, and interpret data. Planning tools assure that we have a comprehensive plan to ensure the greatest likelihood of success. Consensus tools assist in getting input, and ultimately agreement, from everyone on a course of action. Another group of tools helps us get to the root cause. These tools are not simply about change, they are about improvement: improvement for all students and all stakeholders.

Employers are seeking workers who have strong problem-solving skills and the ability to communicate and work effectively as part of a team. At a more immediate level, teachers and parents are seeking self-motivated students who have both the desire and the skill to fully engage in their education through active participation and problem solving. It is our hope that these lessons, in combination with the utilization of effective instructional strategies and a classroom climate conducive to participation and exploration, will create dynamic learners now and in the future.

# Acknowledgments

I wish to acknowledge the Rock Island School District teachers, Board of Education, and administrators who have embraced the quality movement. I particularly want to thank the Rock Island School District teachers who serve in the capacity of quality facilitators. Their dedication to continuous improvement inspires me.

Thanks to the American Society for Quality (ASQ) for their confidence in Ann and me. Thanks to Ann Haggerty Raines for her insight and expertise of quality tools and processes and special thanks to Crista Kautz for her support and assistance in the project. Many thanks to the pioneers of quality in the Rock Island School District—the teachers who have authored the lesson plans in this book. It is an honor to be associated with such dedicated professionals.

Lastly, I would like to thank Dr. David Markward, superintendent of the Rock Island School District. His visionary leadership, mentoring, encouragement, and support has helped me grow personally and professionally.

—J. M.

Many thanks to the teachers of Rock Island, Illinois, and all the other staff and administrators I've had the pleasure to work with and learn from. Special thanks to Jay Marino for saying yes, and then doing a job any choreographer would envy! To all the folks at ASQ, Crista Kautz, Suzanne Keely, and John Van Slyke who had faith and provided support, *thank you!*

—A. H. R.

# About the Authors

J. JAY MARINO is an American Society for Quality (ASQ) Koalaty Kid trainer and consultant for continuous improvement. He also serves as the assistant superintendent for Instruction and School Improvement in the Rock Island School District in Rock Island, Illinois. Marino received his bachelor's degree in elementary education from the University of Northern Iowa and his master's degree in educational administration from Arizona State University. He has served as an elementary and middle school classroom teacher, elementary school administrator, special education coordinator, director of technology, and director of instruction. You may contact him by visiting his Web site at www.jmarino.ws.

ANN HAGGERTY RAINES began her career as a classroom teacher of English in 1978, and continues to work as a trainer and consultant in the areas of continuous improvement, organizational development, and leadership. Over the past 25 years, her career has taken her through quality training with a wide variety of organizations, including manufacturing, service industries, human services, and ultimately back to education in 1993. She is a 1978 graduate of Mount Holyoke College, and received certification from The Association for Quality and Participation in Quality Management. Additionally, she is an Authorized Trainer-of-Trainers for both the American Society for Quality's Koalaty Kid initiative and PQ Systems.

Raines lives in Bethlehem, Pennsylvania, with her husband, Pete, and children, Gillian and Evan. She is active in her community, serving on the boards of directors of Celtic Fest, Inc., The Bethlehem YMCA, Leadership Lehigh Valley, and Historic Bethlehem, Inc.

# Contributing Authors

CYNTHIA ARKEBAUER currently teaches fourth grade. She has taught third through sixth grades: two years in Carbon Cliff/Barstow School District and 10 years in Rock Island School District. Arkebauer is a graduate of Marycrest University and received her master's degree from Saint Xavier University. You may contact her at cindy.arkebauer@risd41.org.

ANGELA BROWNSON currently teaches second grade. She has taught first through third grades for 10 years in the Rock Island School District. Brownson is a graduate of St. Ambrose University. You may contact her at angie.brownson@risd41.org.

BERNADETTE L. CARMACK currently teaches first/second grade multi-age. She has taught for 23 years in the Rock Island School District: 11 years in the Special Kids in Preschool Program and 12 years in elementary. Carmack is a graduate of Illinois State University and received her master's degree from Western Illinois University. You may contact her at berni.carmack@risd41.org.

CHARLOTTE HARTMANN currently teaches third/fourth grade multi-age. She has been teaching in the Rock Island School District for three years. Hartmann is a graduate of Northern Iowa University and is seeking her master's degree from Western Illinois University. You may contact her at charlotte.hartmann@risd41.org.

CAROL SCHOENING currently teaches an intermediate special education and a fifth/sixth grade multi-age integrated technology class. She has taught for 24 years in the Rock Island School District. Shoening is a graduate of Illinois State University and received her master's degree from Western Illinois University. You may contact her at carol.schoening@risd41.org.

CATHERINE SLININGER currently teaches in a looping third/fourth grade classroom. She has taught third through sixth grades in the Rock Island School District for nine years. Slininger is a graduate of St. Ambrose University and received her master's degree from Western Illinois University. You may contact her at katy.slininger@risd41.org.

PATRICIA WALLS currently teaches fourth grade. She has been teaching for four years in Rock Island and previously taught in inner-city Chicago. Walls is a graduate of Western Illinois University. You may contact her at patricia.walls@risd41.org.

# How To Use This Book

In order to get the most out of this book, the following suggestions are recommended:

- Select the lesson that contains the content area and learning standard that integrates with an existing unit of study. Lessons are best received by students when real-world connections can be made and the lesson is seen as a natural extension of classroom instruction.

- Review the entire lesson plan to gain understanding of the lesson and the identified objectives.

- Review the lesson format and pre-lesson materials needed.

- Review the quality tool(s) used and the application to the PDSA cycle. Information about the quality tools can be found in the Tool Appendix section. The lessons only reference the quality tools and require that the teacher familarize him/herself with the tool. It is critical that the teacher has a basic understanding of the tool purpose and procedure for implementation prior to delivering the lesson.

- Obtain all materials needed for the lesson, including the lesson worksheets found on the accompanying CD-ROM.

- Modify the lessons to meet the academic, social, and behavioral needs of the students. Lessons are designed to be a guide, and individualized customization is encouraged.

- Deliver the lesson to students. Utilize the assessments identified in the lesson and be sure to seek feedback on how the lesson was received by students. Student feedback can be utilized to improve the next lesson.

# Lesson Plan Format

Each lesson is designed to prepare the teacher for conducting instruction and activities aligned to learning standards. In addition to estimated time for the session and the number of associated worksheets, you will find a consistent format under each lesson heading. There is also a tool icon that provides the teacher with a visual cue of the quality tools utilized in the lesson (see the tool icon key for further clarification).

**Quality tool/PDSA linkage**—indicates which tool or tools are used in the lesson and where within the PDSA these tools are most likely used

**Lesson overview**—a brief summary of what will happen during the lesson

**Lesson objectives**—what specific activities will be and learning you can expect as an outcome of this lesson

**Pre-lesson activities**—suggested activities that will provide readiness for the content of this specific lesson

**Material needed**—including worksheets, transparencies, routine classroom supplies, and other special equipment of materials necessary to conduct the lesson

**Lesson delivery/Procedure**—specific step-by-step instructions to conduct the lesson

**Guided practice**—additional work for the class and teachers to reinforce the learning of the lesson, during the session or as a follow-up session

**Assessment**—suggested activities to evaluate student performance on a specified task and determine additional instructional requirements

**Post-lesson/Follow-up activities/Extensions**—additional activities outside the current instruction that may support or expand the content of this lesson

**Supporting resources**—worksheets, books, Web sites, and other sources of information related to the lesson that may be useful to the teacher

**Worksheets/CD-ROM**—All lessons contain student activity and/or data collection worksheets that reinforce instructional objectives. Worksheets are labeled either "Example" or "Template." Example worksheets help guide the teacher and students through a task or activity and are appropriately referenced in the lesson. Template worksheets are utilized by students for data collection or student response. All worksheets are available on the accompanying CD-ROM that is included with the book.

# Tool Icon Key

| | | | | |
|---|---|---|---|---|
| | Affinity Diagram | | NGT | Nominal Group Technique (NGT)/Light Voting |
| | Bar Chart | | Define | Operational Definition |
| | Brainstorming | | | Pareto Diagram |
| | Cause-and-Effect Diagram | | | Plus/Delta Chart |
| | Check Sheet/Matrix | | | Radar Chart |
| | Flowchart | | | Relations Diagram |
| | Force-Field Analysis | | | Run/Control Charts |
| | Gallery Walk | | | Scatter Diagram |
| | Lotus Diagram | | | Systematic Diagram/Tree Diagram |
| | Multivoting | | | WWW Chart/Action Plan |

# Quality Across the Curriculum

# MATH

## K-1

### LESSONS

Time . . . . . . . . . . . . . . . . . . . 3

Measurement . . . . . . . . . . . . . 5

Patterns . . . . . . . . . . . . . . . . 9

Number Sense . . . . . . . . . . . . 11

Addition . . . . . . . . . . . . . . . . 15

Subtraction . . . . . . . . . . . . . . 17

Probability . . . . . . . . . . . . . . 19

Sort and Classify . . . . . . . . . . 21

Geometric Figures . . . . . . . . . 23

# Time

Measure units of time using appropriate instruments.

**Estimated Time:** 40 minutes          **Worksheets:** 1 and 2

## Quality Tool/PDSA Linkage

☐ Students will use the Multivoting/Nominal Group Technique.

  • Multivoting is a technique to assist groups in reaching consensus by conducting one or more votes during any portion of the PDSA cycle.

## Lesson Overview

☐ The teacher will facilitate goal setting with use of Multivoting discussing the number of students who will be able to tell time during a chosen time period.

## Lesson Objectives

☐ Students will set goals discussing the number of students who will be able to tell time during a chosen time period.

☐ Students will use the Multivoting quality tool to set classroom goals.

## Pre-Lesson Activities

☐ Obtain copies of worksheets 1 and 2 that go with the lesson.

☐ Create a poster-size replica of worksheet 2.

☐ Obtain all materials needed for this lesson.

☐ Review the importance of the concept of time.

☐ Utilize a time worksheet to be used as pre- and post-assessment. (Worksheets can be found on www.edhelper.com/time.htm.)

☐ Students will take a preassessment on the concept of time.

☐ The teacher will grade the preassessments.

## Materials Needed

☐ Pencils (for each student).

☐ Poster-size replica of worksheet 2.

## Lesson Delivery/Procedure

☐ The teacher will read the book *Telling Time with Big Mama Cat* by Dan Harper to the class.

☐ The teacher will announce the results of the preassessments discussing the number of students who showed an understanding of the concept of time.

☐ The teacher will ask the class: "In two weeks, how many students do you think should be able to tell time?" (During this time, the teacher should emphasize that the number of students who will be able to tell time in two weeks should be larger than the current number of students who know how to tell time.)

☐ The teacher will review the Multivoting/Nominal Group Technique tool with students.

- [ ] The teacher will distribute copies of worksheet 1. Using worksheet 1, students will vote on how many students they think should be able to tell time.

- [ ] The teacher will collect worksheet 1 from the students and calculate the votes.

- [ ] Using the poster-size replica of worksheet 2, the teacher will facilitate the class in making a goal of increasing the number of students to understand the concept of time and the things that they will do to reach this goal.

- [ ] The poster will be displayed.

- [ ] During the next two weeks, the concept of time will be taught.

## Assessment

- [ ] The students will take a post-assessment on the concept of time. This assessment can be teacher-created or taken from a textbook.

- [ ] The teacher will analyze student work to gauge understanding of the concept.

## Post-Lesson/Follow-Up Activities/Extensions

- [ ] Post-assessment results should be compared to the goal to see if the goal has been met.

- [ ] A barchart could be used comparing pre- and post-assessment results.

## Supporting Resources

- [ ] *Telling Time with Big Mama Cat* by Dan Harper

- [ ] *Telling Time* by Jules Older

- [ ] *Big Hand, Little Hand: Learn to Tell Time!* by Judith Herbst

- [ ] *www.edhelper.com*

- [ ] Worksheets 1 and 2

# Measurement

Estimate measurements and determine acceptable levels of accuracy. Measure and compare quantities using appropriate units, instruments, and methods.

**Estimated Time:** 45 minutes          **Worksheets:** 3 and 4

## Quality Tool/PDSA Linkage

☐ Students will learn about the Check Sheet.

• The Check Sheet/Matrix is a tool to collect and organize data in the Plan portion of the PDSA cycle.

## Lesson Overview

☐ This is a hands-on lesson designed to enrich the student's measurement skills while learning about circumference.

☐ The student will estimate the circumference of a pumpkin, then cut a length of string that is the size he or she estimates to be the appropriate length.

☐ Following their estimates, the students will measure their strings and compare their estimates to the actual length of their string.

## Lesson Objectives

☐ The students will learn appropriate measurement techniques using a standard tape measure, yardstick, meter stick, and/or ruler.

☐ The students will compare inches to centimeters.

☐ The students will estimate and compare their estimates to actual measurements.

☐ The students will understand and define circumference.

☐ The students will use the Check Sheets to determine the strength and accuracy of their predictions compared to actual measurements.

## Pre-Lesson Activities

☐ Obtain copies of the worksheets that go with the lesson.

☐ Obtain all materials needed for the lesson.

☐ Review measurement vocabulary and concepts with students such as inch, foot, yard, centimeter, and meter.

☐ Measure the actual circumference of the pumpkin.

## Materials Needed

☐ One tape measure (that is, inches, feet, yard) per five-student group.

☐ Pencil or pen for appropriate recording of data.

☐ Graph paper or plain paper for appropriate recording of data.

☐ A large pumpkin.

☐ String.

☐ Scissors.

☐ Large graph paper.

☐ Markers.

## Lesson Delivery/Procedure

- ☐ The teacher will display a large pumpkin for the class to view.
- ☐ The teacher will ask the students to try to wrap their arms around the pumpkin to see if their fingers can touch behind the pumpkin.
- ☐ The teacher will introduce/review the concept of circumference.
- ☐ The teacher will ask the students to estimate how many inches/centimeters/feet/yards long a piece of string would need to be in order for it to measure the circumference of the pumpkin.
- ☐ The teacher will review the Check Sheet tool with students.
- ☐ The teacher will record student estimates on the chart for later comparison.
- ☐ The students will work in groups to record their estimates/measurements on one chart (worksheet 3) if the ability level of the group allows.

## Guided Practice

- ☐ The students will estimate the length of string necessary to reach around the circumference of the pumpkin.
- ☐ The students will cut the string at the appropriate place without using a ruler or any other measuring instrument.
- ☐ After all students have cut their piece of string, each will try his or hers around the circumference of the pumpkin.
- ☐ The students will tape their piece of string on the Check Sheet in the categories of "too long," "too short," or "just right." Use worksheet 4 for this purpose.
- ☐ The students will measure their piece of string using either nonstandard measurements, or using standard measurements (that is, ruler/ tape measure/yard stick/meter stick).

## Assessment

- ☐ The students will record their estimates and actual measurements on worksheet 3.
- ☐ The students will determine the number of students who were correct in their estimates by reviewing the Check Sheet.
- ☐ The students will determine how many of their estimates were "too long" vs. "too short," "too long" vs. "just right," and "too short" vs. "just right."
- ☐ The students will measure their length of string accurately.
- ☐ The students will determine how close their estimates were to their actual measurements using subtraction.

## Post-Lesson/Follow-Up Activities/Extensions

- ☐ Read aloud books: *The Berenstain Bears and the Prize Pumpkin* by Stan and Jan Berenstain; *The Biggest Pumpkin Ever* by Steven Kroll.
- ☐ Estimate and then measure the circumference of a smaller pumpkin.
- ☐ Estimate and then measure the circumference of your pumpkin at home.
- ☐ Estimate and then measure the circumference of another round object.
- ☐ Use a calculator to add up all the estimates.
- ☐ Use a calculator to average the estimates from a small group (four to five students).

## Supporting Resources

- [ ] *The Pumpkin Fair* by Eve Bunting
- [ ] *From Seed to Pumpkin* by Gail Gibbons
- [ ] *Too Many Pumpkins* by Linda White
- [ ] Worksheets 3 and 4

# Patterns

Solve problems involving pattern identification and completion of patterns.

**Estimated Time:** Two 30-minute sessions      **Worksheets:** 5, 6, and 7

## Quality Tool/PDSA Linkage

☐ Students will use the Affinity Diagram, Check Sheet, and the Pareto Diagram.

- The Affinity Diagram is a tool to generate, organize, and consolidate information gathered through Brainstorming, and is used in many portions of the PDSA cycle.

- The Check Sheet/Matrix is a tool to collect and organize data in the Plan portion of the PDSA cycle.

- The Pareto Diagram is a bar chart that ranks categorical data from largest to smallest to find the "significant few" in the Plan portion of the PDSA cycle.

## Lesson Overview

☐ This lesson is designed to give students practice in creating and identifying patterns.

☐ The students will be given a collection of objects. (They need to have more than one of each type.)

☐ The students will use the Affinity Diagram to come up with a list of categories (example: big, little, round, and so on).

☐ The students will create a tally sheet to count their items by category.

☐ The students will use the Pareto Diagram to chart the information from their tally sheets. (Remember the highest value is charted first.)

☐ The students will create three patterns using their groups of objects; they will record these on a Check Sheet.

## Lesson Objectives

☐ The students will understand and use the Affinity Diagram, Check Sheet, and Pareto Diagram.

☐ The students will understand how to categorize objects using the Affinity Diagram.

☐ The students will organize their objects using a Check Sheet.

☐ The students will plot their data on a Pareto Diagram.

☐ The students will use a Check Sheet to show patterns created with their set of objects.

## Pre-Lesson Activities

☐ The students should have some basic practice with patterns.

☐ Gather various objects or manipulatives for this lesson. Students should have worked with these manipulatives previously.

☐ Obtain copies of the worksheets that go with the lesson.

☐ Obtain all materials needed for the lesson.

## Materials Needed

☐ Chart paper.

☐ Markers.

- [ ] Post-It notes.
- [ ] Manipulatives (variety of items—several of each kind).

## Lesson Delivery/Procedure

- [ ] The students will be seated in cooperative groups.
- [ ] The students will work independently with manupulatives in the center of the table.
- [ ] As a whole group, the students will come up with categories for their objects on chart paper.
- [ ] The teacher will review the Check Sheet tool with students.
- [ ] The students will compare a Check Sheet to count and classify their manipulatives (worksheet 5).
- [ ] The teacher will review the Pareto Diagram tool with students.
- [ ] The students will chart their data on a Pareto Diagram using information recorded on the Check Sheet (worksheet 5).
- [ ] The teacher will review the Affinity Diagram tool with students.
- [ ] The students will create an Affinity Diagram to draw three specified patterns using their manipulatives.

## Guided Practice

- [ ] Each student will apply his or her understanding of patterns in order to complete the Affinity Diagram (worksheet 5).

## Assessment

- [ ] The students will use the Affinity Diagram, Check Sheet, and Pareto Diagram to demonstrate understanding of patterns and categories.

## Post-Lesson/Follow-Up Activities/Extensions

- [ ] Apply these quality tools in other areas of academic work.
- [ ] Identify patterns found in the classroom or school.

## Supporting Resources

- [ ] Worksheets 5, 6, and 7

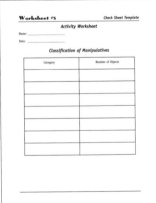

# Number Sense

Demonstrate and apply a knowledge and sense of numbers, including numeration and operations (addition, subtraction, multiplication, division), patterns, ratios, and proportions.

**Estimated Time:** 30 minutes          **Worksheet:** 8

## Quality Tool/PDSA Linkage

☐ Students will use the Check Sheet.

- The Check Sheet/Matrix is a tool to collect and organize data in the Plan portion of the PDSA cycle.

## Lesson Overview

☐ This lesson helps students build a stronger sense of numbers by comparing whole numbers between one and one hundred using the > "greater than," < "less than," and = "equal to" signs.

☐ The students will draw numbers from a can or envelope and chart the number in the appropriate column on a Check Sheet while learning how to use this quality tool.

☐ It is recommended that this lesson be conducted later in the school year so that children have previously been introduced to printed numbers 1–100 and have some sense of place value.

## Lesson Objectives

☐ The students will identify whole numbers between one and one hundred.

☐ The students will compare whole numbers between one and one hundred using the symbols and words >"greater than," < "less than," and = "equal to."

☐ The students will understand and use the Check Sheet quality tool.

## Pre-Lesson Activities

☐ Conduct a variety of lessons to introduce students to the printed numbers 1–100.

☐ Conduct lessons to introduce place value: tens and ones.

☐ Create an overhead transparency of the Check Sheet (worksheet 7).

☐ Obtain copies of worksheet 8 that goes with the lesson.

☐ Obtain all materials needed for the lesson.

## Materials Needed

☐ Worksheet 8—one copy per student.

☐ Multiple sets of printed numbers 1–100—one set per student or cooperative pair (can photocopy a hundreds chart found in many math resource books and cut numbers apart).

☐ Small cans or envelopes—one per set of numbers 1–100.

☐ Writing utensils for students; overhead transparency marker for teacher.

☐ Overhead transparency of Check Sheet (worksheet 8).

## Lesson Delivery/Procedure

- ☐ The teacher will review the concepts of the words "greater than," "less than," and "equal to" as they apply to comparing whole numbers.

- ☐ The teacher will introduce the symbols used with these words: >, <, =.

- ☐ The teacher will review the Check Sheet tool with students.

- ☐ The teacher will explain the lesson by modeling use of a Check Sheet to compare whole numbers (use of overhead worksheet 8).

- ☐ After observing teacher modeling and asking questions for clarification, the students will compare numbers using individual Check Sheets.

- ☐ Slips of numbers 1–100 will be placed in a small can or envelope. The first number drawn will be written in the circle at the top of the Check Sheet. Each consecutive number will be written in the correct column on the Check Sheet. Is the number >, <, or = to the number in the circle? (Drawn numbers are not returned to the can or envelope until activity is finished.)

- ☐ Students continue drawing numbers for approximately 10–15 minutes or until an adequate amount of numbers are drawn to show understanding or misunderstanding of the math concept.

- ☐ Observations are made as to what column had the most numbers listed in the given time period.

- ☐ At the end of the activity, cut-up numbers are all returned to the can or envelope for further use.

## Guided Practice

- ☐ In another class session, students can draw a new "beginning" number, write this number in the circle, and compare to successive numbers drawn.

- ☐ The students can draw all numbers and glue the numbers in the correct column to create a more permanent document.

- ☐ The students can complete a similar Check Sheet as a homework assignment.

- ☐ The students will learn to use symbols only (without the corresponding words) when comparing numbers.

- ☐ The students will begin to recognize that the number in the tens place should be compared first.

## Assessment

- ☐ The students will correctly identify 25 random numbers between 1–100.

- ☐ Individual Check Sheets will be collected and checked to ensure numbers are written in the correct column.

- ☐ The students will demonstrate the ability to compare numbers in different math lessons by using the correct terms (more than, less than, equal to).

- ☐ Given the symbols, the students will use and write the correct symbol to compare numbers.

- ☐ The students will compare numbers on a teacher-made test to show understanding and transference of knowledge.

## Post-Lesson/Follow-Up Activities/Extensions

- ☐ The students will draw 10 numbers from the can or envelope and order the numbers from smallest to greatest.

- ☐ More competent students will work in cooperative pairs with classmates who have difficulty comparing numbers to complete the Check Sheet together.

- ☐ The students can participate in this activity on the 100th day of school.

## Supporting Resources

- [ ] *The 100th Day of School* by Angela Shelf Medearis
- [ ] *100 Hungry Ants* by Elinor J. Pinczes
- [ ] Worksheet 8

**Worksheet #8**     *Check Sheet Template*

### Activity Worksheet

Name: _____

Date: _____

#### Comparing Numbers

Write the first number selected in the circle. Compare the rest of the numbers selected to the number in the circle and place it in the correct column below.

| "greater than" | "less than" | "equal to" |
|---|---|---|
| | | |
| | | |
| | | |
| | | |
| | | |
| | | |

# Addition

Demonstrate and apply a knowledge and sense of numbers, including numeration and operations.

**Estimated Time:** 45 minutes          **Worksheets:** 9, 10, and 11

## Quality Tool/PDSA Linkage

- ☐ Students will use Force-Field Analysis and the Scatter Diagram.

    - Force-Field Analysis is a tool used to evaluate the forces driving and restraining a desired change and is used during the plan portion of the PDSA cycle to generate the most comprehensive plan possible to test the improvement theory.

    - The Scatter Diagram is a tool used to show the relationship between two factors in the plan portion of the PDSA cycle.

## Lesson Overview

- ☐ This lesson is designed to allow students to determine the reasons for their scores on addition assignments.

- ☐ Over time, students will graph their scores compared to the amount of time they have studied their addition facts.

## Lesson Objectives

- ☐ The students will determine the reasons for their scores on addition assignments.

- ☐ The students will graph their scores compared to the amount of time they have studied their addition facts.

- ☐ The students will understand and use the Force-Field Analysis quality tool.

- ☐ The students will understand and use the Scatter Diagram quality tool.

## Pre-Lesson Activities

- ☐ Obtain copies of the worksheets that go with the lesson.

- ☐ Obtain all materials needed for the lesson.

## Materials Needed

- ☐ A blank worksheet for each student group.

- ☐ Any addition worksheet from a student textbook or other source.

## Lesson Delivery/Procedure

- ☐ The teacher will provide the change statement, "Improve performance on addition assignments."

- ☐ The teacher will review the Force-Field Analysis tool with students.

- ☐ Together, students and the teacher will discuss what helps them to improve their performance on their addition assignments, and what keeps them from improving. These are the driving and the restraining forces. See example on worksheet 9.

- ☐ The students will offer driving forces and restraining forces for their addition assignment scores.

- ☐ In collaborative groups, or as a class, students will fill in the Force-Field Analysis chart placing the driving and restraining forces in their appropriate places on the chart (worksheet 10).

- [ ] The teacher will review the Scatter Diagram tool with students.
- [ ] Students will keep track of the amount of time they studied for use on the Scatter Diagram (worksheet 11).

## Guided Practice

- [ ] After reviewing together the Force-Field Analysis, the students and the teacher will create an action plan to be implemented.
- [ ] As a class, after each subsequent assignment, students will graph their scores as compared to the amount of time they spent studying their addition facts on a Scatter Diagram.
- [ ] The students will realize that, in general, the greater amount of time spent studying, the greater their percentage on their assignments.

## Assessment

- [ ] The students will show growth in their scores by following through on their action plan(s).
- [ ] The teacher will assess the worksheets and determine if students are following through on their action plan.
- [ ] The students will use Scatter Diagram correctly.

## Post-Lesson/Follow-Up Activities/Extensions

- [ ] Read aloud several of the books listed below.
- [ ] Use the Internet sites listed below for practice at home and at school.
- [ ] The students could keep an individual Run Chart to show progress in their scores over time.

## Supporting Resources

- [ ] *www.aaamath.com/B/add.htm*
- [ ] *www.aplusmath.com/Flashcards/addition.html*
- [ ] *www.aplusmath.com/games/matho/AddMatho.html*
- [ ] *The Hershey's Kisses Addition Book* by Jerry Pallotta
- [ ] *Each Orange Had 8 Slices* by Paul Giganti Jr.
- [ ] Worksheets 9, 10, and 11

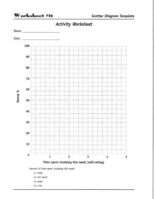

# Subtraction

Demonstrate and apply a knowledge and sense of numbers, including numeration and operations.

**Estimated Time:** 45 minutes          **Worksheets:** 12 and 13

## Quality Tool/PDSA Linkage

☐ Students will use the Radar Chart and the Pareto Diagram.

- The Radar Chart is a graph with multiple scales to report self-assessed knowledge or competence, often over time and is used during both the plan and study portions of the PDSA cycle.

- The Pareto Diagram is a bar chart that ranks categorical data from largest to smallest to find the "significant few" in the plan portion of the PDSA cycle.

## Lesson Overview

☐ This lesson is designed to allow students to self-assess their abilities to use various subtraction strategies.

☐ The teacher will analyze the types of errors students are making by observing their responses and interviewing individual students as necessary.

☐ This lesson should be used after students are familiar with several subtraction strategies.

## Lesson Objectives

☐ The students will self-assess their abilities to use various subtraction strategies.

☐ The teacher will analyze the types of errors being made by students to direct instructional focus.

☐ The students will understand and use the Radar Chart quality tool.

☐ The students will understand and use the Pareto Diagram quality tool.

## Pre-Lesson Activities

☐ Obtain copies of the worksheets that go with the lesson.

☐ Obtain all materials needed for the lesson.

## Materials Needed

☐ A blank worksheet for each student group.

☐ Any subtraction worksheet, that is, from a student textbook or other source that contains a variety of types of subtraction problems (doubles, counting up, counting back, number families, making a 10, and so on).

## Lesson Delivery/Procedure

☐ The teacher will provide an example for the students to review each subtraction strategy, that is, a subtraction problem that demonstrates doubles, another that demonstrates one less, another that demonstrates counting up, and so on.

☐ The students will use the strategies (listed above) to practice.

☐ The teacher will review the Radar Chart tool with students.

☐ The students will use the Radar Chart (worksheet 12) provided to assess their abilities to use each subtraction strategy. This can be done individually or as a whole class.

☐ If a student feels confident in using the doubles strategy, for example, he or she will mark a "6" on the Radar Chart for that strategy. Continue for all strategies listed on the worksheet.

## Guided Practice

☐ The teacher will ask individuals to share their individual Radar Charts with the class, or will display the class' Radar Chart.

☐ The teacher will discuss with students which strategies they feel the most comfortable with, and which they feel the least comfortable with as evident by the self-scored Radar Charts.

☐ The teacher will assign students to complete a subtraction worksheet where they use a variety of strategies.

## Assessment

☐ Students will use the Radar Chart accurately.

☐ The students and teacher will assess the worksheets and determine the kinds of errors being made.

☐ In some cases, the teacher may need to ask the student, "How did you get this answer?" to determine if he or she is using his or her fingers, a number line, counting up, or counting back.

☐ The teacher will review the Pareto Diagram tool with students.

☐ The students and teacher will graph the kinds of errors on the Pareto Diagram (worksheet 13). Remember to graph the largest bar first.

☐ The teacher will use the information gathered to direct instructional focus, that is, students may understand doubles in subtraction but not making a 10 or number families.

## Post-Lesson/Follow-Up Activities/Extensions

☐ Read aloud several of the books listed below.

☐ Play the "one less" game—the teacher shows the student a number on a flash card and the students tell the number that is one less than that number.

☐ Play the "magic 10" game—the teacher shows a number on a flash card and students tell which number goes with that number to make 10.

## Supporting Resources

☐ *www.aaamath.com*

☐ *www.aplusmath.com/Flashcards/subtraction.html*

☐ *www.superkids.com/aweb/tools/math/subtract/*

☐ *Twenty is Too Many* by Kate Duke

☐ *Hershey's Kisses Subtraction Book* by Jerry Pallotta

☐ Worksheets 12 and 13

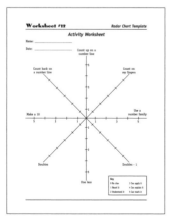

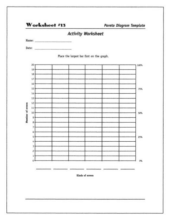

# Probability

Students will collect, organize, and analyze data using statistical methods, predict results, and interpret uncertainty using concepts of probability.

**Estimated Time:** 50 minutes          **Worksheets:** 14 and 15

## Quality Tool/PDSA Linkage

- ☐ Students will use the Bar Chart and the Check Sheet.
  - • The Bar Chart is a graph of categorical data plotted by frequency, and is used in the plan portion of the PDSA cycle.
  - • The Check Sheet/Matrix is a tool to collect and organize data in the plan portion of the PDSA cycle.

## Lesson Overview

- ☐ This is a hands-on lesson designed for students to demonstrate understanding of the concept of probability.
- ☐ Students will use a Bar Chart and a Check Sheet to keep track of their findings.

## Lesson Objectives

- ☐ The students will conduct several probability experiments.
- ☐ The students will determine when it is more likely to achieve a given result, when it is less likely to achieve a given result, and when it is not possible to achieve a given result.
- ☐ The students will use the Bar Chart and Check Sheet quality tools to record their results.

## Pre-Lesson Activities

- ☐ Obtain copies of the worksheets that go with the lesson.
- ☐ Obtain all materials needed for the lesson.
- ☐ Review with the students the concept of probability.

## Materials Needed

- ☐ A copy of the Bar Chart and Check Sheet for each group.
- ☐ Five paper bags for each group, labeled.
- ☐ Linker cubes or other small, colored objects, sorted as described in the Check Sheet.

## Lesson Delivery/Procedure

- ☐ The teacher will review the concept of probability with the students and model an example of its use.
- ☐ The teacher will display five bags and describe the contents of each.
- ☐ The teacher or student volunteer will pull one object from bag one.
- ☐ The teacher will review the Check Sheet tool with students.
- ☐ The teacher will model and demonstrate how to record findings on the Check Sheet (worksheet 14).

## Guided Practice

- ☐ Each cooperative group will be given five bags as described and a copy of the Check Sheet and Bar Chart.

- [ ] The student groups will pull linker cubes from their bags and record findings on the Check Sheet. (Alternatively, this could be done as a whole-class activity.)

- [ ] After the class or groups of students have recorded their results on the Check Sheet, the teacher will remind students of the contents of each bag.

- [ ] As a class, or in groups, students will try to pull a yellow cube from bag 1.

- [ ] The teacher will review the Bar Chart tool with students.

- [ ] The teacher will demonstrate how to record number of tries on the Bar Chart (worksheet 15).

- [ ] Continue this process for the remaining bags.

- [ ] The teacher and students will discuss how to record results from bag 5 on the Bar Chart. (Filling in the entire chart, or writing "impossible" across the column are two possibilities.) There are no yellows, so students could try indefinitely to pull a yellow with no success. Students should understand that it is impossible to pull a yellow cube from bag 5.

## Assessment

- [ ] The students will self-assess their assignment to see that the charts have been filled in correctly.

- [ ] The students will answer questions on worksheet 14 accurately to demonstrate understanding.

- [ ] The student will understand when something is "possible" and when something is "not possible" or "impossible."

- [ ] The students will complete a Bar Chart accurately as a result of probability experiment.

- [ ] Students will complete a Check Sheet accurately as a result of probability experiment.

## Post-Lesson/Follow-Up Activities/Extensions

- [ ] Change the variables of each bag for alternative results.

- [ ] Use candy or toys instead of linker cubes.

## Supporting Resources

- [ ] *nces.ed.gov/nceskids/probability/*

- [ ] *www.mathleague.com/help/percent/percent.htm*

- [ ] *Do You Wanna Bet?: Your Chance to Find Out About Probability* by Jean Cushman

- [ ] Worksheets 14 and 15

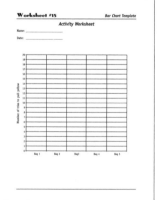

# Sort and Classify

Sort, classify, and compare familiar shapes. Collect, organize, and analyze data.

**Estimated Time:** 60 minutes          **Worksheets:** 16 and 17

## Quality Tool/PDSA Linkage

- ☐ Students will use the Nominal Group Technique/Light Voting and the Bar Chart.

  - • Nominal Group Technique/Light Voting is a structured group process (ranked voting) used to make decisions during any portion of the PDSA cycle.

  - • The Bar Chart is a graph of categorical data plotted by frequency, and is used in the plan portion of the PDSA cycle.

## Lesson Overview

- ☐ This is a hands-on lesson designed to help students sort and classify objects by their characteristics and attributes.

- ☐ The students will create a list of attributes by which to sort their classmates.

- ☐ The students will vote on one way to sort/classify the class after having made a list of possibilities.

- ☐ After class has been sorted, students will use a Bar Chart to record their data.

## Lesson Objectives

- ☐ The students will sort and classify their classmates by similar characteristics.

- ☐ The students will organize data.

- ☐ The students will understand and use the Nominal Group Technique/Light Voting quality tool.

- ☐ The students will understand and use the Bar Chart (worksheet 17) quality tool.

## Pre-Lesson Activities

- ☐ Obtain copies of the worksheets that go with the lesson.

- ☐ Obtain all materials needed for the lesson.

- ☐ Create a blank Bar Chart for the class.

## Materials Needed

- ☐ A blank worksheet for each student.

- ☐ Poster board or butcher paper.

- ☐ Markers.

- ☐ Chalkboard.

- ☐ Sticky dots (for Light Voting).

## Lesson Delivery/Procedure

- ☐ The teacher will call two students to the front of the room.

- ☐ The teacher will ask students to list ways that the students are the same, and ways they are different.

- ☐ The teacher will identify three (or so) students with similar characteristics as identified by the class (such as eye color).

- ☐ The students will give the reason that the teacher chose those three students to be called at the same time (the color of their eyes is the same).

- ☐ The teacher will continue using several different characteristics and several groups of students trying to find some categories that are not obvious immediately to students (in order to emphasize various characteristics and attributes).

## Guided Practice

- ☐ The students will list several different ways that the class can be sorted/classified.

- ☐ The teacher will review the Nominal Group Technique tool with students.

- ☐ The students will use Nominal Group Technique/Light Voting to choose one way to sort classmates. See example on worksheet 16.

- ☐ The teacher will review the Bar Chart tool with students.

- ☐ Having chosen one way, the class will create a Bar Chart (worksheet 17) to represent their data.

## Assessment

- ☐ The students will use NGT/Light voting technique accurately.

- ☐ The students will organize their data accurately and appropriately.

- ☐ The students will complete the Bar Chart to reflect their data accurately.

## Post-Lesson/Follow-Up Activities/Extensions

- ☐ Small groups of students could make a Bar Chart of a different characteristic (that is, shirt color).

- ☐ Read aloud *Sorting* by Henry Pluckrose.

- ☐ The students could sort pattern or attribute blocks.

- ☐ Play a game such as "change one" or "change two" with attribute blocks.

- ☐ Sort candy by color or shape and make a Bar Chart according to the data.

## Supporting Resources

- ☐ *Sorting* by Henry Pluckrose

- ☐ *First Words: Sorting and Matching Fun* by Silver Dolphin

- ☐ *www.eduplace.com/math/mathsteps/k/b/*

- ☐ Worksheets 16 and 17

# Geometric Figures

Demonstrate and apply geometric concepts involving points, lines, planes, and space.

**Estimated Time:** 50 minutes        **Worksheets:** 18 and 19

## Quality Tool/PDSA Linkage

☐ Students will use the Lotus Diagram.

• The Lotus Diagram is a tool to expand thinking around a single topic or theme and is used at any portion of the PDSA to generate additional thoughts.

## Lesson Overview

☐ This is a hands-on lesson designed for students to demonstrate and apply knowledge of geometric figures.

☐ Utilizing a Lotus Diagram, students will create a collage of geometric figures.

## Lesson Objectives

☐ The students will be able to recognize geometric shapes and structures found in collections of magazines, newspapers, and discarded books.

☐ The students will understand and use the Lotus Diagram quality tool to create a collage of geometric figures.

## Pre-Lesson Activities

☐ Obtain copies of the worksheets that go with the lesson.

☐ Obtain all materials needed for the lesson.

☐ Obtain a variety of magazines, newspapers, and discarded books to be used in cooperative group settings.

☐ Review geometric shape structures.

☐ Obtain at least 10 precut pictures that contain images of geometric figures (such as squares, rectangles, circles, spheres, cubes, rectangular prisms, pyramids, and triangles).

☐ Create a poster board size Lotus Diagram (worksheet 19).

☐ Place posters on the walls discussing the various shapes and their qualifications. (These could be manufactured by the teacher after the initial shape lesson or store bought.)

## Materials Needed

☐ A basket of assorted magazines, newspapers, and discarded books per four-student group.

☐ Lotus Diagram for each student.

☐ Scissors.

☐ Glue sticks.

## Lesson Delivery/Procedure

☐ The teacher will review the definitions and features of the following figures: squares, rectangles, circles, triangles, spheres, rectangular prisms, pyramids, and cubes using posters displayed in the classroom as guides.

☐ The teacher will review the Lotus Diagram tool with students.

- ☐ The teacher will display the poster size Lotus Diagram and explain that their goal will be to find the aforementioned shapes in the magazines, books, and newspapers.
- ☐ The teacher will label the middle box, "Geometric Figures."
- ☐ The teacher will ask the students to aid him or her in labeling the outer boxes by asking what are the different types of geometric figures (refer to worksheet 18 as an example of finished product).
- ☐ Displaying the precut pictures of geometric figures, the teacher will enlist the students' help in placing the pictures in the appropriate boxes.

## Guided Practice

- ☐ Each cooperative group will be given their assortment of magazines, books, newspapers, glue, scissors, and copies of worksheet 18.
- ☐ Using their resources, each student will be required to find at least one example of each geometric figure.

## Assessment

- ☐ Each student will self-assess his or her assignment, checking to see if each box has at least one picture of a geometric figure according to each box's label.
- ☐ The students will examine the commonalities of the picture in each box and the example displayed on the posters utilized in the classroom.
- ☐ The teacher will check to see if each student was able to find an example of each geometric figure placed in the appropriate boxes.

## Post-Lesson/Follow-Up Activities/Extensions

- ☐ As a homework assignment, students will be required to find eight examples of one geometric figure of their choice. Use worksheet 19.

## Supporting Resources

- ☐ *mathforum.org/*
- ☐ *The Greedy Triangle* by Marilyn Burns, Gordon Silveria (Illustrator)
- ☐ Worksheets 18 and 19

# Math

## 2-3

### LESSONS

Counting Money . . . . . . . . . . 27

Division . . . . . . . . . . . . . . . . 29

Story Problems . . . . . . . . . . . 31

Geometry/Angles. . . . . . . . . . 35

Problem Solving . . . . . . . . . . 39

Telling Time . . . . . . . . . . . . . 41

Regrouping. . . . . . . . . . . . . . 43

Fact Families. . . . . . . . . . . . . 45

Geometry/Solid Figures . . . . . . 49

# Counting Money

Identify and describe the relative values and relationships among coins and solve addition and subtraction problems using currency.

**Estimated Time:** two or more 45-minute sessions     **Worksheets:**   20, 21, 22, and 23

## Quality Tool/PDSA Linkage

☐   Students will use the Check Sheet, Radar Chart, and Bar Chart.

- The Check Sheet/Matrix is a tool to collect and organize data in the plan portion of the PDSA cycle.

- The Radar Chart is a graph with multiple scales to report self-assessed knowledge or competence, often over time and is used during both the plan and study portions of the PDSA cycle.

- The Bar Chart is a graph of categorical data plotted by frequency, and is used in the plan portion of the PDSA cycle.

## Lesson Overview

☐   This lesson is designed to allow students to self-assess their confidence level with counting money.

☐   After assessing their confidence level, students will find various ways to show a given amount of money.

☐   The students will also determine the number of different coin combinations possible to show given amounts of money.

## Lesson Objectives

☐   The students will self-assess their confidence level with counting money.

☐   The students will understand that the greater amount of money, the greater the possibilities of coin combinations there are to show that amount.

☐   The students will make a Check Sheet that shows various coin combinations for making a given amount of money.

☐   The students will understand and use the Radar Chart quality tool.

☐   The students will understand and use the Check Sheet quality tool.

☐   The students will understand and use the Bar Chart quality tool.

## Pre-Lesson Activities

☐   Obtain copies of the worksheets that go with the lesson.

☐   Obtain all materials needed for the lesson.

## Materials Needed

☐   A blank worksheet for each student group.

☐   Money manipulatives.

☐   Chart paper or overhead.

## Lesson Delivery/Procedure

☐   The teacher will review the Radar Chart tool with students.

☐   The students will use the Radar Chart (worksheet 20) provided to assess their current confidence level with counting money.

- [ ] In collaborative groups, students will find as many ways as possible to combine coins that equal a given amount of money.
- [ ] The teacher will review the Check Sheet tool with students.
- [ ] The students will record their findings on the Check Sheet (worksheet 22) provided.
- [ ] The students will share their findings with the class.

## Guided Practice

- [ ] The teacher will guide students toward realization that the greater the amount of money, the greater the number of coin combinations that are possible to show that amount.
- [ ] The teacher will review the Bar Chart tool with students.
- [ ] The students will work collaboratively to complete the Bar Chart (worksheet 23) for the number of coin combinations to represent 5 cents, 10 cents, and so on.

## Assessment

- [ ] The teacher will assess the Bar Chart and the Check Sheet for accuracy.
- [ ] The students will complete the Check Sheet accurately to demonstrate understanding.
- [ ] The students will complete the Bar Chart accurately.

## Post-Lesson/Follow-Up Activities/Extensions

- [ ] Complete a Check Sheet for another amount of money collaboratively.
- [ ] Complete a Check Sheet for a new amount of money independently.

## Supporting Resources

- [ ] *The Coin Counting Book* by Rozanne Lanczak Williams
- [ ] *The Monster Money Book* by Loreen Leedy
- [ ] www.edu4kids.com/money/
- [ ] www.playtolearn.com/coins.asp
- [ ] Worksheets 20, 21, 22, and 23

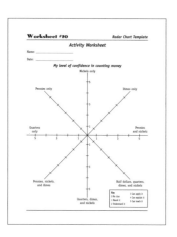

# Division

Solve one- and two-step problems with whole numbers using addition, subtraction, multiplication, and division.

**Estimated Time:** 30–40 minute lesson     **Worksheets:** 24 and 25

## Quality Tool/PDSA Linkage

- ☐ Students will use a Flowchart.

  - • The Flowchart is a drawing of any process used to document the process flow during the plan portion of the PDSA cycle.

## Lesson Overview

- ☐ This is a lesson designed for students to demonstrate and apply knowledge of dividing even two-digit numbers by two.

- ☐ Utilizing a Flowchart, students will demonstrate their knowledge of division.

## Lesson Objectives

- ☐ The students will be able to recognize and demonstrate the steps of dividing an even two-digit number by two.

- ☐ The students will understand and use the Flowchart quality tool.

## Pre-Lesson Activities

- ☐ Obtain copies of the worksheets that go with the lesson.

- ☐ Obtain all materials needed for the lesson.

- ☐ Obtain manipulatives for students who are tactile learners.

- ☐ Create a poster board size Flowchart (worksheet 24).

- ☐ Review the definitions: divisor, dividend, quotient, and product.

## Materials Needed

- ☐ Worksheets.

- ☐ Manipulatives.

- ☐ Overhead or poster paper.

## Lesson Delivery/Procedure

- ☐ The teacher will review the definitions: divisor, dividend, quotient, and product.

- ☐ The teacher will review the Flowchart tool with students.

- ☐ The teacher will display the poster-size Flowchart and explain that their goal will be able to write the steps that they should follow to divide an even two-digit number by two.

- ☐ The teacher will use a sample problem and go through the steps of the Flowchart with the students.

- ☐ The teacher will ask the students to aid him or her in putting the correct information for completing the problem in the Flowchart.

## Guided Practice

- ☐ The students will make their own copies of the classroom Flowchart (worksheet 24).
- ☐ Using the Flowchart, the students will complete the practice problems on worksheet 25.

## Assessment

- ☐ Each student will self-assess his or her assignment, checking to see if he or she has copied the classroom Flowchart correctly.
- ☐ The students will be able to explain how they followed the Flowchart to get an answer of one of their practice problems.
- ☐ The teacher will evaluate to see if each student was able to answer the practice problems correctly.

## Post-Lesson/Follow-Up Activities/Extensions

- ☐ The students may create Flowcharts for other types of problems.
- ☐ The students may create problems for classmates to solve using the Flowchart.

## Supporting Resources

- ☐ *mathforum.org*
- ☐ *teachers.net*
- ☐ *users.black-hole.com*
- ☐ *One Hungry Cat* (Hello Math Reader, Level 3) by Joanne Rocklin and Rowan Barnes-Murphy
- ☐ Worksheets 24 and 25

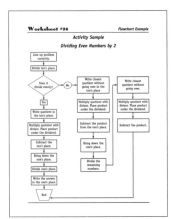

# Story Problems

Demonstrate and apply a knowledge and sense of numbers, including numeration and operation (addition, subtraction, multiplication, division).

**Estimated Time:** Two 60-minute periods   **Worksheets:** 26, 27, and 28

## Quality Tool/PDSA Linkage

☐ Students will use the Relations Diagram, Force-Field Analysis, and Flowchart.

- The Relations Diagram is a picture of the cause and effect relationships between elements of the problem and is used to determine root cause in the plan portion of the PDSA cycle.

- The Force-Field Analysis is a tool used to evaluate the forces driving and restraining a desired change and is used during the plan portion of the PDSA cycle to generate the most comprehensive plan possible to test the improvement theory.

- The Flowchart is a drawing of any process used to document the process flow during the plan portion of the PDSA cycle.

## Lesson Overview

☐ This is a lesson designed to help students discover why they are having difficulty solving story problems.

☐ The students will use a Relations Diagram to discover the root cause.

☐ The students will use a Force-Field Analysis to identify driving and restraining forces and to develop an action plan.

☐ The students will develop a Flowchart to provide a step-by-step process for solving a story problem.

## Lesson Objectives

☐ The students will understand and use the Relations Diagram, Force-Field Analysis, and Flowchart.

☐ The students will use the Relations Diagram to identify the root causes of solving story problems.

☐ The students will use the Force-Field Analysis to identify driving and restraining forces in solving story problems.

☐ The students will develop a Flowchart to demonstrate a step-by-step process for solving story problems.

☐ The students will understand the basic concepts of solving a story problem.

## Pre-Lesson Activities

☐ Obtain copies of the worksheets that go with the lesson.

☐ The students should have had some experience solving story problems.

☐ The students should have some experience with the quality tools used in this lesson.

☐ Obtain all materials needed for the lesson.

## Materials Needed

☐ Chart paper.

☐ Markers.

☐ Post-It notes.

## Lesson Delivery/Procedure

- ☐ The teacher will review the Relations Diagram tool with students.
- ☐ The students and the teachers together will list causes (limit 5) to the question "Why do we have trouble with story problems?" and then list them in the boxes on the Relations Diagram (see worksheet 26).

```
┌─────────────────┐          ┌─────────────────┐
│                 │          │                 │
│                 │          │                 │
└─────────────────┘          └─────────────────┘

           ┌──────────────────────────┐
           │   Why do we have trouble │
           │   with story problems?   │
           └──────────────────────────┘

┌─────────────┐     ┌─────────────┐     ┌─────────────┐
│             │     │             │     │             │
│             │     │             │     │             │
└─────────────┘     └─────────────┘     └─────────────┘
```

- ☐ The teacher will lead a discussion to dentify the main or root cause or causes of the problem.
- ☐ The five main root causes will be placed in the outer boxes of the Relations Diagram (worksheet 26).
- ☐ The teacher will lead the students through the completion of the Relations Diagram.
- ☐ The teacher will review the Force-Field Analysis tool with students.
- ☐ Together as a group, students will use the Force-Field Analysis tool to define the restraining and driving forces to solve story problems as evident by the root cause they discovered in the Relations Diagram and use this information to create an Action Plan.
- ☐ The class will complete the Force-Field Analysis (worksheet 27) with guidance from the teacher.
- ☐ Students will develop a step-by-step process for solving story problems using a Flowchart using information generated from the Force-Field Analysis.

## Guided Practice

- ☐ The students will implement the Action Plan developed using the Force-Field Analysis.
- ☐ The students will develop a Flowchart showing the step-by-step process for solving story problems.

## Assessment

- ☐ The students will use the Relations Diagram, Force-Field Analysis, and Flowchart to develop an action plan to help students solve story problems.
- ☐ The students will evaluate implementation of the Action Plan and determine if it made a difference in their process for solving story problems.
- ☐ The students will give feedback to the group on the usefulness of the Flowchart and decide on changes that need to be made.
- ☐ Students will reflect in written form on how the action plan worked.

## Post-Lesson/Follow-Up Activities/Extensions

☐ Continue to review and re-evaluate Action Plan.

☐ Describe how the Action Plan changed scores in math story problems.

## Supporting Resources

☐ Worksheets 26, 27, and 28

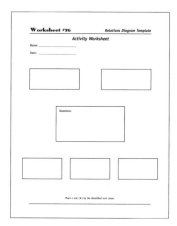

# Geometry/Angles

Use geometric methods to analyze, categorize, and draw conclusions about points, lines, and angles.

**Estimated Time:** Two 60-minute sessions          **Worksheets:** 29, 30, and 31

## Quality Tool/PDSA Linkage

☐ Students will learn about the Check Sheet, Brainstorming, Operational Definition, Lotus Diagram, and Pareto Diagram.

- The Check Sheet/Matrix is a tool to collect and organize data in the plan portion of the PDSA cycle.

- The Brainstorming technique is the generation of ideas by a group and is used at any portion of the PDSA cycle when every person needs to be heard from and many ideas need to be generated.

- Operational Definition is a standard process for measuring our critical quality characteristics used before gathering data in the plan portion of the PDSA cycle.

- The Lotus Diagram is a tool to expand thinking around a single topic or theme and is used at any portion of the PDSA cycle to generate additional thoughts.

- The Pareto Diagram is a bar chart that ranks categorical data from largest to smallest to find the "significant few" in the plan portion of the PDSA cycle.

## Lesson Overview

☐ The students will develop an Operational Definition for each type of angle: right, acute, and obtuse.

☐ The students will use a Check Sheet to identify the various types of angles.

☐ The students will use a Pareto Diagram to record the results.

☐ The students will further define each type of angle using a Lotus Diagram.

## Lesson Objectives

☐ The students will understand and use the Check Sheet, Brainstorming, Operational Definition, Lotus Diagram, and Pareto Diagram quality tools.

☐ The students will clearly identify the characteristics of acute, right, and obtuse angles.

☐ The students will demonstrate and utilize a protractor.

☐ The students will be able to report out their findings to another group of students.

## Pre-Lesson Activities

☐ The students should have some working knowledge of geometry.

☐ The students should have some practice working with a protractor and identifying angles.

☐ The teacher needs to make sure that the area of the room assigned to the students has examples of all types of angles.

☐ Obtain copies of the worksheets that go with the lesson.

☐ Obtain all materials needed for this lesson.

## Materials Needed

- ☐ Chart paper.
- ☐ Markers.
- ☐ Post-It notes.
- ☐ Protractors.

## Lesson Delivery/Procedure

- ☐ The teacher will review the Operational Definition tool with students.
- ☐ The students will meet as a whole group in order to create an Operational Definition for each type of angle.
- ☐ The teacher will review the Brainstorming tool with students.
- ☐ The students will brainstorm a list of characteristics for each angle; this will be the basis for the Operational Definition.
- ☐ The Operational Definition should be posted for students to refer to during this unit.
- ☐ Divide the students into pairs.
- ☐ Assign each pair of students a section of the room or a certain area of your school.
- ☐ The teacher will review the Check Sheet tool with students.
- ☐ The students will count the number of angles that they find in their area and record on a Check Sheet (worksheet 29).
- ☐ The teacher will review the Pareto Diagram tool with students.
- ☐ The students will graph their results on a Pareto Diagram (worksheet 30).
- ☐ The teacher will review the Lotus Diagram tool with students.
- ☐ The students will create a Lotus Diagram for each type of angle. Students will draw examples (worksheet 31).
- ☐ The students will share in small groups their Pareto Diagrams and Lotus Diagram.
- ☐ The teacher will review the Operational Definitions of angles.

## Guided Practice

- ☐ Each student will utilize the Operational Definition to help them identify different types of angles.
- ☐ The students will create a Pareto Diagram and Lotus Diagram to further demonstrate understanding of the different types of angles.

## Assessment

- ☐ The students will use the Operational Definition, Check Sheet, Pareto Diagram, and Lotus Diagram tools to develop a clear understanding of the concepts of angles.
- ☐ The students will share their Pareto Diagram and Lotus Diagrams with other groups within the classroom to demonstrate understanding of the quality tools and their use.

## Post-Lesson/Follow-Up Activities/Extensions

- ☐ As a homework assignment, students can take their Check Sheet home and see how many angles they can find.
- ☐ The students can complete a Pareto Diagram using home data.

# Supporting Resources

☐ Worksheets 29, 30, and 31

**Worksheet #31**      *Lotus Diagram Template*

**Activity Worksheet**

Name: _____

Date: _____

|  |  |  |
|---|---|---|
|  |  |  |
|  | *(Name of Angle)* |  |
|  |  |  |

# Problem Solving

Solve problems using systems of numbers and their properties.

**Estimated Time:** 45 minutes          **Worksheets:** 32 and 33

## Quality Tool/PDSA Linkage

☐  Students will use Force-Field Analysis.

  • Force-Field Analysis is a tool used to evaluate the forces driving and restraining a desired change and is used during the plan portion of the PDSA cycle to generate the most comprehensive plan possible to test the improvement theory.

## Lesson Overview

☐  This is a lesson designed for students to demonstrate and apply knowledge of problem solving.

☐  Utilizing the Force-Field Analysis tool, students will distinguish between necessary (driving forces) and extra (restraining forces) information.

## Lesson Objectives

☐  The students will be able to recognize the difference between necessary and extra information in problem solving.

☐  The students will understand and use the Force-Field Analysis quality tool.

## Pre-Lesson Activities

☐  Obtain copies of the worksheets that go with the lesson.

☐  Obtain all materials needed for the lesson.

☐  Review problem-solving strategies.

☐  Create a poster board size or overhead transparency of the Force-Field Analysis tool (worksheet 32).

☐  Create and post posters on the walls discussing the different problem-solving strategies.

## Materials Needed

☐  Worksheets for each student.

☐  Force-Field Analysis worksheet.

## Lesson Delivery/Procedure

☐  The teacher will review the processes for problem solving and discuss the difference between necessary and extra information.

☐  The teacher will display the poster-size Force-Field Analysis and explain that their goal will be to find the problem that needs to be solved and decide what information in the problem is necessary to solve the problem and what information provided is extra.

☐  The teacher will review the Force-Field Analysis tool with students.

☐  The teacher will use one of the given problems as an example and complete a Force-Field Analysis with the class by using an overhead or poster board.

☐  The teacher will ask the students to aid him or her in solving the problem using the completed Force-Field Analysis.

## Guided Practice

☐ Each student will be given a Force-Field Analysis (worksheet 32) and the worksheet of sample problems (worksheet 33).

☐ Using their resources, each student will be required to complete the Force-Field Analysis and solve the given problems.

☐ Each student will create his or her own word problem that contains extra information, along with a completed Force-Field Analysis and the problem's answer.

☐ The students will then exchange and solve each other's problems.

## Assessment

☐ Each student will self-assess their assignment checking to see if each part of the Force-Field Analysis is correctly filled out.

☐ The teacher will evaluate if each student was able to correctly identify the extra information in the problems and correctly answer each problem.

## Post-Lesson/Follow-Up Activities/Extensions

☐ The students will use the Force-Field Analysis in future problem-solving assignments.

## Supporting Resources

☐ *mathcounts.org*

☐ *www.mav.vic.edu.au/PSTC/general/strategy.htm*

☐ *100 Great Problems of Elementary Mathematics* by Heinrich D-Orrie

☐ *How to Solve It* by George Polya, Gyorgy Polya

☐ Worksheets 32 and 33

# Telling Time

Measure units of time using appropriate instruments, both analog and digital.

**Estimated Time:** 45 minutes          **Worksheets:** 34 and 35

## Quality Tool/PDSA Linkage

☐ Students will use a Radar Chart.

  • The Radar Chart is a graph with multiple scales to report self-assessed knowledge or competence, often over time and is used during both the plan and study portions of the PDSA cycle.

## Lesson Overview

☐ The students will learn how to determine their level of understanding with different elements of time.

## Lesson Objectives

☐ The students will learn or review how to tell time using digital and analog instruments.

☐ The students will also review the importance of knowing how to identify their comfort level with a particular concept.

☐ Each student will complete a Radar Chart expressing the level of knowledge of a particular concept of time.

☐ The class will average the results from the individual Radar Charts and then make a class Radar Chart reflecting the consensus of the class.

☐ The students will share experiences they have had in making the Radar Chart and will state other instances where a Radar Chart could be used.

## Pre-Lesson Activities

☐ Obtain copies of the worksheets that go with the lesson.

☐ Obtain all materials needed for the lesson.

☐ The teacher or class will study the information about telling time with analog and digital clocks and tools.

☐ Review with the class how to determine their comfort level in assessing their level of knowledge with telling time.

☐ Review with the class how to complete the Radar Chart.

## Materials Needed

☐ A copy of a blank Radar Chart (worksheet 35).

☐ Pencils for students.

☐ Markers for teacher use.

## Lesson Delivery/Procedure

☐ The teacher will introduce or review with students how to use the Radar Chart.

☐ Each student will evaluate his or her comfort and knowledge level with time and record the value on the Radar Chart.

☐ The teacher will review the different aspects of analog and digital instruments.

☐ The students will reevaluate their comfort and knowledge level of analog and digital time on the Radar Chart.

- ☐ The students and the teacher will discuss which of the aspects of time will be useful in making the Radar Chart.
- ☐ The class will make a Radar Chart together on the overhead or board using the aspects of time as discussed in class (worksheet 35).

## Guided Practice

- ☐ The teacher will review with students how to use the Radar Chart.
- ☐ The students will create their own Radar Chart reflecting their knowledge of time.
- ☐ The teacher and the class will discuss the Radar Charts and then create a class consensus Radar Chart which represents the class average.
- ☐ The class will review telling time on analog and digital clocks. The teacher will review the key concepts of telling time.
- ☐ Each student will look at the Radar Chart he or she created and, using a different color of dot or marker, all students will reevaluate their comfort and knowledge levels with the concept of time. (This will occur after the review.)
- ☐ The class will then figure a new class average on the Radar Chart to see if understanding improved.

## Assessment

- ☐ The students will make notes of their understanding of the different elements of the Radar Chart.
- ☐ The students will review their work, discussion, and findings to gauge level of understanding.
- ☐ The teacher will summarize the lesson objective, findings, and key concepts of the lesson to remember with students.

## Post-Lesson/Follow-Up Activities/Extensions

- ☐ The students can take the Radar Chart concept home to share with family and friends.
- ☐ The students can challenge themselves by developing a Radar Chart to help them assess their comfort level with new concepts being introduced in class.
- ☐ The students can visit another grade with their Radar Chart and teach younger or older students how to use the tool.

## Supporting Resources

- ☐ Hands-on materials about time such as clocks for student use
- ☐ *Telling Time with Tickety Tock* by Sandy Lutzky
- ☐ Worksheets 34 and 35

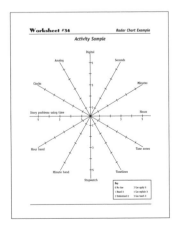

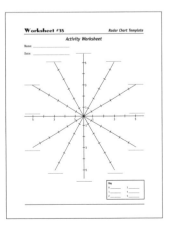

# Regrouping

Demonstrate and apply a knowledge and sense of numbers, including numeration and operations.

**Estimated Time:** 60 minutes          **Worksheets:** 36, 37, and 38

## Quality Tool/PDSA Linkage

- ☐ Students will use a Flowchart and Scatter Diagram.
  - • The Flowchart is a drawing of any process used to document the process flow during the plan portion of the PDSA cycle.
  - • The Scatter Diagram is a tool used to show the relationship between two factors in the plan portion of the PDSA cycle.

## Lesson Overview

- ☐ In this lesson, the students and the teacher will work together to create a Flowchart to visually organize the steps in regrouping.
- ☐ This lesson should begin when regrouping is introduced for the first time in a given year.
- ☐ The students will measure their confidence in regrouping using the Scatter Diagram at the beginning of the unit and at several other points during the year as instruction/remediation continue.
- ☐ One Scatter Diagram could be used for "regrouping" or a separate Scatter Diagram could be used for regrouping in addition and regrouping in subtraction.

## Lesson Objectives

- ☐ The students will be able to break a process down into simple steps.
- ☐ The students will measure their confidence with regrouping.
- ☐ The students will understand and use the Flowchart quality tool.
- ☐ The students will understand and use the Scatter Diagram quality tool.

## Pre-Lesson Activities

- ☐ Obtain copies of the worksheets that go with the lesson.
- ☐ Obtain all materials needed for the lesson.
- ☐ Create the beginning of a blank Flowchart on the overhead or on poster board.
- ☐ Create or obtain a poster or overhead of the symbols used when creating the Flowchart.

## Materials Needed

- ☐ Markers.
- ☐ Sticky dots for the Scatter Diagram.

## Lesson Delivery/Procedure

- ☐ The teacher will discuss with the students their level of confidence with regrouping vs. the amount of time the students have spent practicing regrouping. This should be done at the beginning of the regrouping unit and repeated weekly or as the teacher feels is appropriate.

- ☐ The teacher will review the Scatter Diagram tool with students.
- ☐ The students could keep their own Scatter Diagram (worksheet 38) and color code it over time, and/or the class could create one Scatter Diagram.
- ☐ The students will realize that as their practice increases, their level of confidence will also increase.

## Guided Practice

- ☐ The students and the teacher will discuss the steps in regrouping.
- ☐ The teacher will review the Flowchart tool with students.
- ☐ Individually, in groups, or as a class, students will develop a Flowchart for the steps taken when regrouping. See examples listed on worksheets 36 and 37.

## Assessment

- ☐ The students will use the proper symbols in the Flowchart.
- ☐ The students will list the steps for regrouping correctly and in the proper order.

## Post-Lesson/Follow-Up Activities/Extensions

- ☐ The class could conduct a Force-Field Analysis to answer the question, "Why aren't we sure when to regroup?"

## Supporting Resources

- ☐ *Addition and Subtraction with Regrouping* by Sara Freeman
- ☐ *Addition and Subtraction with Regrouping: With Ocean Animals* (Puzzles and Practice Series) by H. S. Lawrence
- ☐ *www.mathplayground.com/wpindex.html*
- ☐ *www.dositey.com/addsub/subra4.htm*
- ☐ Worksheets 36, 37, and 38

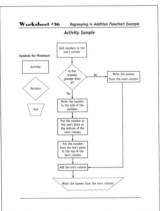

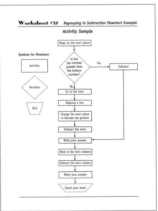

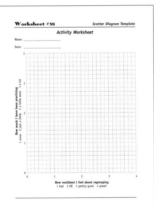

# Fact Families

Demonstrate knowledge and use of numbers and their representations in a broad range of theoretical and practical settings.

**Estimated Time:** 30–45 minutes          **Worksheets:** 39, 40, and 41

## Quality Tool/PDSA Linkage

☐ Students will use the Lotus Diagram and a Flowchart.

- The Lotus Diagram is a tool to expand thinking around a single topic or theme and is used at any portion of the PDSA cycle to generate additional thoughts.

- The Flowchart is a drawing of any process used to document the process flow during the plan portion of the PDSA cycle.

## Lesson Overview

☐ In this lesson, students will learn about fact families.

☐ The students will be actively engaged in a hands-on activity to learn about a fact family.

## Lesson Objectives

☐ The students will review the definition of a number sentence.

☐ The students will learn about fact families.

☐ The students will learn about the Lotus Diagram and Flowchart quality tools.

☐ The students will learn how to use manipulatives to understand fact families.

## Pre-Lesson Activities

☐ Review number sentences.

☐ Copy mats for each set of partners.

☐ Obtain a transparency of the mat for the overhead.

☐ Obtain copies of the worksheets that go with the lesson.

☐ Obtain all materials needed for the lesson.

☐ Make a large Lotus Diagram on chart paper for whole class modeling.

## Materials Needed

☐ Number cube for each set of partners.

☐ Counters of two different colors.

☐ Mat for each set of partners.

☐ Paper.

☐ Pencils.

☐ Chart paper.

☐ Overhead projector.

- ☐ Colored counter chips for the overhead projector.
- ☐ Copy of student mat on transparency.

## Lesson Delivery/Procedure

- ☐ The teacher will ask the students, "What is a fact family?"
- ☐ The students will make predictions as to what they think a fact family is.
- ☐ The teacher will record predictions on chart paper.
- ☐ The teacher will tell the students that he or she is going to model what they are going to do for math that day.
- ☐ The teacher will roll a number cube and tell the class what number came up.
- ☐ The teacher will put that amount of counters on the "part" section of transparency that looks like the student's mats (see worksheet 41).
- ☐ The teacher will then roll the number cube again.
- ☐ The teacher will put the second colored counters in the "part" section on the chart paper.
- ☐ The teacher will show the students that if you move all the counters together they equal the whole.
- ☐ The teacher will model how to move the counters to the whole section.
- ☐ The teacher will ask the students what two addition number sentences they can make with the colored counters.
- ☐ Once the students have given the two addition number sentences, the teacher will write the number sentences down on a chalkboard or chart paper.
- ☐ The teacher will then tell the students that to make a complete fact family, they need to add the subtraction problems.
- ☐ Keeping all the counters in the whole section, ask them to take out the first color of counters.
- ☐ The teacher will ask, "How many counters did you start with?"
- ☐ The teacher will ask, "How many counters did you take away?"
- ☐ The teacher will ask, "How many counters are left?"
- ☐ The teacher and students write the subtraction sentences under the addition number sentences.
- ☐ The teacher explains that they have just completed a fact family.
- ☐ The teacher will review the Flowchart tool with students.
- ☐ The teacher will now introduce the Flowchart that the teacher already made (worksheet 40).
- ☐ The teacher will explain that the students need to follow the Flowchart to complete the activity.

## Guided Practice

- ☐ The teacher will tell the students that they are going to work with a partner to complete a fact family in the same manner the teacher just did. Students refer to the Flowchart for help.
- ☐ The teacher will have one person pass out one color of counters and another person to pass out the second color.
- ☐ The teacher will hand out the mats and number cubes.
- ☐ The students will roll the number cubes and get started with the activity.
- ☐ The teacher will review the Lotus Diagram tool with students.
- ☐ Once the students have had time to practice, the teacher can have the students complete a fact family Lotus Diagram (worksheet 39).

## Assessment

☐ The teacher will informally assess students understanding during manipulating the counters.

☐ The teacher can formally assess the students' work by looking at their fact family recording sheet.

## Post-Lesson/Follow-Up Activities/Extensions

☐ The teacher and students will check their predictions of what a fact family was.

☐ The students can write in their math journals or paper how knowing a fact family can help you add and subtract.

## Supporting Resources

☐ Worksheets 39, 40, and 41

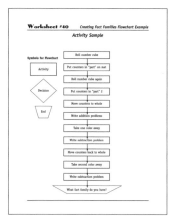

# Geometry/Solid Figures

Identify, describe, classify, and compare relationships using points, lines, planes, and solids.

**Estimated Time:** 45 minutes          **Worksheets:** 42 and 43

## Quality Tool/PDSA Linkage

☐ Students will learn about the Check Sheet and Brainstorming.

  • The Check Sheet/Matrix is a tool to collect and organize data in the plan portion of the PDSA cycle.

  • The Brainstorming technique is the generation of ideas by a group and is used at any portion of the PDSA cycle when every person needs to be heard from and many ideas need to be generated.

## Lesson Overview

☐ This is a hands-on lesson designed to allow students to explore geometric solids.

☐ To begin the lesson, students will Brainstorm vocabulary terms they already know about geometric solid figures.

☐ As a result of their exploration, students will work in groups to compare the number of sides, corners, and edges of each solid figure.

☐ Students will use a Check Sheet/Matrix to record their findings.

## Lesson Objectives

☐ The students will compare the number of sides of solid figures.

☐ The students will compare the number of corners of solid figures.

☐ The students will compare the number of edges of solid figures.

## Pre-Lesson Activities

☐ Obtain copies of the worksheets that go with the lesson.

☐ Obtain all materials needed for the lesson including solid figures, that is, oval, sphere, cube, triangular prism, rectangular prism.

☐ Review vocabulary with students: solid figure, plane figure, side, corner, edge.

## Materials Needed

☐ One set of solid figures for each group.

☐ Pencil or pen for appropriate recording of data.

☐ Large graph paper on an easel or overhead transparency of graph paper to use as a tool for student demonstration.

☐ Markers.

## Lesson Delivery/Procedure

☐ The teacher will display each solid figure and elicit the name of each figure from the students.

☐ The students will tell which plane figures can be found on each solid figure.

☐ The teacher will review the Brainstorming tool with students.

- [ ] The students will Brainstorm all the geometric terms (vocabulary) they know that go with solid figures (corner, edge, side, angle, and possibly names of plane figures) using worksheet 43.
- [ ] The teacher will review concepts of corner, edge, and side with a visual demonstration.

## Guided Practice

- [ ] In small groups, students will review various geometric figures and determine the number of sides, corners, and edges.
- [ ] The teacher will review the Check Sheet tool with students.
- [ ] Each group will record their data on the Check Sheet/Matrix (worksheet 42).
- [ ] The students will record if figure rolls or slides.
- [ ] The teacher will monitor group work and assist as needed.

## Assessment

- [ ] The students will summarize their findings by reporting out and sharing their findings with the class.
- [ ] The students will complete the Check Sheet accurately to demonstrate understanding.

## Post-Lesson/Follow-Up Activities/Extensions

- [ ] The students can discuss which of the figures used in today's lesson are good for building.
- [ ] The students can discuss/predict how tall of a tower could be built with the figures.
- [ ] The students can build such a tower and check predictions.
- [ ] The students can discuss what interesting building could be designed using these shapes and build them.
- [ ] The students can trace around the faces of each shape.
- [ ] The students can define angles and determine the number of angles on each figure.

## Supporting Resources

- [ ] *The Missing Piece* by Shel Silverstein
- [ ] Worksheets 42 and 43

# MATH

4-5

## LESSONS

Multiplication PDSA: Part A . . . 53

Multiplication PDSA: Part B . . . 57

Multiplication PDSA: Part C . . . 59

Multiplication PDSA: Part D . . . 61

Multiplication PDSA: Part E . . . 63

Collecting Data . . . . . . . . . . . . 65

Division . . . . . . . . . . . . . . . . 67

Organizing Data . . . . . . . . . . . 71

Multiplication—Single Lesson . . 73

# Multiplication PDSA: Part A

Investigate, represent, and solve problems using number facts and operations and their properties, algorithms, and relationships.

**Estimated Time:** 45 minutes initially then again after a predetermined time by the teacher

**Worksheet:** 44

## PDSA Background Information

Students have been scoring poorly on their multiplication timed tests and have not been able to transfer their knowledge of basic multiplication facts over to two-digit by two-digit multiplication problems in a timely manner. Students were given a Radar Chart to help gather baseline data in the area needing improvement. (The Radar Chart is a graph with multiple scales to report self-assessed knowledge or competence, often over time, and is used during both the plan and study portions of the PDSA.) Students showed they had a varying range of knowledge of their basic multiplication facts thus indicating to the teacher that improvement was needed in this area. The teacher, together with the class, developed an Operational Definition to help specify the aspects of needed improvement. (The Operational Definition is a clear, concise, and detailed definition of measure.)

The Operational Definition contained the following information:

Characteristic of interest—Time spent studying multiplication facts.

Measuring instrument—Record of time spent studying multiplication facts. (Clock)

Method of test—Record time spent studying multiplication facts each night at home.

Calculate minutes between start and stop time.

Decision criteria—Students will deduct time spent getting a snack, eating dinner, or talking on the phone from total study time to get total time studied.

## Quality Tool/PDSA Linkage

☐ Students will use a Scatter Diagram.

• The Scatter Diagram is a tool used to show the relationship between two factors in the plan portion of the PDSA cycle.

## Lesson Overview

☐ This lesson is designed to help students and the teacher gather baseline data by analyzing possible reasons why students aren't achieving well on their math timed tests and not transferring their knowledge of basic math facts to two-digit by two-digit multiplication problems.

☐ The students will use the Scatter Diagram to help them determine how much time students study and how that information may correlate to the score they receive on the timed math test for each week during the study.

☐ The students and teacher will use the Scatter Diagram to help determine if the amount of time students have spent on studying their math facts contributes to their weekly math achievement scores on timed tests.

## Lesson Objectives

- [ ] The students will create a Scatter Diagram to help them identify the amount of time spent studying and the scores students receive on their weekly timed tests.

- [ ] The students will document on their Scatter Diagram how much time is spent studying their multiplication facts each night before the day of the multiplication timed test.

- [ ] The students will take a timed multiplication test one day a week for six weeks.

- [ ] The students will document their score on their Scatter Diagram after taking the timed test.

- [ ] The students will assess the situation after documenting their scores vs. time spent studying for a six-week time period.

- [ ] In the next lesson, the class will move on to analyze possible causes of why they haven't been doing well on their timed math tests.

## Pre-Lesson Activities

- [ ] Obtain copies of the worksheet that goes with the lesson.

- [ ] Obtain all materials needed for the lesson.

## Materials Needed

- [ ] Graph paper or plain white paper for students to create the Scatter Diagram.

- [ ] Chart paper or overhead and transparency to demonstrate how to complete the diagram.

- [ ] Pens, pencils, and overhead markers.

## Lesson Delivery/Procedure

- [ ] The students and the teacher will discuss the possible reasons why scores are not very high on the weekly timed multiplication tests.

- [ ] The class will also discuss why students are having a tough time completing two-digit by two-digit multiplication facts.

- [ ] The teacher will review the Scatter Diagram tool with students.

- [ ] The teacher will demonstrate how to make a Scatter Diagram.

- [ ] The students will mark on their individual Scatter Diagrams the amount of time spent studying and the scores students received on their weekly timed tests (worksheet 44).

- [ ] The students will mark their progress for a six-week time period.

- [ ] The class will analyze the results after the six-week time period and then move on to analyze possible causes of why they haven't been doing well on their timed math tests.

## Guided Practice

- [ ] The students will be instructed on how to complete the Scatter Diagram.

- [ ] The students will complete their Scatter Diagram independently.

- [ ] The teacher will monitor weekly documentation of students marking their Scatter Diagrams.

- [ ] After the six-week time period is up the teacher will guide the students in analyzing the results of the Scatter Diagram.

## Supporting Resources

- ☐ *The Hershey's Milk Chocolate Multiplication Book* by Jerry Pallotta and Rob Bolster
- ☐ *Amanda Bean's Amazing Dream: A Mathematical Story* by Cindy Neuschwander
- ☐ *www.naturalmath.com/mult/*
- ☐ *www.mathforum.org*
- ☐ Worksheet 44

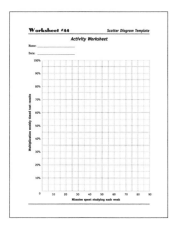

# Multiplication PDSA: Part B

Investigate, represent, and solve problems using number facts and operations and their properties, algorithms, and relationships.

**Estimated Time:** 45 minutes initially, then again after a predetermined time by the teacher

**Worksheets:** 45, 46, and 47

## PDSA Background Information

Up to this point, students have completed the Scatter Diagram to gather baseline data in the PDSA cycle. The next step is to determine root cause.

## Quality Tool/PDSA Linkage

- ☐ Students will use a Cause-and-Effect Diagram.

  - The Cause-and-Effect Diagram is a picture of the output of a brainstorming session that asks, "What causes . . .", and is used to determine root causes in the plan portion of the PDSA cycle.

## Lesson Overview

- ☐ The students will analyze possible root causes of why they haven't been doing well on their timed math tests.

- ☐ The students will use the Cause-and-Effect Diagram to list the possible causes of not knowing their multiplication facts.

- ☐ The students and teacher will create an improvement theory based on root causes identified in the Cause-and-Effect Diagram.

## Lesson Objectives

- ☐ The students will analyze the causes and effects identified leading to why they may not be doing well on their timed multiplication timed tests.

- ☐ The students will also identify reasons why they may not be doing well on completing two-digit by two-digit multiplication problems in a timely manner.

- ☐ The students will create an improvement theory based on what was learned from the Cause-and-Effect Diagram.

## Pre-Lesson Activities

- ☐ The class should have completed Multiplication PDSA: Part A.

- ☐ Obtain copies of the worksheets that go with the lesson.

- ☐ Obtain all materials needed for the lesson.

## Materials Needed

- ☐ Cause-and-Effect Diagram to analyze the cause and effect issues (worksheet 46).

- ☐ Piece of plain white poster-size paper to make a classroom size chart of the improvement theory that was developed by the class.

- ☐ Individual lined paper for students to write down the improvement theory so they may keep it with them and share it at home with the people who may help them study.

- ☐ Pens, pencils, and overhead markers.

- ☐ Worksheets.

## Lesson Delivery/Procedure

- ☐ The students will review with the teacher the Scatter Diagram results from the previous lesson (Multiplication PDSA: Part A).
- ☐ The teacher will model and review how to make a Cause-and-Effect Diagram to help analyze a cause-and-effect relationship (example on worksheet 45).
- ☐ The teacher and students will work on creating a Cause-and-Effect Diagram to help analyze the how the class as a whole can improve (worksheet 46).
- ☐ The students will first create a Cause-and-Effect Diagram with the teacher guiding them through the steps.
- ☐ The students will then create a Cause-and-Effect Diagram on their own to help them discover what the causes to their problem with multiplication might be.
- ☐ The students will then create an improvement theory for the class as a whole.
- ☐ The students will then create an individualized improvement theory for themselves.

## Guided Practice

- ☐ The students will review with the teacher the Scatter Diagram results from the previous lesson.
- ☐ The teacher will lead the class in making a large Cause-and-Effect Diagram of the causes and effects of the problems identified with multiplication.
- ☐ The students will then create their own Cause-and-Effect Diagram analyzing their own causes and effects for the multiplication problem.
- ☐ The students will then have an opportunity to share what they came up with on their Cause-and-Effect Diagrams.
- ☐ The large Cause-and-Effect Diagram will be posted for all students to see.
- ☐ The class will work together to create an improvement theory based on what was learned in the Cause-and-Effect Diagram.
- ☐ The improvement theory will be displayed next to the Cause-and-Effect Diagram so students will be able to view them at different times during the day.

## Supporting Resources

- ☐ *The Hershey's Milk Chocolate Multiplication Book* by Jerry Pallotta and Rob Bolster
- ☐ *Amanda Bean's Amazing Dream: A Mathematical Story* by Cindy Neuschwander
- ☐ *www.naturalmath.com/mult/*
- ☐ *www.mathforum.org*
- ☐ Worksheets 45, 46, and 47

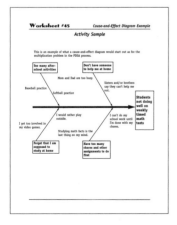
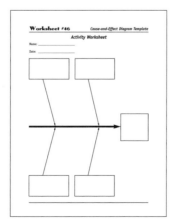

# Multiplication PDSA: Part C

Investigate, represent, and solve problems using number facts and operations and their properties, algorithms, and relationships.

**Estimated Time:** 45 minutes initially, then again after a predetermined time by the teacher

**Worksheets:** 48 and 49

## PDSA Background Information

Up to this point, students have completed the Scatter Diagram and the Cause-and-Effect Diagram in the PDSA cycle. The next step is to test the improvement theory.

## Quality Tool/PDSA Linkage

☐ Students will use the Force-Field Analysis and WWW Chart/Action Plan.

- The Force-Field Analysis is a tool used to evaluate the forces driving and restraining a desired change and is used during the plan portion of the PDSA cycle to generate the most comprehensive plan possible to test the improvement theory.

- The WWW Chart/Action Plan is a description of the actions necessary to create a desired change and is used in the plan portion of the PDSA cycle when preparing to test the improvement theory.

## Lesson Overview

☐ The students will analyze the factors that may be helping or hindering them in learning their multiplication facts though the Force-Field Analysis.

☐ The students will create an Action Plan based on what is learned from the Force-Field Analysis.

☐ The students will take the Action Plan and then use that information to complete the WWW Chart/Action Plan.

## Lesson Objectives

☐ The students will determine what driving forces and restraining forces are factors in learning their multiplication facts.

☐ The students will use these factors to help them determine an Action Plan that will try and allow them to become more successful with learning their facts.

☐ The students will then complete the WWW Chart/Action Plan to help the class know who should be responsible for what in the improvement theory developed in the lesson.

## Pre-Lesson Activities

☐ The class should have completed Multiplication PDSA: Part B.

☐ Obtain copies of the worksheets that go with the lesson.

☐ Obtain all materials needed for the lesson.

☐ Discuss with students what the terms "driving" and "restraining" forces mean.

## Materials Needed

- ☐ Force-Field Analysis (worksheet 48).
- ☐ WWW Chart (worksheet 49).
- ☐ Pens, pencils, and overhead markers.

## Lesson Delivery/Procedure

- ☐ The students will review the improvement theory from the previous lesson (Multiplication PDSA: Part B) with the teacher.
- ☐ The teacher will review the Force-Field Analysis tool with students.
- ☐ The students will complete the Force-Field Analysis, identifying driving and restraining forces.
- ☐ The students will then make an Action Plan based on what was learned from the Force-Field Analysis.
- ☐ The teacher will review the WWW tool with students.
- ☐ The students will create a WWW Chart to help the class and the students stayed focused.

## Guided Practice

- ☐ The teacher will review the improvement theory with students.
- ☐ The teacher will review with the students the definitions of driving and restraining forces.
- ☐ The teacher will lead the class in making a Force-Field Analysis.
- ☐ The class will analyze the material that was contributed to the Force-Field Analysis and make an Action Plan for all to try and follow.
- ☐ The students will then take the Action Plan and create a WWW Chart to plan out the steps to be taken.

## Supporting Resources

- ☐ *The Hershey's Milk Chocolate Multiplication Book* by Jerry Pallotta and Rob Bolster
- ☐ *Amanda Bean's Amazing Dream:A Mathematical Story* by Cindy Neuschwander
- ☐ *www.naturalmath.com/mult/*
- ☐ *www.mathforum.org*
- ☐ Worksheets 48 and 49

# Multiplication PDSA: Part D

Investigate, represent, and solve problems using number facts and operations and their properties, algorithms, and relationships.

**Estimated Time:** 45 minutes initially.
then again after a
predetermined time
by the teacher

**Worksheets:** 50, 51, and 52

## PDSA Background Information

Up to this point, students have completed the Scatter Diagram, the Cause-and-Effect Diagram, the Force-Field Analysis, and the WWW Chart to test the improvement theory. It is now time to move into the study portion of the PDSA cycle, and check the new data against the prior data.

## Quality Tool/PDSA Linkage

☐ Students will use a Pareto Diagram, a Radar Chart, and a Run Chart.

• The Pareto Diagram is a bar chart that ranks categorical data from largest to smallest to find the "significant few" in the plan portion of the PDSA cycle.

• The Radar Chart is a graph with multiple scales to report self-assessed knowledge or competence, often over time and is used during both the plan and study portions of the PDSA cycle.

• The Run/Control Chart graphically reports system performance over time and is used to compare performance before and after changes in both the plan and study portions of the PDSA cycle.

## Lesson Overview

☐ The students will mark the Radar Chart based on how they feel about knowing their multiplication facts.

☐ The students will then take the data from their timed multiplication tests and plot it on a Run Chart.

☐ Finally, the students will help the teacher compile the information into a Pareto Diagram.

## Lesson Objective

☐ The students will determine what factors of multiplication are still difficult to learn and then transfer that data to a Pareto Diagram to help determine if the improvement theory worked.

## Pre-Lesson Activities

☐ The class should have completed Multiplication PDSA: Part C.

☐ Obtain copies of the worksheets that go with the lesson.

☐ Obtain all materials needed for the lesson.

☐ Discuss with students the importance of knowing if improvement has been made with the problems they have been trying to improve on.

## Materials Needed

☐ Worksheets 50, 51, and 52.

☐ Pens, pencils, and overhead markers.

## Lesson Delivery/Procedure

- ☐ The students will recall the improvement theory already created in the previous lesson.
- ☐ The teacher will review the Radar Chart tool with students.
- ☐ The students will complete the Radar Chart, gauging their current level of knowledge.
- ☐ The teacher will review the Run Chart tool with students.
- ☐ The students will then make a Run Chart, charting their progress on the weekly time tests (worksheet 51).
- ☐ The teacher will review the Pareto Diagram tool with students.
- ☐ The students and the teacher will then create a Pareto Diagram together, identifying which factors were missed most (worksheet 52).

## Guided Practice

- ☐ The teacher will review with the students how to mark the Radar Chart indicating how students feel about their knowledge of multiplication facts. Students may work individually or with a partner.
- ☐ The teacher will guide students in charting their results on their individualized Run Chart.
- ☐ The class will then give their information to the teacher so that the information can be complied into a Pareto Diagram.
- ☐ Students will indicate which factors were missed most in the weekly time tests.
- ☐ The class will analyze the material that was contributed to the Pareto Diagram and decide if the improvement theory worked or if parts of it need to be reworked to have a greater success.

## Supporting Resources

- ☐ *The Hershey's Milk Chocolate Multiplication Book* by Jerry Pallotta and Rob Bolster
- ☐ *Amanda Bean's Amazing Dream A Mathematical Story* by Cindy Neuschwander
- ☐ *www.naturalmath.com/mult/*
- ☐ *www.mathforum.org*
- ☐ Worksheets 50, 51, and 52

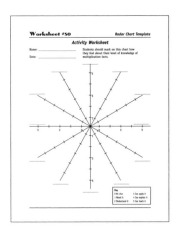
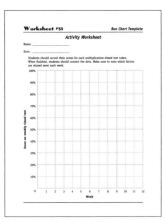
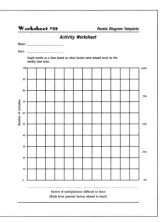

# Multiplication PDSA: Part E

Investigate, represent, and solve problems using number facts and operations and their properties, algorithms, and relationships.

**Estimated Time:** 45 minutes initially, then again after a predetermined time by the teacher

**Worksheet:** 53

## PDSA Background Information

Up to this point, students have completed the Scatter Diagram, Cause-and-Effect Diagram, Force-Field Analysis, and the WWW Chart in the PDSA cycle. To compare the baseline data prior to implementing the improvement theory with the current data, the class completed the Radar Chart, Run Chart, and the Pareto Diagram. The final step of the PDSA cycle is to Act to make improvements a standard part of the process. This will be done by creating a Flowchart.

## Quality Tool/PDSA Linkage

☐ Students will use a Flowchart.

  • The Flowchart is a drawing of any process used to document the flow of activities during the plan portion of the PDSA cycle.

## Lesson Overview

☐ The class will create a Flowchart of the improved process in order to document the new and improved process for multiplication.

## Lesson Objectives

☐ The class will identify strategies that helped them become successful with their timed multiplication tests.

☐ The students will create a Flowchart indicating which steps to take to be successful and what to do if they get stuck in one area.

## Pre-Lesson Activities

☐ The class should have completed Multiplication PDSA: Part D.

☐ Obtain copies of the worksheet that goes with this lesson.

☐ Obtain all materials needed for the lesson.

☐ Discuss with students the importance of knowing if improvement has been made with the process students have been trying to improve.

## Materials Needed

☐ Pens, pencils, and overhead markers.

☐ Worksheet 53.

## Lesson Delivery/Procedure

- ☐ The students will review with the teacher the improvement theory already created.
- ☐ The teacher will review with the students the steps in making a Flowchart.
- ☐ The class will discuss ideas that helped them become successful with learning their multiplication facts.
- ☐ The students will take into consideration the helpful ideas, as well as the items that got them confused, so students will know what to watch out for when creating their Flowchart.
- ☐ The class will create a Flowchart that documents the new multiplication process.

## Guided Practice

- ☐ The teacher will guide students in the final stages of making their Flowchart.
- ☐ Students will complete the Flowchart (worksheet 53) and share it with another student.

## Assessment

- ☐ Students will share the key steps in the PDSA process and the key tools used.
- ☐ Students will utilize the new process for multiplication in their daily work.

## Supporting Resources

- ☐ *The Hershey's Milk Chocolate Multiplication Book* by Jerry Pallotta and Rob Bolster
- ☐ *Amanda Bean's Amazing Dream: A Mathematical Story* by Cindy Neuschwander
- ☐ *www.naturalmath.com/mult/*
- ☐ *www.mathforum.org*
- ☐ Worksheet 53

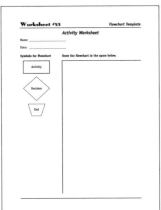

# Collecting Data

Collect, organize, and display data using tables, charts, bar graphs, line graphs, circle graphs, line plots, and stem-and-leaf graphs.

**Estimated Time:** 45 minutes          **Worksheets:** 54 and 55

## Quality Tool/PDSA Linkage

☐ Students will use the Scatter Diagram.

- The Scatter Diagram is a tool used to show the relationship between two factors in the plan portion of the PDSA cycle.

## Lesson Overview

☐ This is a hands-on lesson designed to demonstrate how to collect and interpret data.

☐ The students will participate in an activity that will provide data to collect.

☐ The students will then make a Scatter Diagram of their results and analyze their data.

## Lesson Objectives

☐ The students will learn appropriate techniques for collecting data.

☐ The students will learn how to analyze the collected data.

☐ The students will use a Scatter Diagram to display and predict outcomes.

## Pre-Lesson Activities

☐ Obtain copies of the worksheets that go with the lesson.

☐ Obtain all materials needed for the lesson.

☐ Review graphing vocabulary with the students.

## Materials Needed

☐ One stop watch.

☐ Worksheets for each student.

## Lesson Delivery/Procedure

☐ After reviewing the procedure for graphing data, the teacher will announce that the students will be conducting an experiment.

☐ The teacher will call two students to the front of the room (enough space will eventually be needed for everyone in the class to get in the circle). The two students should hold hands.

☐ The teacher will designate a student as timekeeper. When the timekeeper says "now," the first person should squeeze the hand of the second person who then squeezes the other hand of the first person. The last person will say "now" when the hand squeeze has come back to him or her.

☐ The teacher has the students record the number of seconds on their data table (worksheet 54).

☐ The teacher then has the students predict what will happen as they add more students to the circle.

- ☐ The teacher will select two more students for the circle and the process of passing the hand squeeze around the circle is repeated. The number of seconds is recorded.
- ☐ This process is repeated until all students are in the circle.
- ☐ Record data on data collection sheet (worksheet 54).
- ☐ The teacher will review the Scatter Diagram tool with students.
- ☐ The teacher will model how the students should plot their points on the Scatter Diagram (worksheet 55) by demonstrating the first point letting the *x* axis represent the number of students and the *y* axis represent the number of seconds.

## Guided Practice

- ☐ The teacher will observe as the students plot the rest of the data on the Scatter Diagram.

## Assessment

- ☐ The students will look at the relationship between length of time and number of students and draw conclusions.
- ☐ The students will review their predictions and use their Scatter Diagrams to explain if their predictions were correct or not.
- ☐ The students will summarize their findings by reporting out and sharing their findings with another student.
- ☐ The students will predict how many seconds it would take to pass squeezes between 100 students. They will then convert that number to minutes.
- ☐ The teacher will evaluate student work, discussion, and findings to gauge the level of understanding.

## Post-Lesson/Follow-Up Activities/Extensions

- ☐ Another activity could be timed using the same number of people.
- ☐ Students could use a computer program to create their Scatter Diagram.
- ☐ One hundred students could participate in this activity on the 100th day of the year or school year.

## Supporting Resources

- ☐ nces.ed.gov/nceskids/graphing/index.asp
- ☐ Worksheets 54 and 55

# Division

Investigate, represent, and solve problems using number facts and operations (addition, subtraction, multiplication, division), and their properties, algorithms, and relationships.

**Estimated Time:** 45 minutes        **Worksheets:** 56, 57, and 58

## Quality Tool/PDSA Linkage

☐ Students will use a Flowchart and Force-Field Analysis.

- The Flowchart is a drawing of any process used to document the process flow during the plan portion of the PDSA cycle.

- Force-Field Analysis is a tool used to evaluate the forces driving and restraining a desired change and is used during the plan portion of the PDSA cycle to generate the most comprehensive plan possible to test the improvement theory.

## Lesson Overview

☐ In this lesson the students will be learning how to complete simple division number sentences.

☐ The students will use the Flowchart to assist in the steps to be taken when completing a division problem.

☐ The students and the teacher will complete a Force-Field Analysis to help students identify why they have difficulty with division facts.

## Lesson Objectives

☐ The students will review their multiplication facts.

☐ The students will explain that division is the opposite operation from multiplication.

☐ The students will learn how to complete division problems.

☐ The students will learn how to use the Flowchart and Force-Field Analysis.

## Pre-Lesson Activities

☐ Review with the students their multiplication facts using flash cards.

☐ Obtain copies of the worksheets that go with the lesson.

☐ Obtain all materials needed for the lesson.

☐ Create a large poster-size blank Flowchart (similar to worksheet 56) to be filled in with the students during the lesson.

☐ Write the vocabulary words on large index cards to use in the lesson (dividend, divisor, quotient).

☐ Write the stages of the Flowchart onto large index cards.

## Materials Needed

☐ Multiplication flashcards.

☐ Tape.

☐ Chart paper.

☐ Markers.

☐ Index cards.

☐ Division problems.

## Lesson Delivery/Procedure

- ☐ The teacher will write a simple addition problem on the board (5 + 3 = ?).
- ☐ The teacher will ask the students to first solve the addition problem, and then ask them how they can check the problem. What is the opposite of addition?
- ☐ The teacher will ask the students how division is related to multiplication.
- ☐ The teacher will give the students a simple multiplication problem to solve (4 × 3 = ?).
- ☐ The students will answer that 4 × 3 = 12.
- ☐ The teacher can then write on the board the problem 4 × ? = 12.
- ☐ The students can answer 3.
- ☐ Now the teacher can write the division problem 12 ÷ 3 = ?
- ☐ The students will answer 4.
- ☐ The teacher will keep the problem up on the board and explain that just like in multiplication, each number has a name.
- ☐ The teacher will read the three name cards as they place them on the chalkboard ledge.
- ☐ The teacher will ask the students to predict what each of the numbers in the problem is called.
- ☐ The teacher will explain what each of the words mean using the problem above.
      12 = dividend, 3 = divisor, 4 = quotient
- ☐ The teacher will give several more practice division problems (use problems from the division worksheet 58).
- ☐ The teacher will review the Flowchart tool with students.

## Guided Practice

- ☐ The teacher and students will look at the large Flowchart (worksheet 56) at the front of the room.
- ☐ The teacher will explain that the Flowchart is used to show a process.
- ☐ The teacher will show the index cards with the different stages of the Flowchart on them.
- ☐ Students will try to place the index cards in the correct place on the Flowchart by talking through the process of how to do a division problem.
- ☐ Once the students think they have the cards in the correct place, the teacher will have the students complete a division problem using the Flowchart they completed.
- ☐ If the steps are not in the correct place then the students can rearrange as needed.
- ☐ Give the students a basic division worksheet to complete (see worksheet 58).

## Assessment

- ☐ The student will apply the knowledge gained to solve division facts.
- ☐ The teacher will be able to judge, based on the worksheet, their level of understanding of basic division facts.
- ☐ The teacher will also be able to judge the students' understanding of the division process when the teacher and students completed the Flowchart.

## Post-Lesson/Follow-Up Activities/Extensions

- ☐ As a class, complete a Force-Field Analysis to analyze the driving and restraining forces that surround the students learning of division facts (see worksheet 57). The teacher will need to review the Force-Field Analysis tool with students.

# Supporting Resources

- [ ] *Nimble with Numbers* by Leigh Childs and Laura Choate
- [ ] *Skill Drill Math* by Frank Schaffer Publications
- [ ] Worksheets 56, 57, and 58

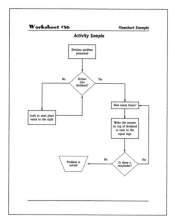

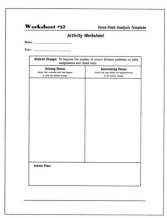

# Organizing Data

Estimate measurements and determine acceptable levels of accuracy. Measure and compare quantities using appropriate units, instruments, and methods.

**Estimated Time:** Day 1: 20 minutes  
Day 2–5: 10 minutes (Data collection)  
Day 6: 60 minutes

**Worksheets:** 59, 60, and 61

## Quality Tool/PDSA Linkage

☐ Students will use the Check Sheet, Run Chart, and Pareto Diagram.

- The Check Sheet/Matrix is a tool to collect and organize data in the plan portion of the PDSA cycle.

- The Run/Control Chart graphically reports system performance over time and is used to compare performance before and after changes in both the plan and study portions of the PDSA cycle.

- The Pareto Diagram is a bar chart that ranks categorical data from largest to smallest to find the "significant few" in the plan portion of the PDSA cycle.

## Lesson Overview

☐ The students will use blowing bubbles with bubble gum in order to work with the quality tools.

☐ The students will use the Check Sheet, Pareto Diagram, and Run Chart to collect and organize their data.

## Lesson Objectives

☐ The students will understand and use the Check Sheet, Run Chart, and Pareto Diagram.

☐ The students will chart the number of bubbles they can blow in two minutes.

☐ The students will collect data for five days.

☐ The students will work with a partner.

☐ The students will collect their data on a Check Sheet.

☐ The students will use an individual Pareto Diagram to show how many bubbles were blown in two minutes.

☐ A class Run Chart will be completed. Each student will use a different color; this will show comparison from student to student.

## Pre-Lesson Activities

☐ The students should have some experience with charting and data collection.

☐ The students should have some experience in organizing and interpreting data.

☐ Obtain copies of the worksheets that go with the lesson.

☐ Obtain all materials needed for the lesson.

## Materials Needed

☐ Chart paper.

☐ Bubble gum.

☐ Markers.

☐ Post-It notes.

## Lesson Delivery/Procedure

- ☐ The teacher will review the Check Sheet and its use. The teacher will demonstrate how the Check Sheet (worksheet 59) is used with an example.
- ☐ The teacher will explain the bubble gum activity.
- ☐ The students will create ground rules for this activity.
- ☐ The teacher will post the ground rules and review them daily.
- ☐ The teacher will divide the students in pairs and distribute bubble gum and the Check Sheet template (worksheet 59).
- ☐ The students will follow this same procedure for the five days of data collection.
- ☐ The teacher will introduce the Run Chart and Pareto Diagram. The teacher will give students examples of the use of these two quality tools in organizing their data so the students understand the tools.
- ☐ The students will use a Pareto Diagram (worksheet 60) to chart their data.
- ☐ The students will each chart their data on a classroom Run Chart (worksheet 61) using different colors. This will show comparison from student to student.
- ☐ The teacher and students will discuss high, lows, and averages. Together they will brainstorm conclusions that can be drawn from their data. They will record their observations on chart paper.

## Guided Practice

- ☐ Each student will complete his or her own Check Sheet from data collected daily.
- ☐ The students will organize the Data they have collected on a Pareto Diagram and a classroom Run Chart.

## Assessment

- ☐ The students will be able to use and apply the data collection tools: Check Sheet, Run Chart, and Pareto Diagram.
- ☐ The student will self-evaluate individual Check Sheets and Pareto Diagram to determine understanding of tools and concepts of working with data.
- ☐ The students will reflect on their learning; they will write about their experience with this project.

## Post-Lesson/Follow-Up Activities/Extensions

- ☐ The students could take this process one step further and collect data on the circumference of the bubble blown.
- ☐ The students can design their own method for data collection of a project using the quality tools learned.

## Supporting Resources

- ☐ Worksheets 59, 60, and 61

# Multiplication—Single Lesson

Investigate, represent, and solve problems using number facts and operations and their properties, algorithms, and relationships.

**Estimated Time:** 45 minutes
(and then another 45 minutes
at another time)

**Worksheets:** 62 and 63

## Quality Tool/PDSA Linkage

☐ Students will use a Radar Chart and a Force-Field Analysis.

- The Radar Chart is a graph with multiple scales to report self-assessed knowledge or competence, often over time and is used during both the plan and study portions of the PDSA cycle.

- Force-Field Analysis is a tool used to evaluate the forces driving and restraining a desired change and is used during the plan portion of the PDSA cycle to generate the most comprehensive plan possible to test the improvement theory.

## Lesson Overview

☐ This lesson is designed to help students analyze which facts they are having problems with in timed multiplication facts.

☐ The students will use the Radar Chart to help them determine their comfort level with the multiplication facts before and after different strategies are taught to the students.

☐ The students and teacher will use the Force-Field Analysis to help determine the factors that keep the students from remembering their multiplication facts.

## Lesson Objectives

☐ The students will complete the Radar Chart to help them identify their comfort level with the different set of facts they are expected to know.

☐ The students will take a timed multiplication test for each of the factors 0–12 to get a baseline for their current achievement levels.

☐ The students will complete the Force-Field Analysis as a class to determine what things help students learn facts and what elements hurt students when they are trying to learn their facts.

☐ The students will learn the multiplication facts from 0–12 through strategies taught by the teacher and the use of flashcards.

☐ The students will learn different strategies to help them retain the facts they have learned.

☐ The students will chart their progress in taking the timed math tests so they can analyze their progress.

☐ The students will complete the Radar Chart again to see where they are with their comfort level at the end of the strategy sessions in learning their facts.

## Pre-Lesson Activities

- ☐ Obtain copies of the worksheets that go with the lesson.
- ☐ Have flashcards ready for students to study their multiplication facts. (If possible, have students make their own set of flashcards to take home or leave as shown.)
- ☐ Obtain all materials needed for the lesson.

## Materials Needed

- ☐ Index cards for students' flashcards.
- ☐ Chart paper for Radar Chart and Force-Field Analysis.
- ☐ Chalkboards and/or dry erase boards for students to practice their facts with partners.
- ☐ Graph paper for students to chart their progress of learning their multiplication facts.
- ☐ Colored dots or markers.

## Lesson Delivery/Procedure

- ☐ The teacher will review the Radar Chart tool with students.
- ☐ The students will obtain baseline data using an individual Radar Chart. Students will indicate what they feel their current level of knowledge is on each of the multiplication facts 0–12 (worksheet 63).
- ☐ The students will be instructed on how to complete the Radar Chart. The teacher will model the process.
- ☐ The students will complete their Radar Chart independently.
- ☐ The class and teacher will average the Radar Chart data to then compile a class Radar Chart to establish a baseline measurement.
- ☐ The teacher will introduce the Force-Field Analysis tool and discuss its purpose.
- ☐ The students will work with the teacher to complete the Force-Field Analysis chart focusing on how to get better at multiplication facts (worksheet 62).
- ☐ The class will complete a Force-Field Analysis to determine the activities that help them learn their facts and the activities that hindered their fact learning.

## Guided Practice

- ☐ The students will develop an Action Plan to help them overcome the restraining forces (identified in the Force-Field Analysis).
- ☐ The students will spend some time carrying out their Action Plan to study their facts.

## Assessment

- ☐ After the given time, students will summarize their findings by reporting out and sharing their results and progress with another student.
- ☐ The students will once again come back together as a class and complete their individual Radar Chart (for the second time) to establish their new comfort level with knowing their facts.
- ☐ The teacher will take out the original Radar Chart and display the new levels (class average) on that same chart but using a different colored marker or dots so that students can compare the baseline data with the new data collected.
- ☐ The teacher will review student work, discussion, and findings to gauge level of understanding.
- ☐ The teacher will summarize the lesson objectives, findings, and key concepts of the lesson to remember with students.

## Post-Lesson/Follow-Up Activities/Extensions

- ☐ The students can spend time studying their multiplication facts with family members.

- ☐ The students can make up story problems involving multiplication facts and share them with other students.

- ☐ The students can share their Force-Field Analysis with family members and try using that strategy to solve some problems at home.

## Supporting Resources

- ☐ *The Hershey's Milk Chocolate Multiplication Book* by Jerry Pallotta and Rob Bolster

- ☐ *Amanda Bean's Amazing Dream: A Mathematical Story* by Cindy Neuschwander

- ☐ *www.naturalmath.com/mult/*

- ☐ *www.mathforum.org*

- ☐ Worksheets 62 and 63

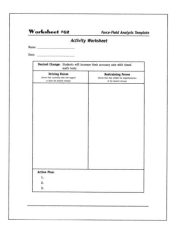

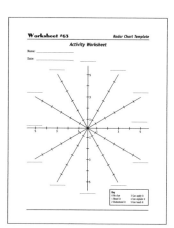

# Quality Across the Curriculum

# SCIENCE

## K-1

### LESSONS

Insects . . . . . . . . . . . . . . . . . 79

Living/Nonliving Things . . . . . 83

Weather . . . . . . . . . . . . . . . . 87

Tree Identification . . . . . . . . 91

Five Senses . . . . . . . . . . . . . . 95

Physical and Chemical
   Changes . . . . . . . . . . . . . . . 99

Rocks . . . . . . . . . . . . . . . . . 103

Dinosaurs . . . . . . . . . . . . . . 105

Simple Machines . . . . . . . . . 109

# Insects

Understand the fundamental concepts, principles, and interconnections of the life, physical, and earth/space sciences.

**Estimated Time:** 15–30 minutes          **Worksheets:** 64 and 65

## Quality Tool/PDSA Linkage

☐ Students will use the Flowchart and Bar Chart.

- The Flowchart is a drawing of any process used to document the process flow during the plan portion of the PDSA cycle.

- The Bar Chart is a graph of categorical data plotted by frequency, and is used in the plan portion of the PDSA cycle.

## Lesson Overview

☐ This lesson is designed for whole class participation in researching the lifecycles of insects. Many insects go through four stages of growth in their lifecycle called metamorphoses. The students and the teacher will read books in shared reading experiences to learn more about the lifecycles of at least five insects.

☐ The students will illustrate and/or label the lifecycles using a Flowchart.

☐ The students will then indicate their favorite insect on a Bar Chart.

## Lesson Objectives

☐ The students will learn basic research skills.

☐ The students will listen attentively during shared reading of nonfiction books about insects.

☐ The students will participate in whole-class discussions about the lifecycles of insects.

☐ The students will identify the four stages of insect lifecycles.

☐ The students will build vocabulary skills.

☐ The students will understand and use the Flowchart quality tool by participating in whole-class completion of the Flowcharts and copying one accurately.

☐ The students will understand and use the Bar Chart quality tool by filling in their own bar (favorite insect), and interpreting the Bar Chart.

## Pre-Lesson Activities

☐ Begin the study of insects at least two weeks prior to this lesson to increase background knowledge.

☐ Obtain a selection of nonfiction books about insects.

☐ Enlarge the Flowchart, worksheet 64. One per insect studied.

☐ Obtain copies of the worksheets that go with the lesson.

☐ Photocopy the Bar Chart, worksheet 65, and add insect names of choice. Either enlarged or one per student.

☐ Obtain all materials needed for the lesson.

## Materials Needed

☐ Nonfiction books about a variety of insects.

☐ Enlarged Flowcharts.

☐ Individual Flowcharts.

☐ Markers.

## Lesson Delivery/Procedure

☐ The teacher will review the definition of an insect and introduce the terms lifecycle and metamorphoses.

☐ The teacher will review the Flowchart tool with students.

☐ The teacher will display the first poster-size Flowchart (worksheet 64) and explain that after reading a book about insects, the class will complete a Flowchart together by labeling and illustrating the lifecycle of each insect.

☐ Common insects to consider are an ant, butterfly, bee, ladybug, grain beetle, and firefly. Others include a fly, grasshopper, walking stick, praying mantis, wasp, moth, cricket, mosquito, or dragonfly.

☐ The teacher will model the process by reading about, labeling, and illustrating the lifecycle of one insect (enlarged worksheet 64). For example, a grain beetle lifecycle would be egg—larva (mealworms)—pupa—adult (grain beetle).

☐ During each consecutive reading session, the class will read about, label, and illustrate the lifecycle of an insect. Students can take turns illustrating the growth stages on the enlarged Flowcharts. (The number of insects researched is determined by the teacher.)

☐ When five to six insect lifecycles are illustrated on the Flowcharts, post the enlarged charts around the classroom.

☐ Distribute the individual Flowchart worksheets to the students. Ask that they select and copy the lifecycle of one insect onto their individual Flowchart. Students may refer back to the books used for the initial drawings.

☐ In the last part of the lesson, students will indicate their favorite insect on the Bar Chart (worksheet 65).

☐ The teacher will review the Bar Chart tool with students.

☐ Display the Bar Chart (worksheet 65) with the five-six previously researched insects listed. (Modifications include enlarging the Bar Chart and/or replicating the chart for a pocket chart format.)

☐ Ask the students to fill in a square above their favorite insect. Before returning to their seats, have the students explain why they made the choice that they did.

☐ Interpret and discuss the Bar Chart by asking such questions as "What insect did most students choose as their favorite?" "What insect was the least favorite?" "Why do you think the (insect name) was not selected as a favorite?"

## Guided Practice

☐ As an option, cooperative groups can research other insects and complete a Flowchart together.

☐ Students can help create a class big book about the lifecycles of insects using the Flowchart as their format.

☐ Students can observe the metamorphoses of grain beetles. Mealworms are readily available at pet stores or bait shops. This activity is included in many resource books about the study of insects. Students keep mealworms in cups on their desks and observe the process of change from the larva stage (mealworms) to the adult stage (grain beetle).

☐ Students can find advantages and disadvantages of insects. For example, we need bees for pollination and honey but do not like to get stung by them!

## Assessment

- ☐ Students will participate in and contribute to whole-class discussions during completion of each insect lifecycle on the enlarged Flowcharts.

- ☐ The students will explain their (copied) insect lifecycle Flowcharts.

- ☐ The students will identify four stages in the lifecycle of the researched insects by matching a picture to its correct term.

- ☐ The students will demonstrate beginning research skills by finding and identifying pictures of insect lifecycles in nonfiction books.

- ☐ The students will interpret the Bar Chart by making two correct statements (verbally or in writing) about the data shown.

- ☐ The students will build vocabulary skills by correctly reading and pronouncing at least two stages of an insect lifecycle.

## Post-Lesson/Follow-Up Activities/Extensions

- ☐ Create three-dimensional insects from common materials (for example, egg carton caterpillars or painted rock ladybugs).

- ☐ The students will learn the difference between insects and spiders.

- ☐ The students will create new insects by combining the names of two insects, for example ladybug + fly = "ladyfly." The students can illustrate their new insects.

- ☐ The students can further their study of insects by discussing the different ways insects move, what they eat, where they live, and what sounds they make.

- ☐ The students can take a nature walk with the teacher or parent/guardian and observe insects in their neighborhood.

## Supporting Resources

- ☐ (Entomology for Beginners) Web site *www.bijlmakers.com/entomology/begin.htm*

- ☐ *The Icky Bug Alphabet Book* by Jerry Pallotta

- ☐ *The Life Cycle of a Praying Mantis* by Andrew Hipp

- ☐ *I'm a Caterpillar* by Jean Marzollo

- ☐ *The Butterfly* and *The Ladybug* by Sabrina Crewe

- ☐ Worksheets 64 and 65

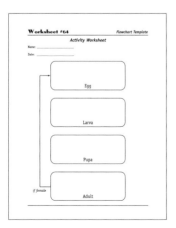

# Living/Nonliving Things

Know and apply concepts that describe how living things interact with each other and with their environment.

**Estimated Time:** 45 minutes     **Worksheets:** 66 and 67

## Quality Tool/PDSA Linkage

☐ Students will use the Affinity Diagram and the Lotus Diagram.

- The Affinity Diagram is a tool to generate, organize, and consolidate information gathered through Brainstorming, and is used in many portions of the PDSA cycle.
- The Lotus Diagram is a tool to expand thinking around a single topic or theme and is used at any portion of the PDSA cycle to generate additional thoughts.

## Lesson Overview

☐ In this lesson, students will use picture cards or real live examples to compare and contrast living and nonliving objects.

☐ In addition to comparing living and nonliving things, students will expand upon their observations of living or nonliving things using the Lotus Diagram.

☐ The students will understand and use the Affinity Diagram tool to organize their ideas.

## Lesson Objectives

☐ The students will state characteristics of living and nonliving things.

☐ The students will sort characteristics of objects as those of living or nonliving things.

☐ The students will use the Affinity Diagram to classify their data.

☐ The students will use the Lotus Diagram to expand upon and organize their data.

## Pre-Lesson Activities

☐ Obtain copies of the worksheets that go with the lesson.

☐ Review the characteristics of living and nonliving things with students, possibly displaying items that fit into each category.

☐ Obtain all materials needed for the lesson.

## Materials Needed

☐ Copies of the Lotus Diagram for each student, or a piece of paper folded into nine sections.

☐ Pencil or writing utensil for appropriate recording of data.

☐ Post-It notes.

☐ Large butcher paper or board space for Affinity Diagram.

☐ Markers.

☐ Pictures or actual representations of living and nonliving things.

## Lesson Delivery/Procedure

- ☐ The teacher will display a living object such as the class pet or a living plant. Alternatively, the teacher will display a picture of a nonliving thing.
- ☐ The teacher will elicit responses from students as to the characteristics of the object.
- ☐ The teacher will display an object such as a pencil or a desk.
- ☐ The teacher will elicit responses from students as to the characteristics of that object.
- ☐ Students will use their observational skills to compare and contrast these items.

## Guided Practice

- ☐ The teacher will distribute Post-It notes to each student.
- ☐ The students will write one word or phrase (or picture) describing a characteristic of a living or a nonliving thing (for example, "moves," "grows")
- ☐ The teacher will review the Affinity Diagram tool with students.
- ☐ After all students have written or drawn two to three responses, they will bring them to the board or the butcher paper and place the Post-It note on the appropriate side (living/nonliving). The poster will look similar to worksheet 67.
- ☐ The teacher will review the Lotus Diagram tool with students.
- ☐ The teacher will distribute Lotus Diagram papers (worksheet 66) to all students. Students will work with a partner and label the center either "living" or "nonliving."
- ☐ The students will fill as many of the other eight spaces with words or pictures depicting the appropriate concept.
- ☐ The teacher will review student work, discussion, and findings to gauge level of understanding.

## Assessment

- ☐ The teacher will review student responses placed on Post-It notes.
- ☐ The students will place Post-It notes in the appropriate side, and group for similarities.
- ☐ The students will again work with their partner from the Lotus activity. Each partnership will work with another pair of students that completed an opposite Lotus Diagram. (If a group of students completed a "living" diagram, they will work with another group of students that completed a "nonliving" diagram.) Students will share their work with the new group of students and compare their work.
- ☐ The teacher will monitor student interactions, making adjustments to the Lotus Diagrams as necessary.

## Post-Lesson/Follow-Up Activities/Extensions

- ☐ Read aloud a nonfiction book about a living thing (see Supporting Resources section). Compare its characteristics against the students' Lotus Diagrams and Affinity Diagrams.
- ☐ Compare the Lotus Diagram of a nonliving item to the sidewalk or to the wall or another nonliving object.
- ☐ Draw pictures of living/nonliving things.
- ☐ More capable students: write an expository paragraph about a living thing or a nonliving thing.
- ☐ Write an expository paragraph as a group language experience activity.

## Supporting Resources

- [ ] *Every Living Thing* by Cynthia Rylant
- [ ] *Each Living Thing* by Joanne Ryder
- [ ] *The Magic School Bus Plants Seeds: A Book About How Things Grow* by Joanna Cole
- [ ] Worksheets 66 and 67

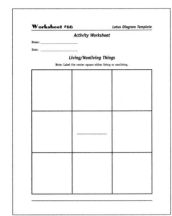

**Worksheet #66**    *Lotus Diagram Template*

**Activity Worksheet**

Name: _____

Date: _____

*Living/Nonliving Things*

Note: Label the center square either living or nonliving.

**Worksheet #67**    *Affinity Diagram Template*

**Activity Worksheet**

Name: _____

Date: _____

*Living/Nonliving Things*

| Living | Nonliving |
|---|---|
| Growing | Does not grow |
| Changing | Does not need water |
| Needs water | Does not die |
| Needs air | Does not need air |

# Weather

Know and apply concepts that describe the features and processes of the earth and its resources.

**Estimated Time:** 15–20 minutes          **Worksheets:** 68 and 69

## Quality Tool/PDSA Linkage

- [ ] Students will use the Affinity Diagram.

    - The Affinity Diagram is a tool to generate, organize, and consolidate information gathered through Brainstorming, and is used in many portions of the PDSA cycle.

## Lesson Overview

- [ ] This lesson is designed to help students Brainstorm what weather means to them and what are some of the elements of weather.

- [ ] The students will use the Affinity Diagram to sort information they have discussed with the teacher.

- [ ] The students and the teacher will put all of the elements that were discussed into groups to aide in further discussion.

## Lesson Objectives

- [ ] The students will learn different elements of weather systems.

- [ ] The students will share experiences they have had with weather.

- [ ] The students will learn how to sort information into different categories.

- [ ] The students will understand and use the Affinity Diagram quality tool.

## Pre-Lesson Activities

- [ ] Ask students if they know what the word "weather" means.

- [ ] Ask why weather is important to the earth.

- [ ] Read about weather-related material to stimulate interest in the topic to be discussed.

- [ ] The students will be given Post-It notes to write or draw an element they know about weather. Teachers may want to allow students to do more than one if possible and time allows.

- [ ] Obtain copies of the worksheets that go with the lesson.

- [ ] Obtain all materials needed for the lesson.

## Materials Needed

- [ ] Post-It notes.

- [ ] Large sheet of paper to put the Post-It notes on.

- [ ] Large sheet of paper to write categories on for discussion.

- [ ] Pencils for students.

- [ ] Markers for teacher.

- [ ] Weather-related books for students to look through to gain more understanding of topics.

## Lesson Delivery/Procedure

- ☐ The students will be given Post-It notes to write or draw an element they know about weather.
- ☐ The teacher may want to allow students to do more than one if possible and time allows.
- ☐ The teacher will read or show each of the student's writings or drawings that were discussed.
- ☐ As the teacher is reading and showing the student's work, it will be out on the large sheet of paper.
- ☐ The teacher, with the class assisting, will then put all of the Post-It notes into categories established by the students (see worksheet 68 as an example).
- ☐ The students will have an opportunity to share what experiences they have had with weather.
- ☐ The teacher will end the lesson by reading a book about weather and make available for students other books for students to view in the classroom at a later time.

## Guided Practice

- ☐ The teacher will review the Affinity Diagram tool with students (see worksheet 69 as an example).
- ☐ The students will write ideas about elements of weather on Post-It notes.
- ☐ The students will share their brainstormed ideas with the class.
- ☐ The class will put the ideas into like categories with teacher guidance.
- ☐ The class will discuss how weather is important to the earth.
- ☐ Depending on the students' level of interest and knowledge, the teacher can carry the conversation on further to include how the weather is helpful and harmful to people.

## Assessment

- ☐ The students will look at the brainstormed ideas and put the notes into related categories to complete the Affinity Diagram.
- ☐ The students will make notes of their understanding of the different elements of weather.
- ☐ The students will review their work, discussion, and findings to gauge level of understanding.
- ☐ The students will list key elements of weather.

## Post-Lesson/Follow-Up Activities/Extensions

- ☐ The students can spend time studying the weather and drawing pictures of what the weather is like each day for a week. Students can share what they learned about their drawings at school when the assignment has concluded.
- ☐ The students can make up a story about the weather and share it with their families.
- ☐ The students can use a make-believe bear and dress a student up in the appropriate clothing for the time of year the student is in currently or draw a card with different seasons and dress the bear according to what they see or read on the card.

## Supporting Resources

- ☐ *The Cloud Book* by Tomie De Paola
- ☐ *The Raindrops' Adventure: From Raindrops to Rainbows* by Kimberly Kerr
- ☐ *faldo.atmos.uiuc.edu/WEATHER/weather.html*
- ☐ Worksheets 68 and 69

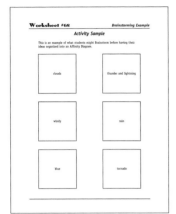

# Tree Identification

Know and apply concepts that explain how living things function, adapt, and change.

**Estimated Time:** 45 minutes          **Worksheets:** 70 and 71

## Quality Tool/PDSA Linkage

- ☐ Students will use a Check Sheet and Bar Chart.
  - The Check Sheet/Matrix is a tool to collect and organize data in the plan portion of the PDSA cycle.
  - The Bar Chart is a graph of categorical data plotted by frequency, and is used in the plan portion of the PDSA cycle.

## Lesson Overview

- ☐ This is a "hands-on" lesson designed to strengthen student's abilities to identify two types of trees while learning about the Check Sheet and Bar Chart quality tools.
- ☐ Following an introduction to the two main types of trees—deciduous and evergreen/coniferous—students are shown examples in books or other media, and then the class will take a walk to identify trees in the school's neighborhood.
- ☐ The students will collect leaves from trees observed on their walk to sort and label in a related lesson.

## Lesson Objectives

- ☐ The students will learn to differentiate between deciduous and coniferous trees.
- ☐ The students will strengthen their identification skills with leaves collected from deciduous and coniferous trees.
- ☐ The students will use a Check Sheet to record and collect data found on their "tree identification" walk.
- ☐ The students will organize the data using a Bar Chart.
- ☐ The students will learn how to analyze the collected data.
- ☐ The students will apply safety skills and demonstrate responsible behaviors on a walk outside of the school.
- ☐ The students will understand and use the Check Sheet and Bar Chart quality tools.

## Pre-Lesson Activities

- ☐ Review differences between deciduous and coniferous trees and their leaves.
- ☐ Obtain copies of the worksheets that go with the lesson.
- ☐ Obtain all materials needed for the lesson.
- ☐ Review ways to demonstrate responsible and safe behaviors while on a class walk.
- ☐ Obtain permission to go on a walk beyond school grounds.
- ☐ Have students predict whether they will see more deciduous or coniferous trees on their walk and record on Check Sheets.
- ☐ Choose groups of four that will work and walk together.

## Materials Needed

- ☐ One Check Sheet per student for recording of data.
- ☐ Pencil for recording of data; clipboard or notebook to write on.
- ☐ Plastic bags for collection of leaves; one bag per group of four students.
- ☐ Appropriate attire for walk outdoors.
- ☐ Bar Chart worksheets copied for use upon return.
- ☐ Large graph paper on an easel or overhead transparency of Bar Chart to use as a tool for student demonstration.
- ☐ Crayons or colored pencils.
- ☐ Adequate space cleared for sorting of leaves.

## Lesson Delivery/Procedure

- ☐ After the teaching of deciduous and coniferous trees, the class will take a walk in the immediate (school) neighborhood to identify such trees. It is suggested that the walk take no more than 15 minutes.
- ☐ The teachers will review the Check Sheet tool with students.
- ☐ Before leaving, students record predictions on their Check Sheet as to whether more deciduous or coniferous trees will be seen in the area.
- ☐ As the class walks together in groups of four, stop at each tree encountered to reach a group/class decision: Is this a deciduous or coniferous tree? How do we know?
- ☐ The students will record these data on their Check Sheets (worksheet 70—tally mark for each type seen).
- ☐ Groups collect one to two leaves from the identified trees.
- ☐ After returning from the tree identification walk, analyze data with students and discuss findings and observations, then check their predictions.
- ☐ The teacher will review the Bar Chart tool with students.
- ☐ The teacher demonstrates on enlarged or overhead transparency of Bar Chart how to transfer data from Check Sheets to individual Bar Chart (worksheet 71).
- ☐ The class will color in bars on the Bar Chart for a visual display of the collected data.
- ☐ The class will summarize data in a whole-class discussion.

## Guided Practice

- ☐ In the same groups of four, students will sort collected leaves into two piles: those that came from deciduous trees or those that came from coniferous trees.
- ☐ The students will note differences between the leaves collected from these two types of trees.
- ☐ The students will further analyze data—does the number of leaves or needles in each pile correlate with the type of trees seen the most on our walk?
- ☐ The students will determine other ways to sort the leaves, for example, by color, shape, size, leaf patterns, and so on.
- ☐ The students will further examine leaves under magnifying glasses and discuss observations.

## Assessment

- ☐ The students will report their findings with another group and compare results.
- ☐ The students will draw and label a deciduous and coniferous tree in science journals.
- ☐ The students will draw and label leaves from deciduous and coniferous trees in science journals.

- [ ] After the teacher models the process, the students will correctly transfer the data from their Check Sheets to their individual Bar Charts.
- [ ] The students will interpret the Bar Chart by giving at least one correct statement about trees on their walk.

## Post-Lesson/Follow-Up Activities/Extensions

- [ ] Homework assignment: Take a walk in your own neighborhood with an older family member to record the number of deciduous and coniferous trees found (can use same worksheet).
- [ ] Create a Bar Chart with these new data (can use same worksheet).
- [ ] Share findings in class and analyze differences between (school and home) Bar Charts, and those from different parts of the city.
- [ ] Use a tree identification book or chart to further identify the trees in your neighborhood: oak, maple, spruce, fir, and so on.
- [ ] Use leaves from different trees to make an interesting mobile.
- [ ] Revisit books read in class to compare the trees in our city to those found in books.
- [ ] Take a follow-up walk to make bark and leaf rubbings of deciduous and coniferous trees.

## Supporting Resources

- [ ] Tree identification guides
- [ ] Important parts of a tree—*www.urbanext.uiuc.edu/trees2/*
- [ ] Learning about conifers—*www.realtrees4kids.org*
- [ ] Identify trees by their name, leaves, or fruit—*www.oplin.lib.oh.us/products/tree/*
- [ ] Worksheets 70 and 71

# Five Senses

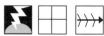

Explain how knowledge can be gained by careful observation.

**Estimated Time:** 45 minutes          **Worksheets:** 72, 73, and 74

## Quality Tool/PDSA Linkage

- ☐ Students will use Brainstorming, the Affinity Diagram, and the Cause-and-Effect Diagram.

  - The Brainstorming technique is the generation of ideas by a group and is used at any portion of the PDSA cycle when every person needs to be heard from and many ideas need to be generated.

  - The Affinity Diagram is a tool to generate, organize, and consolidate information gathered through Brainstorming, and is used in many portions of the PDSA cycle.

  - The Cause-and-Effect Diagram is a picture of the output of a brainstorming session that asks, "What causes . . . ," and is used to determine root causes in the plan portion of the PDSA cycle.

## Lesson Overview

- ☐ This lesson is to be used after students have had instruction in the five senses.

- ☐ The students will use the knowledge they have gained to expand upon and organize their learning.

- ☐ The students will engage in a Brainstorming session at the beginning of the lesson, followed by an Affinity Diagram that will organize the information generated.

- ☐ Having organized the information, students will further organize the information using a Cause-and-Effect Diagram.

## Lesson Objectives

- ☐ The students will list ways that our bodies get information.

- ☐ The students will list attributes they can hear, smell, taste, touch, and see.

- ☐ The students will group these attributes according to the appropriate senses.

- ☐ The students will understand and use the Brainstorming, Affinity Diagram, and Cause-and-Effect Diagram quality tools.

## Pre-Lesson Activities

- ☐ Obtain copies of the worksheets that go with the lesson.

- ☐ Obtain all materials needed for the lesson.

- ☐ Review the five senses by asking questions such as, "What senses do we use when we eat ice cream?" or "What sense are we using when we pet our dogs?"

## Materials Needed

- ☐ Copies of blank Cause-and-Effect Diagram (worksheet 73) for each student, or one blank diagram drawn on the board or butcher paper.

- ☐ Pencil or writing utensil for appropriate recording of data.

- ☐ Post-It notes.

- ☐ Large butcher paper or board space for Affinity Diagram.
- ☐ Markers.

## Lesson Delivery/Procedure

- ☐ The teacher will review the Brainstorming tool with students.
- ☐ The teacher will begin the lesson by asking students what "observe" means. Students will brainstorm several responses.
- ☐ The teacher will distribute Post-It notes to each student.
- ☐ Students will write or draw (depending on ability level) something that people can hear, see, touch, smell, or taste on the Post-It notes.
- ☐ The teacher will review the Affinity Diagram tool with students.

## Guided Practice

- ☐ After students have written several ideas on Post-It notes, they will place them on the butcher paper with the blank Affinity Diagram (worksheet 74). This activity can be done in several small groups or one large group.
- ☐ Students will sort their Post-It notes according to the five senses: things that we use our sense of sight for, things that we use our sense of smell for, and so on.
- ☐ The teacher will review the Cause-and-Effect Diagram with students.
- ☐ After completing the Affinity Diagram, the teacher should direct the students to the Cause-and-Effect Diagram (worksheet 74). Students can fill in their own Cause-and-Effect Diagram (worksheet 73), or the teacher can fill it in as part of a shared writing experience. The teacher can use worksheet 72 as an example.

## Assessment

- ☐ The teacher will give examples from the lesson and students will tell (or point to) which sense they use to observe that item.
- ☐ The teacher will review student work, discussion, and findings to gauge level of understanding.

## Post-Lesson/Follow-Up Activities/Extensions

- ☐ Read aloud the book *My Five Senses* by Aliki.
- ☐ Have a taste-testing party with unusual foods.
- ☐ Open a jar of perfume or vanilla and observe how its smell spreads throughout the room.
- ☐ Play "feel the mystery object" with objects in a paper bag.
- ☐ Put on a blindfold and have a partner lead you around the room or the school.
- ☐ Play "what's that sound?" with prerecorded sounds, such as a door closing, a dog barking, and so on.

# Supporting Resources

- ☐ *The Five Senses* by Keith Faulkner
- ☐ *A Tasting Party* by Jane Belk Moncure
- ☐ *Touch* by Sue Hurwitz
- ☐ Worksheets 72, 73, and 74

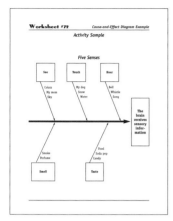
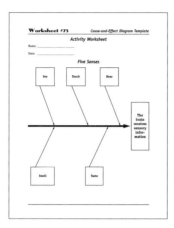

# Physical and Chemical Changes

Know and apply concepts, principles, and processes of scientific inquiry.

**Estimated Time:** 25–30 minutes    **Worksheets:** 75 and 76

## Quality Tool/PDSA Linkage

- ☐ Students will use a Check Sheet/Matrix.
  - • The Check Sheet/Matrix is a tool to collect and organize data in the plan portion of the PDSA cycle.

## Lesson Overview

- ☐ In this lesson, the students will be learning about two changes that occur in science.
- ☐ The students will be engaged in a hands-on activity to experience learning about physical and chemical changes that occur in everyday life.
- ☐ The students will also work together to communicate their results through the use of a Check Sheet and discussion.

## Lesson Objectives

- ☐ The students will learn to work with a partner and share materials.
- ☐ The students will learn different stages of the scientific process.
- ☐ The students will learn about physical and chemical changes.
- ☐ The students will learn how to record data on a Check Sheet.

## Pre-Lesson Activities

- ☐ Obtain materials for the hands-on lab.
- ☐ Obtain copies of the worksheets needed for the lesson.
- ☐ Make a large Check Sheet on chart paper to model the use of a Check Sheet.

## Materials Needed

- ☐ Toast.
- ☐ Chart paper.
- ☐ Markers.
- ☐ Clay.
- ☐ Newspaper.
- ☐ Orange slices.
- ☐ Apples.
- ☐ Ice cubes.
- ☐ Bread.
- ☐ Oil.
- ☐ Matches.
- ☐ Candle.
- ☐ Baby food jars.
- ☐ Toaster.

## Lesson Delivery/Procedure

- ☐ The teacher will gather the students into a central location. Chart paper of Check Sheet should be nearby.
- ☐ The teacher will review the Check Sheet tool with students.
- ☐ The teacher will ask the students what they think is a change and will encourage students to respond.
- ☐ The teacher will then ask students what they think is a physical change.
- ☐ The teacher will ask them what they think is a chemical change.
- ☐ The teacher will gather predictions and ideas generated from the students.
- ☐ The teacher will tell the students that they will be exploring what physical changes and chemical changes are in science today.
- ☐ The teacher will then take a piece of bread and a piece of toast and ask the students what happened to the bread. Students may say things like "the bread was toasted and changed."
- ☐ The teacher will ask the students if they can take the piece of toast and change it back to untoasted bread.
- ☐ The students will say no. This is a physical change—when an object is permanently or physically changed in appearance.
- ☐ The teacher can ask the students if they think making something with clay is a chemical or physical change.
- ☐ The teacher will show the students the Check Sheet (worksheet 75) at this time. The teacher will explain that they will make a prediction first as to whether an item has a physical or chemical change.
- ☐ The teacher will write a tally mark showing whether the students think molding the clay will be a physical or chemical change in the prediction column.
- ☐ The teacher will mold the clay into an object of choice.
- ☐ The teacher will ask the students what they observed and write this in the observation column.
- ☐ The teacher will ask whether this is a physical or chemical change. The teacher will put a tally mark in the box to show their response in the last column of the Check Sheet.

## Guided Practice

- ☐ The teacher will explain to the students that they will be completing a few experiments by themselves. They need to use the Check Sheet (worksheet 75) to help collect the data.
- ☐ The teacher will get the students into partners. The teacher may want to have this previously determined.
- ☐ The teacher will pass out the piece of newspaper.
- ☐ The teacher will ask the students if they think it will be a physical or chemical change to crumple up the paper.
- ☐ The students will predict by placing a tally mark in the column of choice.
- ☐ The students will crumple up the newspaper and write what happened.
- ☐ The students will now write whether it was a chemical or physical change in the last column by talking about it with their partner.
- ☐ The teacher and students will repeat the last five steps with the rest of the materials on the Check Sheet.
- ☐ The teacher will model the experiments that involve burning materials or using fire.

## Assessment

- ☐ The teacher can informally assess the students' understanding of the lesson while walking around during the investigation.
- ☐ The teacher can informally assess students' ability to work with a partner by how much cooperation there was with their partner.
- ☐ The teacher can formally assess the students by using the Check Sheet to check for understanding.

## Post-Lesson/Follow-Up Activities/Extensions

- ☐ The teacher can pull the students together again to discuss the results of the lesson.
- ☐ The teacher can ask questions to follow up with the lesson (see worksheet 76).
- ☐ The teacher can ask the students to look for physical and chemical changes that occur at home. Students can write them down on a paper and bring them to class to share.

## Supporting Resources

- ☐ Worksheets 75 and 76

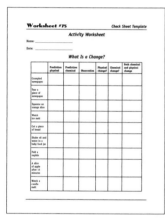

# Rocks

Understand the fundamental concepts, principles, and interconnections of life, physical, and earth/space sciences.

**Estimated Time:** 45–60 minutes          **Worksheets:** 77, 78, and 79

## Quality Tool/PDSA Linkage

- ☐ Students will use an Affinity Diagram, Lotus Diagram, and Bar Chart.

  - The Affinity Diagram is a tool to generate, organize, and consolidate information gathered through Brainstorming, and is used in many portions of the PDSA cycle.

  - The Lotus Diagram is a tool to expand thinking around a single topic or theme and is used at any portion of the PDSA cycle to generate additional thoughts.

  - The Bar Chart is a graph of categorical data plotted by frequency, and is used in the plan portion of the PDSA cycle.

## Lesson Overview

- ☐ This lesson can be used as an introduction to the study of rocks.

- ☐ The students will use the five senses to categorize rocks.

- ☐ The students will use an Affinity Diagram for the process of verifying the following categories: shiny, hard, soft, dull, rough, and smooth.

- ☐ Each student will choose one category to put in the center of the Lotus Diagram.

- ☐ The students will illustrate rocks that go with the category.

- ☐ The students will bring in rocks and use a Bar Chart to keep track of rocks and their categories.

## Lesson Objectives

- ☐ The students will categorize rocks by how they look and feel.

- ☐ The students will use an Affinity Diagram to categorize the rocks.

- ☐ The students will use a Lotus Diagram to demonstrate understanding of a specific category.

- ☐ The students will use a Bar Chart to help categorize and count rocks brought to school by all students.

## Pre-Lesson Activities

- ☐ Obtain copies of the worksheets that go with the lesson.

- ☐ Gather a large collection of rocks.

- ☐ Prepare a large area to lay out the Affinity Diagram with descriptors.

- ☐ Prepare Bar Chart Template (worksheet 79) and post in the classroom.

## Materials Needed

- ☐ Collection of rocks.

- ☐ Cards with descriptors.

- ☐ Chart paper.

- ☐ Markers or crayons.

- ☐ Worksheets 77–79 for each student.

## Lesson Delivery/Procedure

☐ Discuss the meaning of each word (shiny, hard, soft, dull, rough, smooth) and show an example of each.

☐ The teacher will review the Affinity Diagram tool with students.

☐ As a whole group, begin to sort the rocks by category using the Affinity Diagram (worksheet 77).

☐ The teacher will review the Lotus Diagram tool with students.

☐ After the Affinity Diagram is complete, the teacher will demonstrate the use of the Lotus Diagram. Each student will choose one descriptor for the center of their Lotus Diagram.

☐ In the four boxes around the center, students will illustrate four rocks from that category.

## Guided Practice

☐ Students will complete their Lotus Diagram (worksheet 78).

☐ The teacher will review the Bar Chart tool with students.

☐ Students will use the Bar Chart (worksheet 79) to record information as they bring rocks from home.

## Assessment

☐ Students will share their Lotus Diagram with the class, explaining how the rocks fit into the category they chose.

☐ The students will demonstrate an understanding of rocks and the categories as demonstrated on individual Affinity Diagram.

☐ The student and teacher will review the quality tools used, and together determine levels of understanding.

## Post-Lesson/Follow-Up Activities/Extensions

☐ Continue gathering rocks and sorting by classification.

☐ Use rock books to identify the scientific names for your rocks.

## Supporting Resources

☐ *wrgis.wr.usgs.gov/docs/parks/rxmin/rock.html*

☐ *The Magic School Bus Inside the Earth* by Joanna Cole

☐ *Fossils Tell of Long Ago* by Aliki

☐ *Rock Collecting* by Roma Gans

☐ *A First Look at Rocks* by M. Selsman

☐ Worksheets 77, 78, and 79

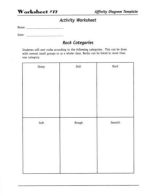

# Dinosaurs

Know and apply concepts that explain how living things function, adapt, and change.

**Estimated Time:** 30–45 minutes          **Worksheet:** 80

## Quality Tool/PDSA Linkage

☐ Students will use Brainstorming and an Affinity Diagram.

- The Brainstorming technique is the generation of ideas by a group and is used at any portion of the PDSA cycle when every person needs to be heard from and many ideas need to be generated.

- The Affinity Diagram is a tool to generate, organize, and consolidate information gathered through Brainstorming, and is used in many portions of the PDSA cycle.

## Lesson Overview

☐ In this lesson, students will learn about the Brainstorming and Affinity Diagram quality tools.

☐ This lesson will help the students identify and describe the body parts of dinosaurs and learn the major functions of these parts.

☐ This lesson should be conducted after time spent reading about and studying dinosaurs to build the students' background knowledge.

☐ The students will brainstorm parts of dinosaurs as they are browsing through books and recalling information learned in previous lessons. (See list of words for reference.)

☐ The teacher will write these brainstormed words on chart paper. Then, each student will copy one word on a Post-It note.

☐ The class will use an Affinity Diagram to organize the words into related groups (see worksheet 80).

☐ The teacher will promote classroom discussion about each body part and its function throughout the lesson.

## Lesson Objctives

☐ The students will identify body parts of dinosaurs.

☐ The students will learn how these body parts function, relate, and work together.

☐ The students will increase their vocabulary skills by learning new dinosaur-related words.

☐ The students will understand and use the Brainstorming and Affinity Diagram quality tools.

## Pre-Lesson Activities

☐ Begin study of dinosaurs at least two weeks prior to conducting this lesson (to build background knowledge and expose the students to different types of dinosaurs).

☐ Obtain books about dinosaurs.

☐ Create an enlarged Affinity Diagram with suggested categories (see worksheet 80).

☐ Obtain all materials needed for the lesson.

☐ Obtain copies of the worksheets that go with the lesson.

## Materials Needed

- ☐ Chart paper for list of brainstormed words.
- ☐ Markers, pen, or pencil.
- ☐ Books about dinosaurs (call #560's), at least one book per student or pair of students.
- ☐ Post-It note pad.
- ☐ Enlarged Affinity Diagram.

## Lesson Delivery/Procedure

- ☐ The teacher will distribute dinosaur books or other printed materials (one book for every one to two students), and one Post-It note per student.
- ☐ The teacher will review the Brainstorming tool with students.
- ☐ The students will browse through books and are directed to look carefully at the pictures to identify body parts of a variety of dinosaurs.
- ☐ The students will brainstorm words and dinosaur body parts as the teacher writes the words on chart paper (worksheet 80). After the teacher lists the word, one student should copy it on his or her Post-It note.
- ☐ The teacher will list one word for every student in the class (see list below for reference).
- ☐ Continue brainstorming words until there aren't any more student responses. (The teacher can add words to the list, if needed.)
- ☐ The teacher will review the Affinity Diagram tool with students.
- ☐ The teacher will display and explain the enlarged Affinity Diagram. Ask the students to help organize the words by their functions, and/or group the body parts by "what works together."
- ☐ The students will post their words under the appropriate category. The teacher will promote discussion as to why the particular category was chosen. Note: Some words may need to be posted in more than one category. For example, jaws—under Eating/Digesting Food and Protection. The teacher can quickly rewrite this word on a Post-It note and have a student add it to the chart.
- ☐ Continue until all words are posted while continually promoting student discussion.
- ☐ Dinosaur body parts:

| | | | | | | | | |
|---|---|---|---|---|---|---|---|---|
| arms | beaks | brain | claws | clubs | crest | duck bill | eyes | frill |
| horn | jaws | knobs | legs | neck | plates | skin | spikes | nostrils |
| tail | teeth | skull | scales | toes | armor | back | | |

## Guided Practice

- ☐ The students and the teacher will use the brainstormed words to create a picture dictionary. (Note: The brain is not an observable body part in a picture or drawing.)
- ☐ The students will label body parts of dinosaurs in pictures (drawn or reproduced).
- ☐ The students and the teacher will discuss ways the dinosaurs adapted to their environments. The teacher may ask, "In what ways did the structure of dinosaurs show their adaptations to the environment?"
- ☐ The teacher will create a dinosaur display with models made by the students.
- ☐ The students and the teacher will compare/contrast dinosaurs to winged reptiles and other prehistoric animals.

## Assessment

- ☐ The students will demonstrate their understanding of dinosaur body parts and functions by adequately explaining their choices when categorizing dinosaur vocabulary words on the Affinity Diagram.

- [ ] The students will gain information about dinosaurs from books and other printed materials by finding a picture identifying at least three body parts.

- [ ] The students will adequately justify their choices when categorizing dinosaur vocabulary words on the Affinity Diagram.

- [ ] The students will correctly label at least three body parts of dinosaurs on reproduced or drawn pictures.

## Post-Lesson/Follow-Up Activities/Extensions

- [ ] Take a class field trip to a local natural history museum.

- [ ] Research what North America was like when the dinosaurs lived.

- [ ] Research the different teeth and jaws of meat eaters and plant eaters.

- [ ] List all of the animals you believe to be descendents of dinosaurs. Good resource book: *Dinosaur Cousins?* by Bernard Most (Voyager Books).

- [ ] Research the function of any words listed in the "other" category. (For example, the crest was a head ornament that allowed the species to identify its own, enhanced the species' sense of smell, and enabled the species to make distinctive noises.)

## Supporting Resources

- [ ] Library book call number for nonfiction dinosaur books: 560's

- [ ] Dinosaur dictionary—*www.dinodictionary.com/index.asp*

- [ ] Worksheet 80

---

**Worksheet #80**   *Affinity Diagram Template*

**Activity Worksheet**

Name: _____

Date: _____

*Dinosaur Body Parts and Functions*

| Eating/ Digesting Food | Walking/Moving | Protection | Other |
|---|---|---|---|
| | | | |

# Simple Machines

Estimate measurements and determine acceptable levels of accuracy. Measure and compare quantities using appropriate units, instruments, and methods.

**Estimated Time:** 30 minutes          **Worksheets:** 81, 82, 83, and 84

## Quality Tool/PDSA Linkage

- ☐ Students will use a Flowchart and Lotus Diagram.
  - The Flowchart is a drawing of any process used to document the process flow during the plan portion of the PDSA cycle.
  - The Lotus Diagram is a tool to expand thinking around a single topic or theme and is used at any portion of the PDSA cycle to generate additional thoughts.

## Lesson Overview

- ☐ In this lesson, the students will be learning about simple machines.
- ☐ The students will be exploring the use of the lever simple machine.
- ☐ The students will use the Flowchart quality tool to decide how to move a heavy box to the table.

## Lesson Objectives

- ☐ The students will review what they know about simple machines.
- ☐ The students will learn about a lever.
- ☐ The students will explore how to get a heavy box to the table.
- ☐ The students will gain knowledge of the Flowchart and the Lotus Diagram.

## Pre-Lesson Activities

- ☐ Obtain copies of the worksheets that go with the lesson.
- ☐ Gather the materials for the lesson.
- ☐ Make a large box too heavy for students to move.
- ☐ Teach about simple machines. Review with the students what they have learned about machines.

## Materials Needed

- ☐ A board for each group.
- ☐ Copy of Flowchart for each group.
- ☐ A box for each group.
- ☐ A triangular piece for the fulcrum for each group.
- ☐ Heavy objects or weights for each box.

## Lesson Delivery/Procedure

- ☐ The teacher will place the large box already filled with weight in front of the room.
- ☐ The teacher will challenge students to lift the box onto a table.
- ☐ When the students realize that they will be unable to lift the box because it is too heavy, invite the students to use their knowledge about simple machines to help.

- ☐ The teacher will ask the students, "What simple machine can you think of to help move this heavy box onto the table?"
- ☐ The teacher will review the Flowchart tool with students.
- ☐ The teacher will show the students the Flowchart that displays the directions that the students would follow while investigating the question posed (see worksheet 81).
- ☐ The teacher will then divide the students into groups of four.
- ☐ The teacher will give each group the materials (board, box, and fulcrum piece).

## Guided Practice

- ☐ The students will use the materials given by the teacher to create a way to get the heavy box that they were given onto the table.
- ☐ When the students are done, each group will need to fill in the Flowchart (worksheet 82). The students will tell what they need to do first, second, third, and so on. The students will use the words that have been provided on the paper to assist them.
- ☐ Once each group has completed the Flowchart, the group will need to try out their procedures.
- ☐ When every group has completed their Flowchart, pull the groups together for sharing and reporting out.

## Assessment

- ☐ Each group will explain their Flowchart.
- ☐ The teacher will analyze the students' level of understanding of the Flowchart.
- ☐ The teacher will ask the students, "What type of simple machine was created today?"
- ☐ The teacher will discuss with the students how a lever is a simple machine.

## Post-Lesson/Follow-Up Activities/Extensions

- ☐ The students and the teacher will discuss other ways that levers are used every day to help people do work.
- ☐ The teacher will review the Lotus Diagram tool with students.
- ☐ The students should complete the Lotus Diagram on levers (worksheet 83).
- ☐ A Super Lotus Diagram is included for extended study of simple machines (worksheet 84).

## Supporting Resources

- ☐ Worksheets 81, 82, 83, and 84

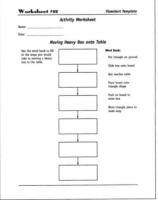
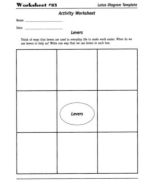

# Quality Across the Curriculum

# SCIENCE

## 2-3

### LESSONS

Endangered Species . . . . . . . . 113

Weather Prediction . . . . . . . . 115

Measurement . . . . . . . . . . . 119

Rain Forest Animals. . . . . . . . 123

Space/Solar System . . . . . . . . 127

Dinosaurs and Fossils. . . . . . . 131

Forms of Energy . . . . . . . . . . 133

Safety During
   Experimentation. . . . . . . . . 137

Renewable and Nonrenewable
   Resources. . . . . . . . . . . . . 139

# Endangered Species

Know and apply concepts that describe how living things interact with each other and with their environment.

**Estimated Time:** Two 45-minute sessions     **Worksheets:** 85, 86, 87, and 88

## Quality Tool/PDSA Linkage

☐ Students will use the Tree Diagram and Cause-and-Effect Diagram.

- The Systematic/Tree Diagram is a tool to guide a group in planning for a broad goal by determining and assigning the different levels of action needed to accomplish the goal and is used in the plan portion of the PDSA cycle.

- The Cause-and-Effect Diagram is a picture of the output of a brainstorming session that asks, "What causes . . . ," and is used to determine root causes in the plan portion of the PDSA cycle.

## Lesson Overview

☐ This is a collaborative lesson designed for use during a study of endangered species.

☐ In this lesson, students will organize the endangered species by the animal group to which each species belongs.

☐ After organizing the information, students will analyze the causes of what makes a species endangered.

## Lesson Objectives

☐ The students will categorize endangered animals.

☐ The students will determine the causes of species endangerment.

☐ The students will understand and use the Tree Diagram quality tool.

☐ The students will understand and use the Cause-and-Effect Diagram quality tool.

## Pre-Lesson Activities

☐ Obtain copies of the worksheets that go with the lesson.

☐ Obtain all materials needed for the lesson.

## Materials Needed

☐ A blank worksheet for each student.

☐ Internet access to Web sites.

☐ Several nonfiction books about endangered species.

## Lesson Delivery/Procedure

☐ The teacher will guide students toward several sources of information (books, Internet sources, encyclopedias) and students will spend time reviewing the materials in their collaborative groups.

☐ The teacher will clarify vocabulary terms that may be found in the materials such as: habitat, habitat destruction, over population, pollution, disease, species, and so on.

☐ The teacher will review the Tree Diagram tool with students.

☐ The teacher will guide student groups to fill out the first column of the Tree Diagram, "endangered species" (worksheet 88).

- [ ] The students and the teacher will then discuss animal groups (that is, birds, reptiles, amphibians, mammals, fish).
- [ ] The teacher will assign the groups to work together to find animals that are extinct and to organize them into their animal groups. The students should have at least three animal groups and at least two animals per group (see example on worksheet 87).
- [ ] After students have found examples of endangered species, they should find specific examples, as in the last column in the example. For example, next to "elephant" students can list "African Elephant" and "Asian Elephant." The Internet sites listed have great information about these.

## Guided Practice

- [ ] The teacher will review the Cause-and-Effect Diagram with students.
- [ ] The teacher will guide students to fill in the main bones of the Cause-and-Effect Diagram (worksheet 86).
- [ ] The students will work collaboratively using a variety of sources to fill in the details of the Cause-and-Effect Diagram (example on worksheet 85). The Internet sites listed contain a vast amount of information on this as well.

## Assessment

- [ ] The student will complete the Tree Diagram accurately (worksheet 88).
- [ ] The student will complete the Cause-and-Effect Diagram (worksheet 86) to demonstrate understanding.

## Post-Lesson/Follow-Up Activities/Extensions

- [ ] Research one endangered animal in depth.
- [ ] Research steps being taken to reduce the threat to animals and/or to their habitats.
- [ ] Create a PowerPoint presentation, a poster, or a written report to share the information learned from this research.

## Supporting Resources

- [ ] *www.endangeredspecie.com/*
- [ ] *www.geocities.com/RainForest/Vines/1460/*
- [ ] *www.tenan.vuurwerk.nl/*
- [ ] *www.amnh.org/nationalcenter/Endangered/*
- [ ] *The Modern Ark: Saving Endangered Species* by Daniel Cohen
- [ ] *Endangered Animals* (First Discovery Books) by Wendy Barish
- [ ] Worksheets 85, 86, 87, and 88

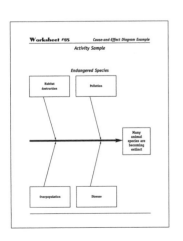
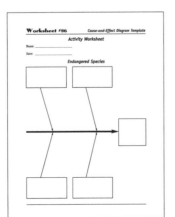
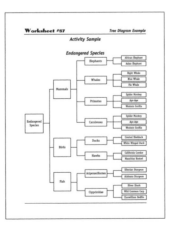
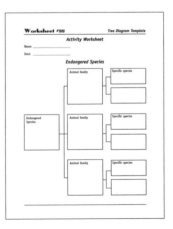

# Weather Prediction

Understand the relationships among science, technology, and society in historical and contemporary contexts.

- Explain why similar results are expected when procedures are done the same way.
- Explain how knowledge can be gained by careful observation.

**Estimated Time:**
- 20 minutes first day
- 10 minutes each day of data collection
- 20 minutes last day

**Worksheets:** 89, 90, and 91

## Quality Tool/PDSA Linkage

☐ Students will use Operational Definition, Check Sheet, and Run Chart.

- Operational Definition is a standard process for measuring our critical quality characteristics used before gathering data in the plan portion of the PDSA cycle.

- The Check Sheet/Matrix is a tool to collect and organize data in the plan portion of the PDSA cycle.

- The Run/Control Chart graphically reports system performance over time and is used to compare performance before and after changes in both the plan and study portions of the PDSA cycle.

## Lesson Overview

☐ This is a hands-on lesson designed to enrich the students' understanding of temperature in their environment and demonstrate the usefulness of an Operational Definition, Check Sheet, and Run Chart in collection of data.

☐ The students will make a prediction of what the temperature will be on a particular day.

☐ The students will be instructed in the use of an outdoor thermometer to measure daily temperature accurately.

☐ The students will use the weather report in the newspaper to determine the actual temperature for the day.

☐ The students will record data collected on a Check Sheet and plot data on a Run Chart.

☐ The students will calculate the average temperature for the week.

## Lesson Objectives

☐ The students will learn how to measure temperature using a thermometer.

☐ The students will understand how to interpret weather data from the newspaper or Internet.

☐ The students will use an Operational Definition to design the quality measures for the process of weather measurement.

☐ The students will use a Check Sheet to record weather data.

☐ The students will use a Run Chart to evaluate and compare weather data for the week.

## Pre-Lesson Activities

☐ Obtain copies of the worksheets that go with the lesson.

☐ Obtain materials needed for the lesson.

## Materials Needed

- ☐ One thermometer per every two students.
- ☐ Pencil or pen.
- ☐ Check Sheet.
- ☐ Markers—three different colors for each group.
- ☐ Chart paper for demonstration of tools.
- ☐ Daily newspapers or access to Internet.

## Lesson Delivery/Procedure

- ☐ The teacher will discuss general vocabulary terms associated with weather, temperature and predictions.
- ☐ The teacher will review the Operational Definition tool with students.
- ☐ Together the class will write the Operational Definition for the process of temperature measurement (worksheet 89).
- ☐ The teacher will review and briefly demonstrate how to use a thermometer.
- ☐ In pairs, students will practice using the thermometer.
- ☐ The teacher will review and demonstrate the use of the Check Sheet (worksheet 90):
  - Students will make a prediction of the current daily temperature
  - Students will record their temperature measurement
  - Students will record the actual temperature from the newspaper or the Internet
- ☐ The teacher will review and demonstrate the use of the Run Chart. Use a different color for each line on the Run Chart (worksheet 91). For example: red—prediction, green—actual temperature, blue—student temperature measurement.
- ☐ The students will complete their first measurement.
- ☐ The teacher will review the Check Sheet and Run Chart tools with students.
- ☐ Record data on Check Sheet and transfer information to the Run Chart.

## Guided Practice

- ☐ The students will continue to make predictions, take temperature measurements, and research actual temperatures for five days and record on Check Sheet and Run Chart.
- ☐ The students will determine the average temperature for the five days and discuss the findings in small groups.

## Assessment

- ☐ The students will be able to explain their data to the class using the Operational Definition, Check Sheets, and Run Charts used in this project.
- ☐ The students will draw conclusions from the data recorded on the quality tools and brainstorm conclusions.
- ☐ Students will successfully complete worksheets 89–91.

## Post-Lesson/Follow-Up Activities/Extensions

- ☐ Students could share what they have learned about weather reports with their family.
- ☐ Students could continue gathering data on daily temperatures.
- ☐ Students could gather data during various seasons in their area.

- [ ] Students could analyze how temperatures fluctuate.
- [ ] Students could compare their region's temperatures with another area of the country.

## Supporting Resources

- [ ] *www.fema.gov/kids/little.htm*
- [ ] Weather Channel: *www.weather.com*
- [ ] *Weather Watch* by Valerie Wyatt
- [ ] *Cloudy with a Chance of Meatballs* by Judi Barrett
- [ ] *Weather Forecasting* by Gail Gibbons
- [ ] *Can Be a Weather Forecaster* by Claire Martin
- [ ] *Looking at Weather* by David Suzuki
- [ ] Worksheets 89, 90, and 91

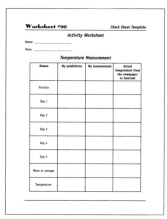

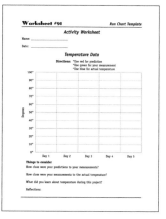

# Measurement

Students will collect data for investigations using measuring instruments and technologies.

**Estimated Time:** 50 minutes          **Worksheets:** 92 and 93

## Quality Tool/PDSA Linkage

- ☐ Students will use the Bar Chart.

    - • The Bar Chart is a graph of categorical data plotted by frequency, and is used in the plan portion of the PDSA cycle.

## Lesson Overview

- ☐ This is a hands-on lesson designed for students to demonstrate and apply knowledge of measurement.

- ☐ The students will use a Bar Chart to graph their results.

## Lesson Objectives

- ☐ The students will form a hypothesis.

- ☐ The students will carry out an experiment using measurement.

- ☐ The students will display their findings using the Bar Chart.

## Pre-Lesson Activities

- ☐ Obtain copies of the worksheets that go with the lesson.

- ☐ Obtain all materials needed for the lesson.

- ☐ Create a poster board size or overhead of the Bar Chart (worksheet 93).

- ☐ Prepare baked popcorn. Preheat the oven to 200° F. Spread out a cup of popping corn in a single layer on a cookie sheet. Bake for two hours.

- ☐ Prepare water soaked popcorn. Put a cup of popping corn in an airtight container (jar) with one tablespoon of water. Shake the jar so that the water coats the seeds. Let the jar stand overnight and shake the jar every few hours to redistribute the water, if possible.

## Materials Needed

- ☐ Three identical clear 8-oz. containers (labeled "baked," "water soaked," and "regular").

- ☐ Bar Chart (worksheet 93).

- ☐ Ruler.

- ☐ *Fresh* popping corn kernels.

- ☐ Oven.

- ☐ Hot-air popper.

- ☐ Airtight jar.

- ☐ Butter/salt if desired.

- ☐ Bowl to catch popcorn.

- ☐ Data sheet (worksheet 92).

## Lesson Delivery/Procedure

☐ The teacher will review what it means to form a hypothesis and to carry out an experiment to test the hypothesis.

☐ The teacher will review the Bar Chart tool with students.

☐ The teacher will display the poster-size or overhead of the Bar Chart and explaining that their goal will be to find which type of popcorn has the highest volume and explain why that is so.

☐ The teacher will display the kernels and let the students observe them. Ask students to form a hypothesis of what will happen to the "baked" kernels, the "water" kernels, and the "regular" kernels once popped. Students should record their hypotheses on the data sheet (worksheet 92).

☐ The teacher will use a hot-air popper to pop the cup of dried corn (from the oven). The teacher will then place the popped corn in a labeled 8-oz. container. Pop the cup of "water" kernels and place them in a separate labeled 8-oz. container. Lastly, pop the cup of kernels that were untreated (regular). Place those in an identical, labeled 8-oz. container. There should now be three identical containers (clear) labeled "baked," "water," and "regular."

☐ The teacher will ask a volunteer to come up and measure (in centimeters) how much the container is filled. Record these answers on the blackboard as well as on the students' data sheets (worksheet 92).

☐ If all works well, the "water" kernels should have popped the best, the "baked" kernels the worst, and the "regular" kernels somewhere in between. The teacher will show the students how to display this information on a Bar Chart.

☐ The teacher will ask the students, "Can anyone explain why these three batches popped differently?" Accept answers and conduct appropriate discussions regarding those answers.

☐ The teacher will tell the students, "Each popcorn kernel contains a certain amount of moisture. The amount of moisture that is inside the kernel will decide how big the kernel will be when popped."

☐ The teacher will ask, "Which kernels used today had the most moisture in them?" The teacher will accept responses and explain, "The kernels that we left in water overnight have the most moisture in them. Since they were sitting in water, they absorbed water, kind of like a sponge." Ask, "Can anyone guess which kernels had the least amount of moisture?" The teacher will accept responses. The teacher will then explain, "The kernels that were baked in the oven had the least amount of moisture. When we baked them, the moisture was released and the heat dried them out. The kernels that we took right from the jar had the average amount of moisture in them."

☐ The teacher will then ask, "We understand now that there is moisture inside of the kernel. But why does the kernel pop?" The teacher will accept appropriate responses. The teacher will then explain, "When the kernel is heated, the moisture inside becomes steam. Once this steam reaches a certain temperature (347° F) the seed coat, or skin, rips open and the inside of the kernel bubbles and becomes solid.

☐ The teacher will direct the students to plot the data on the Bar Chart (worksheet 93).

## Guided Practice

☐ Each student will complete his or her data sheet and Bar Chart.

☐ Each student will write, on the back of their Bar Chart, a simple conclusion from this experiment using the information that he or she collected.

## Assessment

☐ A formative assessment will be determined through teacher questioning and observation.

☐ The teacher will evaluate that the student's data sheet and Bar Chart are properly completed.

## Post-Lesson/Follow-Up Activities/Extensions

☐ Read *The Popcorn Book* by Tomie Paola and let the students eat the popcorn as they listen to the story.

## Supporting Resources

☐ *www.ramseypopcorn.com/popcorn.html*

☐ *The Popcorn Book* by Tomie de Paola

☐ Worksheets 92 and 93

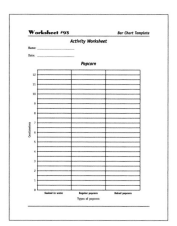

# Rain Forest Animals

Understand world geography and the effects of geography on society.
Understand the fundamental concepts, principles, and interconnections of
life, physical, and earth/space sciences.

**Estimated Time:** 45–60 minutes          **Worksheets:** 94, 95, and 96

## Quality Tool/PDSA Linkage

- ☐ Students will use Brainstorming and the Affinity Diagram.

  - The Brainstorming technique is the generation of ideas by a group and is used at any portion of the PDSA cycle when every person needs to be heard from and many ideas need to be generated.

  - The Affinity Diagram is a tool to generate, organize, and consolidate information gathered through Brainstorming, and is used in many portions of the PDSA cycle.

## Lesson Overview

- ☐ This is a lesson designed to enrich students' knowledge of animals of the rainforest.

- ☐ The students will brainstorm a list of animals found in the rainforest using available research materials.

- ☐ The students will use an Affinity Diagram to differentiate animals and group them by categories they create.

- ☐ A second Affinity Diagram will sort animals by scientific category (mammals, reptiles, amphibians, insects, and birds).

## Lesson Objectives

- ☐ The students will list and identify animals at all levels of the rainforest.

- ☐ The students will categorize animals by observable characteristics and scientific categories.

- ☐ The students will complete an Affinity Diagram in small cooperative groups.

- ☐ The students will use reference materials to assist in completion of the Brainstorming and Affinity Diagram.

## Pre-Lesson Activities

- ☐ Introduce basic information about the Rainforest with students prior to lesson delivery.

- ☐ Gather books or other student materials that contain Rainforest animal information.

- ☐ Obtain copies of the worksheets that go with the lesson.

- ☐ Obtain all materials needed for this lesson.

## Materials Needed

- ☐ Chart paper.

- ☐ Post-It notes.

- ☐ Reference materials on the topic of the rainforest animals.

- ☐ Markers.

## Lesson Delivery/Procedure

- ☐ After the initial introduction of the rainforest concept, distribute rainforest books and other supporting student resources.

☐ Divide students evenly into cooperative groups.

☐ Provide opportunities for students in small groups to look for names of rainforest animals in the books and resources provided.

☐ Each group will come up with a list of rainforest animals that they identified in the books and other resources.

☐ The teacher will review the Brainstorming tool with students.

☐ Briefly discuss the process for using the Brainstorming tool including:

  • All students participate.

  • There are no wrong answers and no criticism is allowed.

  • Generate as many ideas as possible and piggyback off of others' ideas.

☐ The student groups will meet together and share their information with the class and the teacher will record all group findings on a classroom brainstorm list (record on chart paper or worksheet 94).

☐ The teacher will review the Affinity Diagram quality tool with students:

  • Using the Brainstorming data collected, sort ideas into like categories.

  • Name each category of like ideas with a label.

  • Create the Affinity Diagram by organizing all ideas generated from the Brainstorming session and label them by category.

☐ In small groups, students will use their individual lists and come up with a way to sort their animals into categories. (Groups will use Post-It notes and chart paper to categorize animals.)

☐ The students will use the Affinity Diagram (worksheet 95) to create their categorized list of rainforest animals.

## Guided Practice

☐ Each group will share their category groups with the whole class, referring to their Affinity Diagram on chart paper.

☐ The teacher will introduce the scientific categories (birds, mammals, reptiles, insects, and amphibians) to the class.

☐ The students will complete a second Affinity Diagram (worksheet 96) independently sorting their animals into the scientific categories.

## Assessment

☐ The students will be able to identify rainforest animals in each category.

  • Mammals

  • Reptiles

  • Amphibians

  • Insects

  • Birds

☐ The students will choose one animal from each category and explain why the animal meets the characteristics of the scientific category.

☐ The students will share their information with other students (each student will share their information with at least one other student).

## Post-Lesson/Follow-Up Activities/Extensions

☐ Students could choose one animal and research it in depth using other books, Web sites, and resources.

☐ Students could share what they learned about the rainforest with their family.

☐ Students could apply the knowledge learned about animals to help categorize animals from other areas of the world.

## Supporting Resources

☐ *www.enchantedlearning.com*

☐ *The Tropical Rainforest* by Gerard Cheshire

☐ *Rainforest* by Shirley Cook

☐ *The Great Kapok Tree: A Tale of the Amazon Rain Forest* by Lynne Cherry

☐ *Ranger Rick's Nature Scope: Rain Forest: Tropical Treasure* by Chelsea House Publications

☐ Worksheets 94, 95, and 96

# Space/Solar System

Know and apply concepts that explain the composition and structure of the universe and earth's place in it.

**Estimated Time:** 60 minutes          **Worksheets:** 97 and 98

## Quality Tool/PDSA Linkage

☐ Students will use Brainstorming and the Affinity Diagram.

- The Brainstorming technique is the generation of ideas by a group and is used at any portion of the PDSA cycle when every person needs to be heard from and many ideas need to be generated.

- The Affinity Diagram is a tool to generate, organize, and consolidate information gathered through Brainstorming, and is used in many portions of the PDSA cycle.

## Lesson Overview

☐ This is a hands-on lesson designed to introduce our solar system and its planets to the students.

☐ Following a Brainstorming activity where the students will explain everything they know about the solar system, the students will try to simulate a scaled-down solar system.

☐ The students will learn the nine planets' names and their sizes in relation to the sun. They will also learn the order of the planets from the sun.

☐ The students will measure the distance between the planets in relation to the sun.

## Lesson Objectives

☐ The students will identify the names of the nine planets in the solar system.

☐ The students will learn the scaled-down version of each planet. Students will compare distances from various planets.

☐ The students will observe how the planets orbit the sun. They will learn which planets have a longer year and why.

☐ The students will understand and use the Brainstorming and Affinity Diagram quality tools.

## Pre-Lesson Activities

☐ Obtain copies of the worksheets that go with the lesson.

☐ Obtain all materials needed for the lesson.

☐ Set up a large poster paper for the Brainstorming activity.

☐ Before starting the lab activity, have the students brainstorm everything that they know about the solar system.

## Materials Needed

☐ Schedule the gym, cafeteria, or go outside.

☐ One huge 2–3 M diameter balloon (sun).

☐ Two small marbles (Mercury, Pluto).

☐ Two tennis balls (Venus, Earth).

☐ One ping-pong ball (Mars).

☐ One basketball (Jupiter).

☐ One soccer ball (Saturn).

- ☐ Two baseballs (Uranus, Neptune).
- ☐ Paper.
- ☐ Markers.
- ☐ Masking tape.
- ☐ String.
- ☐ Index cards with the names of the planets on each card.
- ☐ Optional: Instead of balls, you can use pieces of cardboard cut to the sizes of the balls.

## Lesson Delivery/Procedure

- ☐ The teacher will review the Brainstorming tool with students.
- ☐ The teacher will record student ideas and comments about their knowledge of the solar system. Student ideas will be placed on a large poster paper.
- ☐ When done with the Brainstorming exercise, the teacher will explain that the class will be making a small model of the solar system.
- ☐ The teacher will share with the students the names of each of the planets.
- ☐ The teacher will ask the students to try to name each of the planets (using the balls or cardboard model that the teacher has supplied). The teacher will remind students that there are 10 balls represented by the nine planets and the sun.
- ☐ The students will role play/act out a model of the solar system. After students have attempted to name the balls (planets), the teacher will select one person to role play as the sun. A student needs to receive the gigantic balloon to represent the sun. Nine other students will role play the "planets." The teacher will tape the name of the planet on the student's chest. The teacher will ask the students several questions, "Are all the planets the same size?" "Which is the largest planet?" "Which is the smallest planet?" "Is it possible to hold more than one 'Mercury' in your hand?" "What about Jupiter?"
- ☐ The students can toss the balls around the group. The teacher will ask if the students can get the balls (planets) back to the correct person.

## Guided Practice

- ☐ The teacher will move the students to the large open area to make the model of the solar system. The teacher will ask the students to get into order from the sun according to the solar system model. (Order of the planets: Sun-Mercury-Venus-Earth-Mars-Jupiter-Saturn-Uranus-Neptune-Pluto). To ensure total class participation, students can either pair up with a planet or sit on the outside and observe what is going on. Later, each "planet" can switch with a person sitting on the outside watching.
- ☐ The teacher will have the students get into relative positions from the sun.

  | Mercury | 4 paces |
  | Venus | 7 paces |
  | Earth | 10 paces |
  | Mars | 15 paces |
  | Jupiter | 52 paces |
  | Saturn | 95 paces |
  | Uranus | 191 paces |
  | Neptune | 301 paces |
  | Pluto | 395 paces |

- ☐ The teacher can scale this down by moving the decimal point one unit left, for example, Mercury 4 paces becomes 0.4 paces.

- ☐ The teacher will have each student mark his or her planet's location with an 'X' made from masking tape.

- ☐ Each student will place his or her ball on the "X." Have the student walk to the sun. When everyone is at the sun, have him or her walk at the same speed to their spot. What do they notice about the distance between planets? From the sun?

- ☐ The teacher will have the students stand at their "X" and try to move in a circle around the sun. Teacher will ask "Why do some orbits take longer?"

## Assessment

- ☐ The students will go back to the classroom to share what they learned with this activity. Students will summarize their findings by reporting out their learning. (This can be done in pairs or small cooperative groups.)

- ☐ The teacher will help students correct any misperceptions they had prior to the lesson, and add any new information they have to the brainstormed list completed prior to the lab.

- ☐ Students can brainstorm in small group or in partners what they learned about the planets. After the students have brainstormed, the students can take the ideas and organize them into an Affinity Diagram (worksheet 97).

- ☐ The teacher will review the Affinity Diagram tool with students.

- ☐ Students can use the information that the students learned to put the planets in order from largest to smallest (worksheet 98).

- ☐ The teacher will review student work and gauge their level of understanding.

- ☐ The teacher will informally assess whether the lesson was successful based on lesson objectives met by the students. The teacher will use this information to guide where he or she takes the students the next day.

## Post-Lesson/Follow-Up Activities/Extensions

- ☐ Students may research information about each of the nine planets.

- ☐ Students may draw or sketch the planets.

## Supporting Resources

- ☐ *www.seds.org/nineplanets/nineplanets/*

- ☐ *www.mines.edu/research/srr/*

- ☐ Worksheets 97 and 98

# Dinosaurs and Fossils

Know and apply the concepts that explain how living things function, adapt, and change.

**Estimated Time:** 40 minutes          **Worksheets:** 99 and 100

## Quality Tool/PDSA Linkage

- ☐ Students will use the Cause-and-Effect Diagram.

  - The Cause-and-Effect Diagram is a picture of the output of a brainstorming session that asks, "What causes . . . ," and is used to determine root causes in the plan portion of the PDSA cycle.

## Lesson Overview

- ☐ The students will learn about the causes of dinosaurs' extinction.
- ☐ The students will work in groups to make skeletal models.

## Lesson Objectives

- ☐ The students will learn theories for the extinction of dinosaurs.
- ☐ The students will learn what adapting to one's environment means.
- ☐ The students will review how scientists learn about dinosaurs.
- ☐ The students will learn and use the Cause-and-Effect Diagram.

## Pre-Lesson Activities

- ☐ Obtain copies of the worksheets that go with the lesson.
- ☐ Obtain all materials needed for the lesson.
- ☐ Obtain resource material that students can use to look for environmental, geographical, food, and climate information of when dinosaurs lived.

## Materials Needed

- ☐ Worksheets.
- ☐ Chart paper.
- ☐ Markers.

## Lesson Delivery/Procedure

- ☐ The teacher leads a discussion with students about why dinosaurs are not around today.
- ☐ When the discussion is completed, the teacher can introduce the word "adapt" and discuss its meaning.
- ☐ The teacher will tell the students that dinosaurs are animals that lived millions of years ago, but no longer exist today because they could not adapt to changes around them.
- ☐ The teacher will ask the following question: How do we know this? What clues do scientists have to support this statement? The teacher should put up the statement about dinosaurs on the overhead projector or on chalkboard.
- ☐ The teacher will show the students books that are located around the room to help them discover how scientists know dinosaurs did not adapt to changes around them.

## Guided Practice

- ☐ The teacher places students in groups of three or four.

- ☐ Each group is then given a particular topic to study, for example, habitat, climate, geography, or food (worksheet 99).

- ☐ The teacher will review the Cause-and-Effect Diagram with students.

- ☐ The students read through the resource books looking for the causes of dinosaurs becoming extinct that covers their topic.

- ☐ The students also will investigate what clues scientists use to help them know this.

## Assessment

- ☐ The teacher will gather groups together to report out their findings.

- ☐ Together the teacher and students will complete the Cause-and-Effect Diagram (worksheet 99).

- ☐ The teacher can collect the students' research for formal assessment or informally assess their understanding during reporting out of information.

## Post-Lesson/Follow-Up Activities/Extensions

- ☐ The students can look at fossils and make observations.

- ☐ The students can make casts and molds to show how fossils are made.

- ☐ The students can also discover what an archaeologist does (worksheet 100).

## Supporting Resources

- ☐ *Digging for Dinosaurs* by Melvin Berger

- ☐ *Dinosaurs* by Gail Gibbons

- ☐ *A Dinosaur Named Sue: The Find of the Century* (Hello Reader! Science. Level 4) by Fay Robinson

- ☐ *Digging up Dinosaurs* by Aliki Brandenberg

- ☐ Worksheets 99 and 100

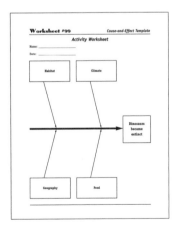

# Forms of Energy

Know and apply concepts that describe properties of matter and energy and the interactions between them.

**Estimated Time:** 40 minutes        **Worksheets:** 101 and 102

## Quality Tool/PDSA Linkage

☐ Students will use a Radar Chart and Brainstorming.

- The Radar Chart is a graph with multiple scales to report self-assessed knowledge or competence, often over time and is used during both the plan and study portions of the PDSA cycle.

- The Brainstorming technique is the generation of ideas by a group and is used at any portion of the PDSA cycle when every person needs to be heard from and many ideas need to be generated.

## Lesson Overview

☐ Using a Radar Chart, students will self-assess their familiarity with scientific terminology involving the various forms of energy.

☐ The students will create a plan to improve their knowledge of scientific terminology discussing the various forms of energy.

## Lesson Objectives

☐ The students will use a Radar Chart to assess knowledge of various forms of energy.

☐ The students will use the Brainstorming quality tool to create goals.

☐ The students will self-assess their familiarity with the forms of energy.

## Pre-Lesson Activities

☐ Obtain copies of the worksheets that go with the lesson.

☐ Obtain all materials needed for the lesson.

☐ Create a transparency of worksheet 101 to be used on the overhead.

## Materials Needed

☐ Pencils (for each student).

☐ Red marker.

☐ Overhead projector.

☐ Folder for each student.

☐ Chart paper.

☐ Black marker (for the chart paper).

☐ Dictionaries (optional).

☐ Science books (optional).

## Lesson Delivery/Procedure

- ☐ The teacher will announce that they will begin a new study discussing the various forms of energy.
- ☐ The teacher will ask the students "What is energy?"
- ☐ As a class, a definition of energy will be formed. During this time, other sources such as dictionaries and science books might be used.
- ☐ The teacher will review the Radar Chart tool and will pass out red markers to each student.
- ☐ The teacher will pass out worksheet 101 to each student.
- ☐ The teacher will display the replica of worksheet 101 on an overhead projector.
- ☐ The teacher will ask students to locate the word potential energy. The teacher will ask students to place a dot on the 1, 2, 3, 4, or 5 according to the level of knowledge of the concept (refer to the key on worksheet 101.)
- ☐ The students will mark each line according to level of knowledge of the concept (word) presented on that line.
- ☐ Once all the lines have been marked, the students will connect their dots.

## Guided Practice

- ☐ The class will discuss the results of their Radar Charts. (Some questions to prompt discussion: What kind of shape did you make? Was the shape you created big or small?)
- ☐ The teacher will explain that students will create a plan to help their shape/object grow even larger.
- ☐ The teacher will review the Brainstorming tool with students.
- ☐ The teacher will display a sheet of chart paper. As a class, students will brainstorm what they will need to do as a class to increase their knowledge of concepts (such as conduct experiments and read books about energy).
- ☐ The teacher will ask the class to choose the top three to five activities they will do as a class to become more knowledgeable about the forms of energy.
- ☐ The teacher will distribute a copy of worksheet 102 to students.
- ☐ As a class, brainstorm ideas of what students can do individually to improve their knowledge and application of the forms of energy on chart paper. Each student will complete the assignment.

## Assessment

- ☐ The teacher will monitor and hold conferences with each student to make sure students are choosing realistic items.
- ☐ The teacher will review the classroom goal.

## Post-Lesson/Follow-Up Activities/Extensions

- ☐ The students could complete the items selected from the brainstorm chart to increase knowledge and application of the forms of energy.
- ☐ The students could retake the Radar Chart to see if their level of understanding of the forms of energy has increased.

# Supporting Resources

☐   Worksheets 101 and 102

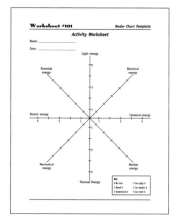

# Safety During Experimentation

Know and apply the accepted practices of science.

**Estimated Time:** 30 minutes          **Worksheets:** 103 and 104

## Quality Tool/PDSA Linkage

☐ Students will use the Cause-and-Effect Diagram and Brainstorming.

• The Cause-and-Effect Diagram is a picture of the output of a brainstorming session that asks, "What causes . . . ," and is used to determine root causes in the plan portion of the PDSA cycle.

• The Brainstorming technique is the generation of ideas by a group and is used at any portion of the PDSA cycle when every person needs to be heard from and many ideas need to be generated.

## Lesson Overview

☐ Using the Cause-and-Effect Diagram, students will determine the causes of conducting safe experiments.

## Lesson Objectives

☐ The students will use a Cause-and-Effect Diagram to organize information gathered.

☐ The students will use the Brainstorming quality tool to determine causes of conducting safe experiments.

☐ The students will enhance their knowledge about cause-and-effect relationships.

## Pre-Lesson Activities

☐ The students should be set up in a cooperative group setting.

☐ Obtain copies of the worksheets that go with the lesson.

☐ A replica of worksheet 103 should be created on a poster board.

☐ Obtain all materials needed for the activity.

☐ Lessons pertaining to cause-and-effect relationships could be performed prior to this relationship, although it is not necessary.

## Materials Needed

☐ Pencils (one per group).

☐ Markers.

☐ Posterboard.

## Lesson Delivery/Procedure

☐ The teacher will explain to the students that they will be conducting experiments to observe, investigate, and draw conclusions as real scientists do.

☐ The teacher will facilitate a discussion on the needs of scientists. (At this time, the teacher will guide the students into realizing the importance of safety.)

☐ The teacher will review or introduce (depending upon students prior knowledge) the concept of cause-and-effect relationships and the purpose of the Cause-and-Effect Diagram tool.

☐ The poster-board replica of the worksheet 103 should be displayed to the class.

- On the Cause-and-Effect Diagram, the teacher will place "safe experiments" in the Effect box.

- The teacher will review the Brainstorming tool with students.

- The teacher will ask the students to brainstorm the causes in the predetermined area of procedure that will lead to conducting safe experiments (for example, having an organized routine to gather the materials needed).

- The teacher will review the Cause-and-Effect Diagram with students.

- Using markers, the teacher will write down the information acquired by students underneath the heading of procedure on the Cause-and-Effect Diagram.

- The teacher will pass out worksheet 103 to each cooperative group.

- The teacher will assign each group a portion of the Cause-and-Effect Diagram to Brainstorm ideas. (Please note: depending upon the number of cooperative groups, some groups might work on the same section.)

## Guided Practice

- The teacher will discuss and add the information gathered by cooperative groups to the poster board replica of the Cause-and-Effect Diagram.

## Assessment

- The class will determine the validity of the Cause-and-Effect Diagram.

- The teacher will review student work, discussions, and findings to gauge level of understanding.

- The teacher will summarize the lesson objectives, findings, and key concepts of the lesson to remember.

## Post-Lesson/Follow-Up Activities/Extensions

- The class will put into action the Cause-and-Effect Diagram during the implementation of science experiments.

- The class could create a Cause-and-Effect Diagram about positive classroom environment (worksheet 104).

## Supporting Resources

- *Safe and Simple Electrical Experiments* by Rudolf F. Graf

- *Barron's Science Wizardry for Kids: Authentic, Safe Scientific Experiments Kids Can Perform!* by Margaret Kenda, et al.

- *www.srpnet.com/safety*

- Worksheets 103 and 104

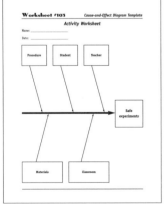

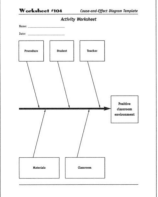

# Renewable and Nonrenewable Resources

Know and apply the concepts that describe the features and processes of the earth and its resources.

**Estimated Time:** 30 minutes          **Worksheets:** 105 and 106

## Quality Tool/PDSA Linkage

- ☐ Students will use a Bar Chart and a Check Sheet.
  - • The Bar Chart is a graph of categorical data plotted by frequency, and is used in the plan portion of the PDSA cycle.
  - • The Check Sheet/Matrix is a tool to collect and organize data in the plan portion of the PDSA cycle.

## Lesson Overview

- ☐ Using the Bar Chart and Check Sheet, students will determine their usage of renewable and nonrenewable resources.

## Lesson Objectives

- ☐ The students will use a Bar Chart quality tool to create a picture of data gathered.
- ☐ The students will use the Check Sheet quality tool to gather data.
- ☐ The students will examine their use of renewable and nonrenewable resources.

## Pre-Lesson Activities

- ☐ Obtain copies of the worksheets that go with the lesson.
- ☐ Obtain all materials needed for the lesson.
- ☐ The students will need knowledge of how to use the Check Sheet quality tool.
- ☐ A lesson identifying the types of renewable and nonrenewable resources should be conducted prior to assigning worksheet 105 for homework.
- ☐ The students should have prior knowledge of tally marks.
- ☐ Poster-size replica of worksheet 106 should be created.
- ☐ Students will need to have their homework assignment of worksheet 105 completed before proceeding with this lesson.
- ☐ Obtain all materials needed for this lesson.

## Materials Needed

- ☐ Crayons.
- ☐ Students' homework—completed worksheet 105.

## Lesson Delivery/Procedure

- ☐ The teacher will review the types of renewable and nonrenewable resources.
- ☐ The teacher will review the Check Sheet tool with students.

- ☐ The teacher will ask the students to obtain their homework assignment (worksheet 105) because they will be utilized in today's lesson.
- ☐ The teacher will lead a discussion of the student homework assignment. (The teacher might ask about the complications about the assignment, the patterns found, and anything interesting that might have occurred.)
- ☐ The teacher will review the Bar Chart tool with students.
- ☐ The teacher will ask students to create a picture of the data gathered by creating a Bar Chart quality tool.
- ☐ The teacher will model how to shade in the Bar Chart quality tool (poster-size replica of worksheet 106) using the data gathered from the Check Sheet (worksheet 105).

## Guided Practice

- ☐ The students will shade their Bar Chart using the data gathered from their Check Sheet.

## Assessment

- ☐ The students will discuss their results with a partner.
- ☐ The teacher will review student work, discussions, and findings to gauge level of understanding
- ☐ The students will self-assess their use of the renewable and nonrenewable resources.

## Post-Lesson/Follow-Up Activities/Extensions

- ☐ The class will come up with a plan to utilize more renewable resources on a daily basis.
- ☐ The students could keep track of their use of resources for longer, extended periods of time.

## Supporting Resources

- ☐ *Economic Renewal Guide: A Collaborative Process for Sustainable Community Development* by Michael Kinsley
- ☐ *www.sitesalive.com/ol/tg/private/oltgRenew.pdf*
- ☐ *www.nationalgeographic.com/xpeditions/lessons/16/gk2/everything.html*
- ☐ Worksheets 105 and 106

# Quality Across the Curriculum

# SCIENCE

4-5

## LESSONS

Simple Machines . . . . . . . . . . 143

Human Body . . . . . . . . . . . . . 145

Ground Water . . . . . . . . . . . 147

Energy . . . . . . . . . . . . . . . . 151

Plants . . . . . . . . . . . . . . . . . 155

Magnetism . . . . . . . . . . . . . . 157

Physical Properties
  of Matter . . . . . . . . . . . . . 159

Rocks and Minerals . . . . . . . . 163

Moon's Surface . . . . . . . . . . 167

# Simple Machines

Estimate measurements and determine acceptable levels of accuracy. Measure and compare quantities using appropriate units, instruments, and methods.

**Estimated Time:** 45 minutes          **Worksheets:** 107 and 108

## Quality Tool/PDSA Linkage

- ☐ Students will use a Check Sheet.

    - • The Check Sheet/Matrix is a tool to collect and organize data in the plan portion of the PDSA cycle.

## Lesson Overview

- ☐ The students will learn how to sort, organize, and analyze data about a related topic.

## Lesson Objectives

- ☐ The students will review or learn about simple machines and their purposes.

- ☐ The students will also review the importance of knowing how to sort information.

- ☐ The students will learn how to make a Check Sheet using the information related to simple machines.

- ☐ The students will share experiences they have had in making the Check Sheet and identify some other instances where using a Check Sheet may be helpful.

## Pre-Lesson Activities

- ☐ The teacher or class will study information about simple machines.

- ☐ Review with the class how to determine if a piece of information is important to include in the Check Sheet.

- ☐ The teacher will review with the class how to create the Check Sheet.

- ☐ Obtain copies of the worksheets that go with the lesson.

- ☐ Obtain all materials needed for the lesson.

## Materials Needed

- ☐ Pencils for students.

- ☐ Markers for teacher use.

- ☐ Worksheet corresponding to the lesson.

## Lesson Delivery/Procedure

- ☐ After the class has finished reading the material about simple machines the class will determine what are the important elements are about each of the machines.

- ☐ The teacher will introduce or review with students the use of the Check Sheet tool.

- ☐ The students and the teacher will discuss which of the details about simple machines will be useful in making the Check Sheet.

- ☐ The class will make a Check Sheet together on the overhead or board using the elements discussed as a class.

## Guided Practice

- [ ] The class will work together to complete the Check Sheet on simple machines (worksheet 107).
- [ ] The class will review what a Check Sheet is and other instances in which it could be used.

## Assessment

- [ ] The students will take notes of the different elements of simple machines and their purposes and will record the information on the Check Sheet.
- [ ] The teacher will review student work, discussion, and findings to gauge level of understanding of how to sort information.

## Post-Lesson/Follow-Up Activities/Extensions

- [ ] The students can take the idea of a Check Sheet home to share with parents and friends and then have them try to use the Check Sheet on their own. This will also promote the idea of thinking things through when needing to make a decision or organize a lot of data (information) that may be confusing or overwhelming.
- [ ] The students can challenge themselves by developing a Check Sheet (worksheet 108) to help them collect and organize data/information in a given subject area or at home with a given issue.
- [ ] The students can visit another grade with their Check Sheet and teach younger or older students how to collect and organize data/information.

## Supporting Resources

- [ ] Reading material about simple machines
- [ ] www.mos.org/sln/Leonardo/InventorsToolbox.html
- [ ] *Science Experiments With Simple Machines* (Science Experiments) by Sally Nankivell-Aston, Dorothy Jackson, and Sally Nankivell-Ashton
- [ ] Worksheets 107 and 108

# Human Body

Know and apply the concepts, principles, and processes of scientific inquiry.

**Estimated Time:** Two 40-minute sessions    **Worksheets:** 109 and 110

## Quality Tool/PDSA Linkage

☐ Students will use Brainstorming and a Bar Chart.

- The Brainstorming technique is the generation of ideas by a group and is used at any portion of the PDSA cycle when every person needs to be heard from and many ideas need to be generated.

- The Bar Chart is a graph of categorical data plotted by frequency, and is used in the plan portion of the PDSA cycle.

## Lesson Overview

☐ This is a hands-on lesson designed for students to demonstrate and apply knowledge of the scientific inquiry.

☐ Utilizing a Bar Chart, students make conclusions about the size of a bone and the weeks needed for it to heal.

## Lesson Objectives

☐ The students will understand the basics of data collection and graphing.

☐ The students will understand the concept of comparing data.

☐ The students will understand that the Bar Chart is used to show how the type of a bone influences healing time.

## Pre-Lesson Activities

☐ Obtain copies of the worksheets that go with the lesson.

☐ Obtain all materials needed for the lesson.

☐ Obtain permission from other teachers for their students to be surveyed.

☐ Review graphing skills.

☐ Create a class-sized poster board graph of the Bar Chart (worksheet 110).

## Materials Needed

☐ Student worksheets.

☐ Pencils.

☐ Markers or dot stickers.

☐ Large construction paper or bulletin board paper for the Bar Chart.

## Lesson Delivery/Procedure

☐ The teacher will facilitate a discussion using the following questions:
- Have any of you ever broken a bone?
- What treatments have you received for broken bones?
- Do you think it takes a large bone longer to heal than it takes a short bone to heal? (Perhaps choose long/short or large/small as a pair.)

- ☐ The teacher will explain what a Bar Chart is and how they are going to use this tool to see if there is a relationship between the size of a bone and the time it takes for it to heal.
- ☐ The teacher will review the Brainstorming tool with students.
- ☐ The class will identify students in the school that have broken a bone.
- ☐ The teacher will instruct the students to brainstorm survey questions to ask students about their broken bones, making sure they include which bone was broken and how many weeks it took for it to heal (worksheet 109).

## Guided Practice

- ☐ The students will then take their survey questions and direct them toward students in the other classes who have had broken bones.
- ☐ Once the data are collected, the information will be organized by the students.
- ☐ The teacher will review the Bar Chart tool with students.
- ☐ The students will then be given turns to plot the healing time of each bone on the Bar Chart (worksheet 110).
- ☐ The teacher will then lead a discussion about the Bar Chart. He or she will ask the class to note whether any conclusions can be made about the size of the bone and the healing time. The teacher will then ask the students to consider why or why not a relationship seems to exist.

## Assessment

- ☐ Each student will self-assess his or her assignment, checking to see if his or her interviewing sheets are complete.
- ☐ The teacher will evaluate if each student completed the survey, his or her own Bar Chart, and participated in the class discussion.

## Post-Lesson/Follow-Up Activities/Extensions

- ☐ The students could use other information from their surveys to make comparisons between things such as age, type of therapy, and so on.

## Supporting Resources

- ☐ *www.school.discovery.com/lessonplans/programs/givemeabreak/*
- ☐ *How the Body Works* by Steve Parker and Dorling Kindersley
- ☐ *Human Body* by Mary J. Wright
- ☐ Worksheets 109 and 110

# Ground Water

Understand the fundamental concepts, principles, and interconnections of the life, physical, and earth sciences.

**Estimated Time:** Day 1: 60 minutes     **Worksheets:** 111 and 112
Day 2–4: 15 minutes
Day 5: 60 minutes

## Quality Tool/PDSA Linkage

- ☐ Students will use a Flowchart and a Bar Chart.

  - The Flowchart is a drawing of any process used to document the process flow during the plan portion of the PDSA cycle.

  - The Bar Chart is a graph of categorical data plotted by frequency, and is used in the plan portion of the PDSA cycle.

## Lesson Overview

- ☐ The students will build an aquifer to demonstrate water seepage.

- ☐ The students will develop a Flowchart showing the step-by-step process to build an aquifer.

- ☐ The students will graph the amount of water added to the aquifer daily for five days.

- ☐ The students will discuss the results of their Bar Chart.

## Lesson Objectives

- ☐ The students will understand and use the Flowchart and Bar Chart.

- ☐ The students will understand how water moves through the ground.

- ☐ The students will construct an aquifer following the directions of the Flowchart.

- ☐ The students will keep a daily graph to show how much water is added to fill the aquifer.

- ☐ The students will discuss the results of their graph and draw conclusions.

## Pre-Lesson Activities

- ☐ Obtain copies of the worksheets that go with the lesson.

- ☐ Students should have some background knowledge of ground water and how it moves through the ground.

## Materials Needed

- ☐ Chart paper.

- ☐ Markers.

- ☐ Shallow box.

- ☐ Plastic wrap.

- ☐ Sand.

- ☐ Water.

- ☐ Small stones.

## Lesson Delivery/Procedure

- [ ] The teacher will discuss general concepts of how water moves through the ground.
- [ ] The teacher will give students directions for making the aquifer.

  1. Line a pan with a double layer of plastic wrap to represent the layer of rock that water cannot get through.

  2. Fill the lined box 3/4 full with sand.

  3. Slowly pour water along the outside of the box until the sand is damp.

  4. Dig a small hole in the center and line it with small stones to make a well.

  5. Watch the water level in the well rise.

  6. Add water each day to replenish the aquifer.

- [ ] The teacher will review the Flowchart tool with students.
- [ ] The students, in groups of three or four, will construct a Flowchart to show the process of constructing an aquifer (see worksheet 111 as an example).
- [ ] The students will construct an aquifer.
- [ ] Each day for five days students will add water to the aquifer.
- [ ] The students will graph the amount of water needed to fill the aquifer.
- [ ] After five days, students will draw conclusions about what happens to ground water.
- [ ] The teacher will review the Bar Chart tool with students.

## Guided Practice

- [ ] The students will use the Flowchart to show how to construct an aquifer.
- [ ] The students will graph data on a Bar Chart (worksheet 112) and draw conclusions about the construction of an aquifer.

## Assessment

- [ ] Small groups of students will explain how the aquifer worked, and the data that was collected.
- [ ] Students will explain Flowcharts and Bar Charts and describe how they were useful in the lesson.

## Post-Lesson/Follow-Up Activities/Extensions

- [ ] Add a pollutant to the aquifer and determine how pollution moves through the ground water.

## Supporting Resources

- [ ] *The River* by David Bellany
- [ ] *A Kid's Guide to How to Save the Planet* by Billy Goodman
- [ ] *Acid Rain* by National Geographic (software)
- [ ] *What Is in Our Water* by National Geographic (software)
- [ ] Worksheets 111 and 112

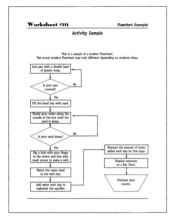

# Energy

Know and apply concepts that describe properties of matter and energy and the interactions between them.

**Estimated Time:** 30–40 minutes    **Worksheets:** 113 and 114

## Quality Tool/PDSA Linkage

- ☐ Students will use a Scatter Diagram.
  - • The Scatter Diagram is a tool used to show the relationship between two factors in the plan portion of the PDSA cycle.

## Lesson Overview

- ☐ This is a hands-on lesson designed for students to demonstrate potential energy.
- ☐ Utilizing a Scatter Diagram, students will see the relationship of height and potential energy.

## Lesson Objectives

- ☐ The students will discover that the higher an object is above the ground, the more potential energy is stored within the object.
- ☐ The students will measure distance in centimeters.
- ☐ The students will make predictions, record observations, and create hypotheses.
- ☐ The students will be able to define potential energy.
- ☐ The students will understand and use the Scatter Diagram quality tool.

## Pre-Lesson Activities

- ☐ Obtain copies of the worksheets that go with the lesson.
- ☐ Obtain all materials needed for the lesson.
- ☐ Set up a demonstration of rolling one marble from different heights down an inclined plane. Place the bottom section of a milk carton at the bottom of the ramp to catch the marble and measure the distance that it moves the carton.
- ☐ Review the definitions of potential energy.
- ☐ Create a poster board size Scatter Diagram (worksheet 114).

## Materials Needed

- ☐ One large marble.
- ☐ Inclined plane.
- ☐ Metric ruler.
- ☐ School milk carton.
- ☐ Worksheet.
- ☐ Posterboard.
- ☐ Marker.

## Lesson Delivery/Procedure

- ☐ The teacher will review the definition of potential energy.
- ☐ The teacher will review the Scatter Diagram tool with students.
- ☐ The teacher will display the poster size Scatter Diagram and explain that their goal will be to find the relationship between the the height that the marble is placed and the distance that the carton is moved.
- ☐ The teacher will have the students make their own prediction of how far the carton will move as the marble changes height.
- ☐ The teacher will ask the students to write their prediction on worksheet 113.
- ☐ The teacher will discuss the predictions with the students and see at which height the marble was predicted to have the most potential energy.

## Guided Practice

- ☐ The school milk carton will be opened and placed near the bottom of the approximately 45 degree inclined plane. The marble will be placed 10 cm from the carton on the first trial, 20 cm on the second trial, and 30 cm on the third trial. (Remember, the same marble will be used for each trial.)
- ☐ The teacher will then ask for volunteers to measure the distance the carton moves during each trial. Each marble will be rolled three times from each height.
- ☐ The students will record their findings on the data sheet (worksheet 113).
- ☐ As a class, the average distance the carton moved will be figured for each height.
- ☐ The averages will then be put on the poster-sized Scatter Diagram (worksheet 114) by chosen students.
- ☐ The teacher will then ask the students to compare their predictions with the actual data collected.
- ☐ The students will complete the Scatter Diagram (worksheet 114) using the actual measurement data from worksheet 113.

## Assessment

- ☐ The students will be asked: At which height did the marble have the most energy? Why?
- ☐ The students will be asked: What are some examples of storing and using energy in our environment? (wrecking ball, elevators, teeter-totters)
- ☐ The teacher will check to see if each student was able to complete the data and Scatter Diagram.

## Post-Lesson/Follow-Up Activities/Extensions

- ☐ The same experiment can be done using the mass of the marble as the variable instead of the initial height.

## Supporting Resources

- ☐ *www.brainpop.com/science/energy/energysources*
- ☐ *www.energyquest.ca.gov/teachers_resources/lesson_plans.html*
- ☐ *Eyewitness: Energy* by Jack Challoner, Clive Streeter
- ☐ Worksheets 113 and 114

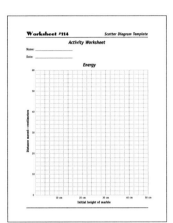

# Plants

Identify physical features of plants and animals that help them live in different environments.

**Estimated Time:** 45 minutes          **Worksheets:** 115 and 116

## Quality Tool/PDSA Linkage

☐ Students will use the Lotus Diagram and Check Sheet.

- The Lotus Diagram is a tool to expand thinking around a single topic or theme and is used at any portion of the PDSA cycle to generate additional thoughts.

- The Check Sheet/Matrix is a tool to collect and organize data in the plan portion of the PDSA cycle .

## Lesson Overview

☐ This is a "hands-on" lesson designed to review students' science vocabulary while learning about the Lotus Diagram and Check Sheet quality tools.

☐ Following a review of the meaning of monocot and dicot to insure consistency, students will name the attributes of each type of plant and organize their information on a Lotus Diagram.

## Lesson Objectives

☐ The students will be able to list the attributes of monocot and dicot plants using a Lotus Diagram and Check Sheet.

☐ By participating in this activity, students will be able to explain and identify the differences between monocot and dicot plants.

☐ The students will understand and use the Lotus Diagram and Check Sheet quality tools.

## Pre-Lesson Activities

☐ Obtain copies of the worksheets that go with the lesson.

☐ Obtain all materials needed for the lesson.

☐ Review monocot and dicot vocabulary with students.

☐ Obtain several kinds of monocot and dicot plants.

## Materials Needed

☐ Lotus Diagrams for each student.

☐ Check Sheets for each student.

☐ If possible, take the class outside to collect flowering plants from the area around the school, or request that the local plant store or nursery donate or loan a variety of flowering plants; supplement the collection with pictures and illustrations.

☐ Numbered cards for each plant in the collection.

## Lesson Delivery/Procedure

☐ The teacher will review the Lotus Diagram tool with students.

☐ The teacher will display, discuss, and list the attributes of each of the two classes of flowering plants with the class by completing the Lotus Diagram.

- [ ] The teacher will explain that botanists divide flowering plants into two classes—monocotyledons (monocots) and dicotyledons (dicots). The first sprout or cotyledon of a monocot has only one leaf, called the seed leaf. A dicot has two seed leaves. Most monocots have leaves with parallel veins and flower petals in multiples of three. Dicots, however, have leaves with veins that run in a netlike pattern and flower petals in multiples of four or five.

- [ ] The teacher will explain that the stems of a monocot have bundles of vascular tissue that are scattered throughout the ground tissue and a dicot's vascular bundles are arranged around a central core of ground tissue.

- [ ] The teacher will instruct the students to use the information from the class discussions and Lotus Diagrams to help them classify each numbered plant as a monocot or a dicot. Students should record the information on the Lotus Diagram worksheets. Students may work with a partner or group.

- [ ] After each student has completed their Lotus Diagram, the teacher will hold up the first plant and have a student volunteer and use the information from their Lotus Diagram to tell whether the plant is a monocot or a dicot and why. Continue with the other plants until they have all been correctly identified.

- [ ] The teacher will display each numbered plant one at a time.

## Guided Practice

- [ ] The teacher will instruct the students to use the information from the class discussions and Lotus Diagrams to help them classify each numbered plant as a monocot or a dicot.

- [ ] The students will record the information on the given Check Sheet Template (worksheet 116).

## Assessment

- [ ] After each student has completed worksheet 116, hold up the first plant and have a student volunteer and use the information from their Lotus Diagram to tell whether the plant is a monocot or a dicot and why. Then continue with the other plants until they have all been correctly identified.

- [ ] The students will record the information correctly on the given worksheets.

## Post-Lesson/Follow-Up Activities/Extensions

- [ ] On a trip to the Botanical Center students can make lists of all of the monocot and dicot plants they encounter on their tour of the center.

- [ ] Have students identify if they have more monocot or dicot plants around their neighborhood.

## Supporting Resources

- [ ] *www.riroe.k12.il.us/riroe/botanical/slininger/examples.html*

- [ ] *Michigan Flora—Gymnosperms and Monocots* by Edward G. Voss

- [ ] *Michigan Flora—Dicots* by Edward G. Voss

- [ ] Worksheets 115 and 116

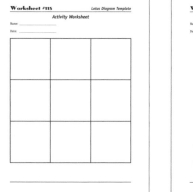

# Magnetism

Know and apply concepts that describe property of matter and energy and the interactions between them.

**Estimated Time:** 40 minutes          **Worksheet:** 117

## Quality Tool/PDSA Linkage

☐ Students will use the Flowchart.

- The Flowchart is a drawing of any process used to document the process flow during the plan portion of the PDSA cycle.

## Lesson Overview

☐ Using a Flowchart, students will create an electromagnet.

## Lesson Objectives

☐ The students will use the Flowchart quality tool.

☐ The students will create an electromagnet.

☐ The students will be able to follow written directions independently.

## Pre-Lesson Activities

☐ Lessons discussing magnets and their magnetic fields should be conducted prior to the implementation of this lesson.

☐ Obtain the materials needed for each student (plus one for demonstration lesson).

☐ Obtain copies of the worksheet that goes with the lesson.

## Materials Needed

☐ Nail

☐ D battery (Caution: Do not use rechargeable batteries because they can become very hot in a short amount of time.)

☐ D battery holder

☐ Wire (14 inches long with stripped ends)

☐ 25 paper clips (to be used in extension lesson)

## Lesson Delivery/Procedure

☐ The teacher will review the concept of magnets and magnetic fields with the class.

☐ The teacher will explain that a magnetic field can become stronger if an electric current is used (electromagnet).

☐ The teacher will review the Flowchart tool with students.

☐ The teacher will inform students that they will be creating electromagnets using a Flowchart.

☐ The teacher will pass out a copy of worksheet 117 (the Flowchart) to each student.

☐ The teacher will acquire the demonstration pack of materials.

- [ ] Using worksheet 117, the teacher will create an electromagnet. (During this time, students might want to take notes on their Flowchart about any questionable items.)
- [ ] After the completion of the demonstration lesson, the teacher and students will discuss the steps of the Flowchart.

## Guided Practice

- [ ] The teacher will pass out materials for each student to create his or her electromagnet.
- [ ] Using the Flowchart provided, students will begin to create their electromagnets.
- [ ] While students are creating electromagnets, the teacher will monitor students' progress and help students in need of assistance.

## Assessment

- [ ] The teacher will review student work by checking to see if the electromagnet is able to attract paper clips.
- [ ] The teacher will summarize the lesson objectives, findings, and key concepts of the lesson to remember.

## Post-Lesson/Follow-Up Activities/Extensions

- [ ] Creating their own Flowchart, students could create a modified electromagnet with more power.

## Supporting Resources

- [ ] *www.howstuffworks.com/electromagnet.htm*
- [ ] *education.jlab.org/beamsactivity/6thgrade/magnetsandelectromagnets*
- [ ] *Magnetism: Permanent Magnets and Electromagnets* by Daniel J. Spero, Gary Shipman
- [ ] *Exploring and Understanding Magnets and Electromagnets* by Edward Victor
- [ ] Worksheet 117

# Physical Properties of Matter

Know and apply concepts that describe property of matter and energy and the interactions between them.

**Estimated Time:** 45 minutes          **Worksheets:** 118 and 119

## Quality Tool/PDSA Linkage

☐ Students will use the Check Sheet and Brainstorming.

  • The Check Sheet/Matrix is a tool to collect and organize data in the plan portion of the PDSA cycle.

  • The Brainstorming technique is the generation of ideas by a group and is used at any portion of the PDSA cycle when every person needs to be heard from and many ideas need to be generated.

## Lesson Overview

☐ Using the Check Sheet quality tool, students will determine the physical properties of preselected objects.

## Lesson Objectives

☐ The students will use a Check Sheet quality tool to gather data.

☐ The students will use the Brainstorming quality tool to acquire data.

☐ The students will be able to describe and classify objects according to their physical properties.

## Pre-Lesson Activities

☐ The students should be set up in cooperative groups.

☐ Obtain copies of worksheet 118 for each cooperative group.

☐ Obtain all materials needed for the activity.

☐ Introduce the concept of matter prior to the implementation of the lesson.

☐ Fill a paper bag with the following items for each group: baseball, unsharpened pencil, rubber band, sponge, tissue, small candle, silly putty, shoe lace, and a rock.

☐ Fill a paper bag with an orange, eraser, and paper clip to be used in a classroom demonstration.

☐ Create a chart-size replica of worksheet 118.

## Materials Needed

☐ Chart paper.

☐ Markers.

☐ Pencils (for each student).

☐ Dictionary.

☐ A paper bag filled with (one for each group): baseball, unsharpened pencil, rubber band, sponge, tissue, small candle, silly putty, shoe lace, and rock.

☐ A paper bag filled with an orange, eraser, and paper clip (for classroom demonstration).

## Lesson Delivery/Procedure

☐ The teacher will review and discuss the concept of matter.

☐ The teacher will introduce the word "property" to students by writing it on the board.

☐ The teacher will ask a volunteer to look up the word "property" in the dictionary. While the volunteer searches for the definition of property, the teacher will ask students to explain what they think the word means.

☐ Using the dictionary definition and the student responses, the class will compose a classroom-friendly definition of the word property.

☐ On a sheet of chart paper, the teacher will write *properties of matter*.

☐ The teacher will review the Brainstorming tool with students.

☐ The class will brainstorm properties of matter (for example, size, shape, color, taste, smell, hardness, length, and weight).

☐ The teacher will review the Check Sheet tool with students.

☐ The teacher will display the chart size replica of worksheet 118.

☐ Using the brainstorm list, the teacher will select four properties of matter that he or she would like to use and will place this information on the chart of worksheet 118.

☐ Using the items from the demonstration bag, the teacher will display an item, making sure to write the name of the item on the chart paper, and discuss its properties according to the ones chosen with class.

☐ The teacher will record the description of the property of the objects in the appropriate boxes.

## Guided Practice

☐ The teacher will pass out worksheet 118 to each cooperative group.

☐ The teacher will pass out bags to each cooperative group.

☐ Each group will select the physical properties that will be used to examine items from the bag. (During this time, discuss any properties that should not be used due to safety concerns.)

☐ Each group will pull items from the bag, discuss and record its physical properties on worksheet 118.

## Assessment

☐ The teacher will review student work, discussions, and findings to gauge level of understanding.

☐ The teacher will summarize the lesson objectives, findings, and key concepts of the lesson to remember.

## Post-Lesson/Follow-Up Activities/Extensions

☐ Students could read the story, *Big and Small* by Christopher Erickson and discuss the physical properties of the objects discussed in the book.

☐ Students could create a Lotus Diagram discussing the properties of an object.

☐ Using worksheet 119, students could find the following items in their home and discuss their properties as a homework assignment.

## Supporting Resources

- [ ] *www.stcms.si.edu/pom/pom_student.htm*

- [ ] *Big and Small* by Christopher Erickson

- [ ] *What Is the World Made Of? All About Solids, Liquids, and Gases (Let's-Read-and-Find-Out Science, Stage 2)* by Kathleen Weidner Zoehfeld (author), Paul Meisel (illustrator)

- [ ] *Gases, Liquids, and Solids: And Other States of Matter* by D. Tabor

- [ ] Worksheets 118 and 119

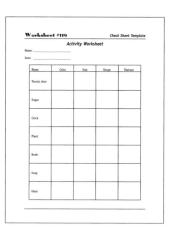

# Rocks and Minerals

Know and apply concepts that describe the features of the earth and its resources.

**Estimated Time:** Two 45-minute sessions     **Worksheets:** 120 and 121

## Quality Tool/PDSA Linkage

☐ Students will use the Check Sheet and Radar Chart.

- The Check Sheet/Matrix is a tool to collect and organize data in the plan portion of the PDSA cycle.

- The Radar Chart is a graph with multiple scales to report self-assessed knowledge or competence, often over time and is used during both the plan and study portions of the PDSA cycle.

## Lesson Overview

☐ This is a hands-on lesson designed to teach the students about rocks and minerals while utilizing the Check Sheet and Radar Chart.

☐ Following the Radar Chart, the students will take notes about rocks and minerals before they start testing different rocks and minerals for their luster, streak, hardness, shininess, color, and other properties identified on their Check Sheet.

☐ The students will also review how to minimize variables when completing the scientific process in this activity.

## Lesson Objectives

☐ The students will learn how rocks are formed.

☐ The students will become familiar with the rock cycle that is always evolving. They will learn how the rocks that they observe are part of the rock cycle.

☐ The students will learn that all rocks are not the same and that they have different properties that make them unique.

☐ The students will observe each rock and record its properties on a Check Sheet.

☐ The students will measure their understanding of the different properties used to classify rocks and minerals by using the Radar Charts both as a pre- and post-lesson activity.

☐ The students will understand and use the Check Sheet and Radar Chart quality tools.

## Pre-Lesson Activities

☐ Obtain copies of the worksheets that go with the lesson.

☐ Obtain all materials needed for the lesson.

## Materials Needed

For each group:

☐ Basalt rock.

☐ Sandstone rock.

☐ Limestone rock.

☐ Igneous rock.

- ☐ Granite rock.
- ☐ Hand lens.
- ☐ Ceramic streak plate.
- ☐ Copper penny.
- ☐ Glass pop bottle.
- ☐ Magnet.
- ☐ Five copies of the Check Sheet or one for each mineral testing.

## Lesson Delivery/Procedure

- ☐ The teacher will review the Radar Chart tool with students.
- ☐ The teacher will have the students complete the initial Radar Chart asking them to identify what they know about each of the terms (worksheet 120).
- ☐ Once students have completed the Radar Chart, the teacher will explain that they will be learning about each of the terms on the Radar Chart with the hands-on activity.
- ☐ The teacher will review the Check Sheet tool with students.
- ☐ The teacher will give each student the lesson's worksheet for taking notes. Students will write down the properties of rocks and minerals and define each of the properties more in depth (worksheet 121). Students should check each of the properties of the rocks and minerals on the worksheet.
- ☐ After students complete the note taking, the class will review each of the properties again (luster, streak, hardness, light transmission, and other properties).
- ☐ The teacher will model the process to complete each test.
  - The luster test is simply looking for shininess.
  - For the streak test, model how to scratch the rock on a ceramic plate. If it leaves a colored streak, then what color is left on the streak plate?
  - For the hardness test, the students will need to scratch the rock on their fingernail, then the copper penny, and, finally, the glass. The students need to observe the scratch made on the three objects. Explain that if they can rub the scratch off the object, then it really isn't a scratch but is residue left by the rock or mineral. The rock must really scratch the surface of the item being rubbed to count.
  - The next test to model is whether the rock transmits light. Demonstrate transparent by using a transparency. Explain that if you can see light but you can't see the item clearly then it is translucent. Opaque lets no light through.
  - Other properties to test for are magnetism, brittleness, and granularity (or does it have grains).
- ☐ Next, the teacher will model the use of the Check Sheet while completing the rock tests.

## Guided Practice

- ☐ Students (in their cooperative groups) will complete each of the tests using the Check Sheet (worksheet 121) to record their data. They will need to look back at their note-taking sheet if they have any questions about what the different rock tests mean.

## Assessment

- ☐ The students will analyze their data by looking for similarities and differences between minerals tested. The teacher will ask, "How are the samples alike?" "How are they different?" "How do you think the samples were formed?" "Why do you think so?"

- [ ] The students will summarize their findings by recording their data on the class Check Sheet and reporting to the class what they discovered about each rock. They will then compare and contrast the physical properties of each type of rock with the other rock types.

- [ ] Once the discussion is completed about the investigation, have students choose a different color of marker to complete the Radar Chart (worksheet 120) again now that they have learned about the different properties of rocks.

- [ ] The teacher can check over student work to observe their level of understanding with this lesson.

## Post-Lesson/Follow-Up Activities/Extensions

- [ ] The teacher will ask other questions such as: Were all the rocks the same? What made them different? Did you know that there are three different types of rocks? Do you know what they are? Why are rocks and minerals important to know about? How do rocks change? What is the rock cycle?

## Supporting Resources

- [ ] *www.realtime.net/anr/minerals.html*

- [ ] Worksheets 120 and 121

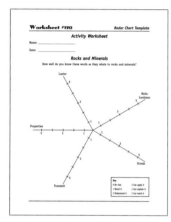

# Moon's Surface

Know and apply concepts that explain the composition and structure of the universe and earth's place in it.

**Estimated Time:** 45 minutes    **Worksheets:** 122, 123, and 124

## Quality Tool/PDSA Linkage

☐ Students will use the Check Sheet and Operational Definition.

- The Check Sheet/Matrix is a tool to collect and organize data in the plan portion of the PDSA cycle.

- Operational Definition is a standard process for measuring the critical quality characteristics used before gathering data in the plan portion of the PDSA cycle.

## Lesson Overview

☐ This is a hands-on lesson designed to educate the students about the surface of the moon while using a quality tool.

☐ The students will observe what the moon's surface looks like and will explore reasons why it appears as it does by simulating meteorites crashing into the moon.

☐ Students will record their findings and then report their data to the class using a Check Sheet.

## Lesson Objectives

☐ The students will review what the surface of the moon looks like.

☐ The students will learn how craters are formed on the moon's surface.

☐ The students will also learn how the height and size of the meteorite determine the size of the craters left on the moon.

☐ The students will understand the importance of minimizing variables in scientific exploration and data collection.

☐ The students will understand and use the Check Sheet and Operational Definition quality tools.

## Pre-Lesson Activities

☐ Gather all materials needed for the lesson.

☐ Obtain copies of the worksheets that go with the lesson.

☐ Gather pictures of the moon's surface to show to the class.

☐ Make the modeling dough for each group.

## Materials Needed

☐ Pictures of the moon's surface.

☐ Aluminum pie pan for each group.

☐ 1/4 c. flour for each group.

☐ Marbles.

☐ Golf balls.

☐ Meter sticks.

☐ Bag of modeling dough for each group.

## Lesson Delivery/Procedure

- [ ] The teacher will show the students pictures of the moon from the Internet. What do the students observe? What do the students think about the different shades? What could have caused the indentations?

- [ ] The teacher will model how to set up the activity. Begin by spreading the dough evenly on the bottom of a pan. Flour should be sprinkled over the dough to represent the moon dust.

- [ ] The teacher will ask what a marble would represent in space. Students would brainstorm ideas.

- [ ] The teacher will demonstrate how to drop the marble onto the dough from the designated heights.

- [ ] The teacher should talk with the students about reducing the amount of variables when completing the lab.

- [ ] The teacher will review the Operational Definition tool with students.

- [ ] The teacher should take the students through the Operational Definition that is provided to minimize the amount of variables when dropping the ball into the dough (see worksheet 124).

- [ ] The teacher will discuss how important it is to drop the items consistantly by using the meter stick to control the height. The teacher should talk about how to drop the marble versus throwing it down.

## Guided Practice

- [ ] The teacher will place the students into groups of four.

- [ ] One student from each group should get the materials for their group.

- [ ] The teacher will review the Check Sheet tool with students.

- [ ] The students will begin the activity and complete the Check Sheet (worksheet 122), recording the data that they discover while dropping the different balls into the dough.

## Assessment

- [ ] The students will look at the relationship between the height from which the ball was dropped, the weight of the ball, and the size of the crater.

- [ ] The groups will report their results to the class.

- [ ] Once students have completed the Check Sheet, they will complete the summary section. The teacher will ask, "What did you (students) observe when analyzing the data?"

- [ ] The teacher will review the students' work, discussion, and findings to gauge their level of understanding.

## Post-Lesson/Follow-Up Activities/Extensions

- [ ] Prepare the students for moon gazing. Have the students record what the moon looks like each day for two weeks (worksheet 123).

- [ ] The teacher will explain that crashing meteorites or space rocks caused most of the depressions on its surface.

- [ ] The teacher will share that the depressions are also caused by the cracks made from the meteorites when lava oozes and fills the craters, and then cools to form smooth, dark rocks. Lava-filled craters are called Maria and are the darkest part of the lunar surface. Some craters are formed by volcanoes too.

- [ ] Follow-up questions may include: "How does the moon change each day?" or "Why does the moon look different each day?"

# Supporting Resources

- [ ] *www.teachspacescience.stsci.edu*
- [ ] *www.lunacity.com*
- [ ] Worksheets 122, 123, and 124

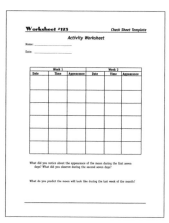

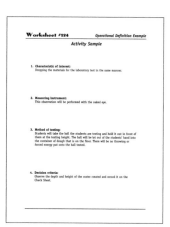

# Quality Across the Curriculum

# SOCIAL STUDIES

## K-1

### LESSONS

Native American Tribes . . . . . 173

Abraham Lincoln . . . . . . . . . . 177

Careers . . . . . . . . . . . . . . . . . 179

Map Skills . . . . . . . . . . . . . . 181

School Rules . . . . . . . . . . . . . 185

Field Trip to the
   Fire Station . . . . . . . . . . . 189

Traditions . . . . . . . . . . . . . . 193

Political Systems/
   Government . . . . . . . . . . . . 195

Families . . . . . . . . . . . . . . . . 199

# Native American Tribes

Understand events, trends, individuals, and movements shaping the history of the state, the United States, and other nations.

**Estimated Time:** 45 minutes          **Worksheets:** 125 and 126

## Quality Tool/PDSA Linkage

☐ Students will use a Lotus Diagram and a Check Sheet/Matrix.

- The Lotus Diagram is a tool to expand thinking around a single topic or theme and is used at any portion of the PDSA cycle to generate additional thoughts.

- The Check Sheet/Matrix is a tool to collect and organize data in the plan portion of the PDSA cycle.

## Lesson Overview

☐ This lesson requires students to use the Lotus Diagram quality tool as a graphic organizer for research of a North American Indian tribe (in the early years).

☐ The students will look in informational books to find eight facts about selected Native American tribes, including the type of dwelling and what region the tribe lived in, as this information will be used later and analyzed with a Check Sheet/Matrix.

☐ The students will use a Check Sheet/Matrix to see if there is a relationship between the type of dwelling and where the tribes lived.

## Lesson Objectives

☐ The students will learn basic research strategies.

☐ The students will identify at least two names of Native American homes.

☐ The students will learn about and appreciate the Native American culture.

☐ The students will compare and contrast the eight main facts about Native Americans on the Lotus Diagram with our current culture, dress, foods, and so on.

☐ The students will build vocabulary skills.

☐ The students will become familiar with states and regions on a map of North America (United States and Canada).

☐ The students will understand and use the Lotus Diagram and Check Sheet/Matrix quality tools.

## Pre-Lesson Activities

☐ Read a variety of fiction and nonfiction picture books about Native Americans who lived in different regions throughout the United States and Canada.

☐ Select common tribes to research (insuring there are adequate materials available for each tribe). List the tribal names on a chart. Assign one tribe per student or cooperative group.

☐ Create a poster board size Lotus Diagram (worksheet 125).

☐ Obtain copies of the worksheets that go with the lesson.

☐ Create a poster board size Check Sheet/Matrix (worksheet 126).

☐ Obtain all other materials needed for the lesson.

## Materials Needed

- ☐ Multiple nonfiction and fiction books about Native American tribes.
- ☐ Enlarged Lotus Diagram.
- ☐ Copies of Lotus Diagram—one per student or cooperative group.
- ☐ Enlarged Check Sheet/Matrix.
- ☐ Chart, markers.
- ☐ Map of North America (laminated, if desired, for reuse).

## Lesson Delivery/Procedure

- ☐ The teacher will review the Lotus Diagram tool with students.
- ☐ The teacher will model use of the Lotus Diagram to research a given Native American tribe.
- ☐ Using the enlarged Lotus Diagram (worksheet 125), the teacher and class will use a variety of books to find and write eight facts about a selected tribe.
- ☐ The teacher should model how to use pictures, captions, charts, and the index (if appropriate) to find these eight facts.
- ☐ The teacher will assign one tribe from the list per student or cooperative group and distribute the (individual) Lotus Diagrams (worksheet 125).
- ☐ The students will be given support and adequate time to find eight facts about their assigned tribe. (Several sessions may be necessary for the students to complete the Lotus Diagrams.)
- ☐ The students will be allowed to write the facts *or draw pictures* to illustrate the facts. (If pictures are drawn, an adult should write the students' dictated labels for each picture.)
- ☐ The students should share the information about each tribe in a whole-class group to familiarize classmates with a variety of tribal cultures.
- ☐ The teacher will review the Check Sheet/Matrix tool with students.
- ☐ In the last part of this lesson, the students will use two facts—the name of the tribal home and the location of the tribe—to complete a whole-class Check Sheet/Matrix. The teacher will help the students connect ideas and try to establish relationships between these two facts.
- ☐ The teacher will display the enlarged Check Sheet/Matrix (worksheet 126).
- ☐ For the purposes of this lesson, common dwellings listed on the Check Sheet/Matrix include teepee, wigwam, longhouse, pueblo, plank house, and "other" for all other types of dwellings. The regions will be divided as Northwest, Southwest, Midwest, Northeast, and Southeast.
- ☐ The students will be asked to identify their tribe's type of home, and locate the tribe's region on the map of North America (with help, as needed).
- ☐ The students will then mark the appropriate square on the Check Sheet/Matrix with an X. (For example, if their tribe lived in longhouses and in the Midwest region, the students would mark an X in that box.) If the dwelling is in the "other" category, the teacher can decide whether to have students mark an X, or to write the name of the dwelling on the Matrix to promote vocabulary.
- ☐ Once all students or groups have contributed, the teacher will promote discussion to make connections about the type of tribal dwellings and where the tribes lived. (For example, tribes may have lived in longhouses in the Midwest due to colder weather.)

## Guided Practice

- ☐ The teacher will decide if other regions can be used such as the "Culture Areas of North America," that is, Northwest Coast; Sub-arctic; Plateau; Great Basin; California; Plains; Southwest; Southeast; and Northeast Woodlands.

- ☐ The teacher will create a modified Check Sheet/Matrix on the map of North America by attaching small pictures of each dwelling to the correct region where each tribe lived.

- ☐ The teacher will research what Native American tribe(s) lived in your state and in what type of dwelling(s). Complete a Lotus Diagram for these tribes as a class and discuss.

- ☐ The teacher will write or dictate a story using the eight facts about the researched tribes.

- ☐ The teacher will write a letter to the tribal council of your researched tribe to tell them about the research, and to ask how their lives have changed (see Web site listed in the Supporting Resources section).

## Assessment

- ☐ The students will draw and label their tribe's home.

- ☐ After the Check Sheet/Matrix is completed, the student will be able to identify the region where his or her researched tribe lived and locate it on a map of North America.

## Post-Lesson/Follow-Up Activities/Extensions

- ☐ More than half of our 50 states' names come from Native American words. Research which states have these names and what they mean. (For example, Alaska is an Aleut word for "great land" or "land not an island.")

- ☐ Create fine arts and crafts representation of each tribe.

- ☐ Learn Native American dances and/or ceremonies of different tribes.

- ☐ Native American names often remind the families of important animals (Running Bear), nature (Whispering Wind), or wishes (She Who Sings with Birds). Students can pick a similar Native American name and explain why the name was chosen.

- ☐ The students will learn and write Native American symbols/sign language.

- ☐ Organize a Native American "food-tasting" party. (Sample foods include buffalo meat, berries, corn, and fish.)

- ☐ Draw and color or paint a tribal scene with the tribe's homes, people, and habitat depicted.

## Supporting Resources

☐ (Addresses of current Native American Tribes of the United States and Canada.)
*www.dickshovel.com/trbindex.html.*

☐ Links to many Native Tribes of the United States and Canada: Yahooligans/School Bell/Social Studies/
Cultures/Native America/Tribes, Nations, and Bands at *www.yahooligans.com.*

☐ *North American Indian Sign Language* by Karen Liptak

☐ *Children of the Earth and Sky: Five Stories About Native American Children* by Stephen Krensky

☐ *Children of the Wind and Water: Five Stories About Native American Children* by Stephen Krensky

☐ Worksheets 125 and 126

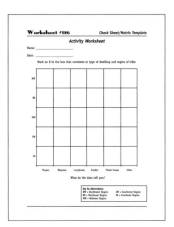

# Abraham Lincoln

## Understand the development of significant political events.

**Estimated Time:** 45 minutes    **Worksheets:** 127, 128, and 129

## Quality Tool/PDSA Linkage

☐ Students will use the Cause-and-Effect Diagram and Affinity Diagram.

- The Cause-and-Effect Diagram is a picture of the output of a brainstorming session that asks, "What causes . . . ," and is used to determine root causes in the plan portion of the PDSA cycle.

- The Affinity Diagram is a tool to generate, organize, and consolidate information gathered through Brainstorming, and is used in many portions of the PDSA cycle.

## Lesson Overview

☐ This lesson is designed to increase students' understanding of the life of Abraham Lincoln.

☐ As a result of this increased understanding, students will understand that Abraham Lincoln was a great leader.

☐ Students will recall details of their instruction and then use the Affinity Diagram and the Cause-and-Effect Diagram to organize their recollections for increased understanding.

## Lesson Objectives

☐ The students will comprehend and retell accurate information about Abraham Lincoln.

☐ The students will understand Abraham Lincoln's contributions to the United States.

☐ The students will understand the events in Abraham Lincoln's life that caused him to become a great leader.

☐ The students will understand and use the Affinity Diagram and Cause-and-Effect Diagram quality tools.

## Pre-Lesson Activities

☐ Obtain copies of the worksheets that go with the lesson.

☐ Have a brief discussion with students about Abraham Lincoln.

☐ Obtain all materials needed for the lesson.

## Materials Needed

☐ *A Picture Book of Abraham Lincoln* by David A. Adler.

☐ *Young Abraham Lincoln* by Andrew Woods.

☐ Markers.

☐ Butcher paper with Cause-and-Effect Diagram outline.

☐ Post-It notes.

## Lesson Delivery/Procedure

☐ The teacher will ask students about their prior knowledge of Abraham Lincoln.

☐ The students will write one thing they know about Abe Lincoln, or alternately the teacher will write students' responses as a shared writing experience—one idea per Post-It note.

☐ The teacher will review the Affinity Diagram tool with students.

☐ Together, students and the teacher will organize and group Post-It notes according to similarities. Use worksheet 129 as a guide.

☐ The teacher will read aloud to students *Young Abe Lincoln* and *A Picture Book of Abraham Lincoln* or another available book about Abe Lincoln.

## Guided Practice

☐ After listening to the stories, students will make necessary additions to the Affinity Diagram.

☐ The teacher will introduce the Cause-and-Effect Diagram tool.

☐ The teacher will refer to the Affinity Diagram to fill in the "headings" of the Cause-and-Effect Diagram.

☐ As a class, the teacher will solicit information to fill in each arm of the Cause-and-Effect Diagram (worksheet 128).

☐ The students will fill in their own Cause-and-Effect Diagram, or may work with a partner, while the teacher completes the whole group example.

☐ The students may also complete the Cause-and-Effect Diagram with a partner or in small groups following the teacher modeling/group activity.

## Assessment

☐ Students will correctly sort Post-It Notes in the Affinity Diagram.

☐ Students will recall/retell five or more events that helped Abraham Lincoln to become a great leader.

☐ Students will share their findings with the group (or with a partner).

☐ Students will complete their Cause-and-Effect Diagram correctly to demonstrate comprehension.

## Post-Lesson/Follow-Up Activities/Extensions

☐ Draw a picture of Abraham Lincoln's log cabin.

☐ Write an expository paragraph about Abraham Lincoln's childhood.

☐ Write a persuasive paragraph listing reasons we should not have slavery.

☐ Write how our country would be different if Abraham Lincoln had never been president.

☐ Make a model of Lincoln's log cabin using pretzels and a milk carton.

## Supporting Resources

☐ *Abe Lincoln's Hat* by Donald Cook

☐ *Abe Lincoln: Log Cabin to White House* by Sterling North

☐ *Abe Lincoln, the Boy Who Loved Books* by Nancy Carpenter

☐ Worksheets 127, 128, and 129

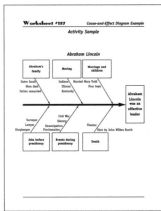
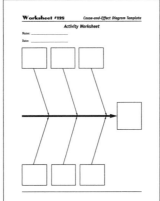

# Careers

Understand the roles and interactions of individuals and groups in society.

**Estimated Time:** 45 minutes          **Worksheets:** 130 and 131

## Quality Tool/PDSA Linkage

☐ Students will use Brainstorming, a Cause-and-Effect Diagram, and an Affinity Diagram.

- The Brainstorming technique is the generation of ideas by a group and is used at any portion of the PDSA cycle when every person needs to be heard from and many ideas need to be generated.

- The Cause-and-Effect Diagram is a picture of the output of a brainstorming session that asks, "What causes . . . ," and is used to determine root causes in the plan portion of the PDSA cycle.

- The Affinity Diagram is a tool to generate, organize, and consolidate information gathered through Brainstorming, and is used in many portions of the PDSA cycle.

## Lesson Overview

☐ This is a lesson that utilizes classroom discussion and sharing of ideas.

☐ Utilizing a Cause-and-Effect Diagram and the Affinity Diagram, students will understand how multiple people are needed to run a business.

## Lesson Objectives

☐ The students will be able to recognize the importance of careers and how people with different jobs are needed to work together to run a business.

☐ The students will understand and use the Cause-and-Effect Diagram, Brainstorming, and Affinity Diagram.

## Pre-Lesson Activities

☐ Obtain copies of the worksheets that go with the lesson.

☐ Obtain all materials needed for the lesson.

☐ Obtain books and pictures about different career choices.

☐ Review the functions of different careers.

## Materials Needed

☐ Post-It notes.

☐ Student worksheets.

☐ Poster-size Cause-and-Effect Diagram.

## Lesson Delivery/Procedure

☐ The teacher will ask the students to recall different careers that they know about.

☐ The teacher will review the Cause-and-Effect Diagram with students.

□ The teacher will display the poster-size Cause-and-Effect Diagram and explain to the students that they are going to use this tool to show the many different people needed to run a certain type of business or do a certain type of job.

## Guided Practice

□ The teacher will decide on a business or job to put in the effect portion of the Cause-and-Effect Diagram.

□ The teacher will ask the students to aid him or her in deciding what tasks need to be done in order to get the given job done.

□ The teacher will review the Brainstorming tool with students.

□ The students will write or draw these tasks on Post-It notes as part of the Brainstorming session.

□ The teacher will review the Affinity Diagram tool with students.

□ The class will work together to sort the tasks according to what person would be doing that task. Then the class will decide on the name of that position. The students will complete the Affinity Diagram.

□ After completing the Affinity Diagram (worksheet 130), the teacher will direct the students to the Cause-and-Effect Diagram. Students can fill in their own Cause-and-Effect Diagram (worksheet 131) or the teacher can fill it in as part of a shared writing experience.

## Assessment

□ The students will explain their completed Cause-and-Effect Diagram and how each career helps in running the given business or job.

## Post-Lesson/Follow-Up Activities/Extensions

□ The students can be divided into cooperative groups and choose a job or business to make a new Affinity Diagram and Cause-and-Effect Diagram for an agreed-upon job or business.

□ The class can write a story about the business used in the Cause-and-Effect Diagram using the activities that were brainstormed as details.

## Supporting Resources

□ Bureau of Labor Statistics Career Information, *www.stats.bls.gov/k12/html/edu_over.htm*

□ Career Day Ideas, *www.etc.i-kan.org/teachers/lesson_plans/tool_of_the_month/apr_el_le_career_day.htm*

□ Community Club, *www.teacher.scholastic.com/commclub/index.htm*

□ Worksheets 130 and 131

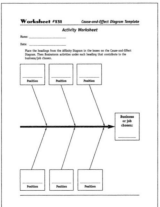

# Map Skills

Understand world geography and the effects of geography on society, with an emphasis on the United States.

**Estimated Time:** 30 minutes for planning purposes; ongoing throughout the school year

**Worksheets:** 132 and 133

## Quality Tool/PDSA Linkage

☐ Students will use the Check Sheet and Bar Chart.

  • The Check Sheet/Matrix is a tool to collect and organize data in the plan portion of the PDSA cycle.

  • The Bar Chart is a graph of categorical data plotted by frequency, and is used in the plan portion of the PDSA cycle.

## Lesson Overview

☐ This is a fun lesson that helps students learn about geographical regions and states.

☐ A stuffed bear (or bears) will travel with families, friends, and extended relatives on vacations or weekend excursions throughout the United States.

☐ Postcards will be sent to school from each destination. The postcards will be read and displayed on a bulletin board that displays a U.S. map.

☐ Destinations will be checked and listed on a Check Sheet, and then located on an enlarged U.S. map with colored pins.

☐ Periodically, the data from the Check Sheet will be transferred to a Bar Chart.

## Lesson Objectives

☐ The students will become more familiar with a U.S. map.

☐ The students will locate the city and state where they live on a U.S. map.

☐ The students will help designate five regions on a U.S. map (Northwest, Southwest, Midwest, Northeast, and Southeast).

☐ The students will locate cities and states on a U.S. map that are vacation destinations.

☐ The students will locate the United States on a world map.

☐ The students will understand and use the Check Sheet and Bar Chart quality tools.

## Pre-Lesson Activities

☐ Acquire one to four stuffed bears (as determined by the class).

☐ Set up a bulletin board with a U.S. map and space for additions of postcards or artifacts, the Check Sheet, and Bar Chart.

☐ Obtain copies of the worksheets that go with the lesson.

☐ Obtain all materials needed for the lesson.

## Materials Needed

☐ Worksheet 132—Check Sheet (enlarged if desired).

☐ Worksheet 133—Bar Chart (enlarged if desired).

- ☐ One to four stuffed bears (number determined by the class).
- ☐ U.S. map, laminated.
- ☐ Overhead transparency pens.
- ☐ Map or colored pins.
- ☐ Notebook paper for letter.

## Lesson Delivery/Procedure

- ☐ The teacher will introduce the lesson by explaining that the bear(s) will be traveling with student families, relatives, or friends throughout the United States. Postcards will be sent to school from the "bears" and the class will chart their destinations on a U.S. map with colored pins. This activity will be an ongoing project throughout the school year.
- ☐ The teacher will review the Bar Chart tool with students.
- ☐ Data will be collected as to regions visited by the bear(s). These data will be transferred to a Bar Chart (worksheet 133) for further analysis.
- ☐ The students will list ways the bear(s) can travel, for example, "When I go to Minnesota to visit my grandparents," "When my cousins take a vacation to Florida," or "When we go to Colorado over winter break."
- ☐ Further discussion can include occupations of relatives or friends that provide more opportunities for travel, for example, flight attendants, truck drivers, or sales representatives.
- ☐ Parents will be informed of this yearlong project by newsletter so that they can begin looking for opportunities to transport the bear(s) as well.
- ☐ The students and teacher will compose a letter in a shared writing experience that will accompany the bear. The letter should explain the project, ask that postcards be sent from destinations along the trip, and tell how this will help the students learn more about the United States.
- ☐ The teacher will review the Check Sheet tool with students.
- ☐ Using overhead transparency pens, divide the (laminated) U.S. map into five regions—Northwest, Southwest, Midwest, Northeast, and Southeast. (All countries outside of the United States can be included in the "other" category on the Check Sheet—worksheet 132.)
- ☐ Recommended regions (to be determined and/or modified by the class):
  - Southwest: Texas, New Mexico, Arizona, Southern California, Nevada, Utah, Colorado, Hawaii
  - Southeast: Arkansas, Louisiana, Mississippi, Alabama, Tennessee, Georgia, Florida, North Carolina, South Carolina, Kentucky
  - Midwest: North Dakota, South Dakota, Nebraska, Kansas, Oklahoma, Illinois, Iowa, Missouri, Minnesota, Wisconsin, Indiana, Michigan
  - Northeast: Ohio, West Virginia, Virginia, Pennsylvania, New Jersey, Delaware, Maryland, New York, Connecticut, Massachusetts, Vermont, Maine, New Hampshire, Rhode Island
  - Northwest: Wyoming, Montana, Idaho, Northern California, Oregon, Washington, Alaska
  - Other: All other countries outside of the United States.
- ☐ As the bear(s) and/or postcards return, the teacher will chart their destinations on the Check Sheet (worksheet 132) displayed on the designated bulletin board. The teacher will read and then display the postcards.
- ☐ The teacher will locate the destination(s) on the U.S. map with a map pin. (Options: String a piece of yarn from the postcard to the location. Use a different color pin for each bear.)

☐ Periodically, the teacher should transfer the data from the Check Sheet to the Bar Chart displayed on the bulletin board. (This is to be determined by the teacher and the school schedule; for example, after school breaks, every nine weeks, or every time a bear returns.)

## Guided Practice

☐ The students will analyze the data from the Check Sheet and Bar Chart. The students will answer questions such as: What region was most visited by the bears? Least visited? Students will also brainstorm ways to get the bears to the less-frequented areas.

☐ The students will compare places the bears visited to the city or state the school is located in and answer questions such as: How far away from your school did the bears travel? In what region is the school located?

☐ The teacher will periodically inform parents/guardians of the status of the project through a class newsletter.

## Assessment

☐ The students will locate the United States on a world map.

☐ The students will locate the state they live in on the U.S. map and point to the general location of their city (if not labeled).

☐ The students will be able to explain the meaning of regions: Northwest, Southwest, Midwest, Northeast, Southeast, and name at least one state in each region.

☐ The students will demonstrate understanding of the Check Sheet by telling how many times a bear visited each region.

☐ The students will demonstrate understanding of the Bar Chart by telling which region was visited the most and which was visited the least by a bear.

## Post-Lesson/Follow-Up Activities/Extensions

☐ Explain how to determine distance between the school and other places visited using the map key.

☐ Visit a Web site that will calculate the distance between the school and another state.

☐ Continue this project (with different classes) each school year.

## Supporting Resources

☐ *mappoint.msn.com/* (map and driving directions)

☐ Rand McNally *Children's Atlas of the United States*

☐ Rand McNally *Kids' U.S. Road Atlas*

☐ Worksheets 132 and 133

# School Rules

Understand the roles and interactions of individuals and groups in society.

**Estimated Time:** 30-45 minutes          **Worksheets:** 134, 135, and 136

## Quality Tool/PDSA Linkage

☐ Students will use the Affinity Diagram, Multivoting/Nominal Group Technique, and the Force-Field Analysis.

- The Affinity Diagram is a tool to generate, organize, and consolidate information gathered through Brainstorming, and is used in many portions of the PDSA cycle.

- Multivoting is a technique to assist groups in reaching consensus by conducting one or more votes during any portion of the PDSA cycle.

- Force-Field Analysis is a tool used to evaluate the forces driving and restraining a desired change and is used during the plan portion of the PDSA cycle to generate the most comprehensive plan possible to test the improvement theory.

## Lesson Overview

☐ Often when young students return to school after summer break or a vacation, they need to be reminded that school is not just like home.

☐ This lesson reminds students that rules help everyone get along better at school.

## Lesson Objectives

☐ The students will understand the importance of rules at school.

☐ The students will design rules for their classroom so everyone can learn and get along better.

☐ The students will understand and use the Affinity Diagram quality tool.

☐ The students will understand and use the Multivoting/Nominal Group Technique.

☐ The students will understand and use the Force-Field Analysis quality tool.

## Pre-Lesson Activities

☐ Obtain all materials needed for the lesson.

☐ Obtain copies of the worksheets that go with the lesson.

## Materials Needed

☐ Post-It notes.

☐ Chart paper.

☐ A fiction book about school.

☐ Sticky dots for Multivoting.

## Lesson Delivery/Procedure

- ☐ The teacher will read aloud a book about school such as *Miss Nelson is Missing* by Harry G. Allard.
- ☐ The teacher and students will discuss why we need rules at school. What happened to the children in the book? Did they learn anything when they did not follow the rules?
- ☐ The teacher will ask, "What rules should we have in our classroom?"
- ☐ The teacher will review the Affinity Diagram tool with students.
- ☐ The students will write or draw one rule on a Post-It note. Students may write as many rules as they can think of, one on each Post-It note.
- ☐ The students will complete the Affinity Diagram (example on worksheet 134) by bringing their Post-It notes to a designated area. Chart paper works well for this.
- ☐ The students and the teacher will sort the Post-It notes using the affinity process, and define categories such as "raise your hand," "keep your hands to yourself," and "no pushing."

## Guided Practice

- ☐ The teacher will list every rule created by students on a new piece of chart paper.
- ☐ The teacher will review the Multivoting tool with students.
- ☐ The students will use the Multivoting technique to vote for the two or three rules they think are the most important rules. Sticky dots work well for this activity.
- ☐ The teacher will review the Force-Field Analysis tool with students.
- ☐ The students and the teacher will complete a Force-Field Analysis (example on worksheet 135) listing driving and restraining forces for behaving at school. Use worksheet 136 or a large poster displaying the information for this activity.
- ☐ After reviewing the Force-Field Analysis, the students and the teacher will develop an Action Plan (as part of the Force-Field Analysis tool) to be implemented in the classroom.

## Assessment

- ☐ Students will sort/group items in Affinity Diagram correctly.
- ☐ Students will explain why rules are important in school.
- ☐ Students will complete the Force-Field Analysis correctly to demonstrate understanding.

## Post-Lesson/Follow-Up Activities/Extensions

- ☐ Students could draw a picture with a behaving class on one half of the paper and a misbehaving class on the other half.
- ☐ The teacher could enlist families to help compile all of the rules of the home.
- ☐ Students could read aloud other school books—see other book titles in the Supporting Resources section.

## Supporting Resources

- ☐ *Miss Nelson Has a Field Day* by Harry G. Allard
- ☐ *Miss Nelson Is Back* by Harry G. Allard
- ☐ *When Dinosaurs Go to School* by Linda Martin
- ☐ *I Am NOT Going to School Today* by Robie Harris
- ☐ *Junie B. Jones and the Stupid, Smelly School Bus* by Barbara Park
- ☐ Worksheets 134, 135, and 136

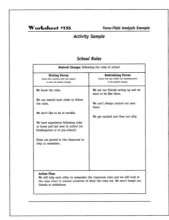

# Field Trip to the Fire Station

Identify goods and services provided by the government.

**Estimated Time:** Two 30-minute sessions before trip; One 15-minute session after trip     **Worksheets:** 137, 138, and 139

## Quality Tool/PDSA Linkage

☐ The teacher and students will use the Affinity Diagram and Cause-and-Effect Diagram before attending a field trip. A Plus/Delta Chart will be used after the trip.

• The Affinity Diagram is a tool to generate, organize, and consolidate information gathered through Brainstorming, and is used in many portions of the PDSA cycle.

• The Cause-and-Effect Diagram is a picture of the output of a brainstorming session that asks, "What causes . . . ," and is used to determine root causes in the plan portion of the PDSA cycle.

• The Plus/Delta Chart is a tool to record feedback about the current state or a recent experience and is used anytime feedback is needed in the PDSA cycle.

## Lesson Overview

☐ This lesson is a structured way to prepare young children for a trip to a fire station. (October is National Fire Prevention Month in the United States.)

☐ Using a (commonly known) Know, Want to Know, Learned (KWL) Chart, students will list what they already *know* about firefighters and fire stations; then list questions in the *want to know* section of the chart.

☐ Sample KWL Chart:

| What we *know* about firefighters/ fire stations | What we *want* to know about firefighters/ fire stations | What we *learned* about firefighters/ fire stations |
|---|---|---|
|  |  |  |

☐ An Affinity Diagram will be used to help students organize these questions generated under the Want To Know section.

☐ The Cause-and-Effect Diagram will help determine elements that ensure a successful field trip to a fire station.

☐ After the field trip, the teacher and students will complete the What We Learned section of the KWL Chart, as well as a Plus/Delta Chart to analyze successes during this field trip and areas in need of improvement before the next field trip is taken.

## Lesson Objectives

☐ The students will use their background information and pictures/text in related books to determine main ideas about firefighters and fire stations.

☐ The students will learn how to formulate questions to ask firefighters about their occupation, the main functions of a fire truck, and the fire station.

☐ The students will determine important elements that can help them have a fun and safe field trip to a fire station.

- [ ] The students will self-assess their field trip in terms of knowledge gained and behaviors exhibited.
- [ ] The students will understand and use the Affinity Diagram and Cause-and-Effect Diagram quality tools prior to the field trip.
- [ ] The students will understand and use a Plus/Delta Chart as a self-assessment tool after the field trip.

## Pre-Lesson Activities

- [ ] Obtain copies of the worksheets that go with the lesson.
- [ ] Obtain all materials needed for the lesson.
- [ ] Obtain a number of books about firefighters and fire stations.
- [ ] Provide shared reading experiences with these books prior to using the Affinity Diagram.
- [ ] Create a poster board size KWL Chart
- [ ] Create a poster board size Affinity Diagram.
- [ ] Create a poster board size Cause-and-Effect Diagram.
- [ ] Create a poster board size Plus/Delta Chart.

## Materials Needed

- [ ] Poster board size charts (see above).
- [ ] Markers and/or writing utensils.
- [ ] Index cards.
- [ ] Theme-related trade books.

## Lesson Delivery/Procedure

- [ ] The teacher will review the theme-related books read with students prior to the first lesson, and elicit background information gained from any previous experiences with firefighters and/or trips to a fire station.
- [ ] In the first lesson, the students will complete the first two sections of the KWL chart, that is, they will list what they already "know" about firefighters and fire stations, and generate questions to list in the *want to know* section of the chart.
- [ ] The teacher will review the Affinity Diagram tool with students.
- [ ] The teacher will then display the poster-size Affinity Diagram and explain that their goal will be to organize these questions to ask firefighters during the field trip to the fire station. (See suggested categories in worksheet 137. Each category should be defined.)
- [ ] The teacher will promote discussion and generation of ideas while allowing each participant to state his or her opinion.
- [ ] After charting, the teacher will write each generated question on index cards.
- [ ] The teacher will take the cards to the fire station to help direct and focus students. If there are not enough questions for each student, group the children in cooperative pairs or groups to find answers to given questions.
- [ ] In the second lesson, the teacher and students will use a Cause-and-Effect Diagram to determine elements of a fun and safe trip to the fire station (see worksheet 138).
- [ ] The teacher will review the Cause-and-Effect Diagram with students.

☐ After the teacher defines the categories of each arm on the Cause-and-Effect Diagram (worksheet 138), the students will help list what is needed for the class to have a fun and safe field trip.

☐ Examples:

> Parents—Drive us to the field trip; Have seat belts for all; Help supervise
>
> Materials—Question cards; First-aid kit
>
> Teacher—Set ground rules; Determine cooperative pairs/groups
>
> Students—Remember behavior expectations; Remain with group and supervisor

☐ The class will review this Cause-and-Effect Diagram before leaving for the field trip to remind students how to have a fun and safe field trip.

☐ The teacher will review the Plus/Delta tool with students.

☐ After the field trip, and in the third part of the lesson, the class will complete a Plus/Delta Chart to determine the successes and areas that need to be improved as demonstrated during the field trip to the fire station (worksheet 139).

## Guided Practice

☐ After the field trip, the class will complete the "Learned" section of the KWL chart in a whole-group setting. Students can use the (question) index cards to guide discussion and promote recall.

☐ The students will modify the Cause-and-Effect Diagram to use for other field trips taken throughout the school year.

☐ The students will complete a "reverse" Cause-and-Effect Diagram, that is, "How to have a perfectly disastrous field trip."

☐ The students will review the completed Plus/Delta Chart before going on another field trip.

## Assessment

☐ The students will contribute one statment to at least one section of the KWL chart before or after the field trip.

☐ The students will contribute at least one idea to the Cause-and-Effect Diagram.

☐ The students will write (or draw) entries in learning logs or writing journals chronicling the field trip to the fire station or listing answers to some of the questions asked of the firefighters.

☐ The students will draw pictures of what they found most interesting on the field trip. They will write (or dictate) a statement explaining the picture.

☐ The students will match labels to common pieces of equipment found at fire stations or on fire trucks, and/or verbally identify parts of a firefighter's uniform.

☐ The students will tell whether their participation and behavior contributed to a fun and safe field trip.

☐ The students will contribute at least one statement to the Plus/Delta Chart.

## Post-Lesson/Follow-Up Activities/Extensions

☐ If there is not enough time to ask all questions from the index cards, leave cards with the firefighters to answer and return their responses by mail.

☐ The teacher will have students write individual thank you letters to the firefighters (or one letter composed in a shared writing experience).

☐ The students will create construction paper firefighter helmets or fire trucks.

☐ The students will have a fire safety (schoolwide) assembly in the month of October.

## Supporting Resources

- ☐ *www.co.kern.ca.us/fire/media/index.htm* (virtual tour of a fire station)
- ☐ *Fire Fighters* by Robert Maass
- ☐ *Firefighters A to Z* by Chris L. Demarest
- ☐ Worksheets 137, 138, and 139

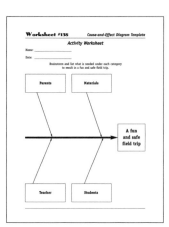

# Traditions

Understand the development of political ideas and traditions in the United States.

**Estimated Time:** 40 minutes          **Worksheets:** 140 and 141

## Quality Tool/PDSA Linkage

☐ Students will use the Affinity Diagram.

• The Affinity Diagram is a tool to generate, organize, and consolidate information gathered through Brainstorming, and is used in many portions of the PDSA cycle.

## Lesson Overview

☐ The students will acquire and organize information involving traditions using an Affinity Diagram.

## Lesson Objectives

☐ The students will interview other students from various classrooms to acquire information about their family traditions.

☐ The students will learn how to use the Affinity Diagram quality tool to organize information.

## Pre-Lesson Activities

☐ Obtain copies of the worksheets that go with the lesson.

☐ Obtain all materials needed for this lesson.

☐ Preselect children for students to interview, prompting them with an understanding of traditions. (If available, use a buddy classroom.)

☐ The children should be familiar with the concept of tradition before the implementation of this lesson.

## Materials Needed

☐ Pencils (for each student).

☐ *Barrio: Josi's Neighborhood* by George Ancona.

☐ Copies of worksheets that go with the lesson.

## Lesson Delivery/Procedure

☐ The teacher will review the concept of "tradition."

☐ The teacher will read the book *Barrio: Josi's Neighborhood* to the class, asking students to pay close attention to the traditions and customs discussed in the book.

☐ The class will briefly discuss any traditions and customs they learned about in the book.

☐ The teacher will announce that each family has its own traditions. The teacher will explain that the students will be interviewing students (in their buddy classrooms) using a survey to find out about the traditions that occur in their family.

☐ Using a student volunteer, the teacher will conduct a model lesson discussing how the students will ask the questions from the survey.

## Guided Practice

- [ ] Each student will interview a student discussing a family's traditions.
- [ ] Each student will record answers on the survey (worksheet 140).
- [ ] The teacher will review the Affinity Diagram tool with students.
- [ ] The teacher and students will complete an Affinity Diagram on a poster paper in class to find commonalities among traditions.

## Assessment

- [ ] The class will discuss the experience of interviewing and their findings.
- [ ] The teacher will review the student work to assess their level of understanding.
- [ ] The teacher will assess the Affinity Diagram.

## Post-Lesson/Follow-Up Activities/Extensions

- [ ] Using worksheet 141, students can survey their parents about a family tradition.
- [ ] Using the findings of the survey, a Bar Chart could be created by the class of common traditions found.
- [ ] Discuss traditions of the United States of America.

## Supporting Resources

- [ ] *Barrio: Josi's Neighborhood* by George Ancona
- [ ] *www.atozteacherstuff.com/lessonsFamilyHistory.shtml/*
- [ ] *Mexico: Culture Kit—Activities, Projects, Poster, Audiotape, and Map* by Linda Scher
- [ ] Worksheets 140 and 141

# Political Systems/ Government

Understand and explain the basic principles of the U.S. government.

**Estimated Time:** 50 minutes        **Worksheets:** 142 and 143

## Quality Tool/PDSA Linkage

☐ Students will use the Operational Definition and Affinity Diagram.

- The Affinity Diagram is a tool to generate, organize, and consolidate information gathered through Brainstorming, and is used in many portions of the PDSA cycle.

- Operational Definition is a standard process for measuring critical quality characteristics used before gathering data in the plan portion of the PDSA cycle.

## Lesson Overview

☐ As a class, a definition of the responsibilities of students will be created and utilized to enhance students' ability to self-assess their roles in the classroom.

## Lesson Objectives

☐ The students will be able to understand and explain basic principles of the U.S. government, utilizing the responsibility of the student's role in a classroom environment as a model.

☐ The students will be able to generate and sort ideas according to common themes.

☐ The students will understand and use the Affinity Diagram and Operational Definition quality tools.

## Pre-Lesson Activities

☐ The concept of responsibility should be introduced and discussed with students prior to this lesson.

☐ Obtain copies of the worksheets that go with the lesson.

☐ Obtain all materials needed for the lesson.

## Materials Needed

☐ Chart paper.

☐ Post-It notes.

☐ Black marker.

☐ White construction paper.

☐ 24-pack of crayons.

☐ Tape.

☐ Worksheet 142.

## Lesson Delivery/Procedure

- ☐ The teacher will review the concept of responsibility with the class.

- ☐ The teacher will introduce the book *Curious George Takes a Job* to the class.

- ☐ As the teacher reads the story, he or she will pause every five or six pages to discuss the responsibilities of Curious George.

- ☐ After completing the book, the teacher will ask students to list ideas of their responsibilities in the classroom. The teacher will collect ideas on a sheet of chart paper for students to refer to during their picture making process that will come later in this lesson.

## Guided Practice

- ☐ The teacher will give each student a piece of white construction paper and pack of crayons.

- ☐ Each student will create a picture displaying student and/or students being responsible or completing tasks of responsibilities.

- ☐ While students work independently, the teacher will conference briefly with each student about the picture being drawn. The teacher will provide a caption for the children's pictures.

- ☐ Once the pictures are completed, the teacher will collect all of the pictures.

- ☐ The teacher will review the Affinity Diagram tool with students.

- ☐ With the assistance of the class, the teacher will create an Affinity Diagram by grouping pictures of common themes together. (For instance, all pictures discussing classroom jobs will be grouped together.)

- ☐ The teacher will provide a header for each group of pictures. (For example: A group of pictures discussing classroom jobs will have the header of "classroom jobs.")

- ☐ The teacher will review the Operational Definiton tool with students.

- ☐ Using the headers provided, the teacher will compose a statement of the responsibilities of students in the classroom setting. This statement is the Operational Definition of a responsible student and will be used as the standard by which students will assess their performance in the area of responsibility.

## Assessment

- ☐ Using Worksheet 142, students will self-assess their ability to be a responsible student according to the Operational Definition created.

## Post-Lesson/Follow-Up Activities/Extensions

- ☐ Using Worksheet 143 and Post-It notes, the parent and students could generate information of what it takes to be a responsible at home. Using these data, the classroom would create an Affinity Diagram of the responsibilities at home.

- ☐ Using the story *It's Not My Job!*, the class could create a Force-Field Analysis entitled "Increasing Student Responsibility."

## Supporting Resources

- ☐ *pbskids.org/adventures/caregivers/parent_guides/responsibilities.html*
- ☐ *It's Not My Job!* by Ted Lish and Charles Jordan
- ☐ *Curious George Takes a Job* by H.A. Rey
- ☐ Worksheets 142 and 143

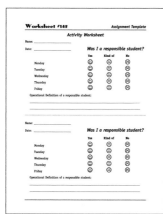

# Families

Understand how social systems form and develop over time.

**Estimated Time:** 20–30 minutes          **Worksheets:** 144 and 145

## Quality Tool/PDSA Linkage

☐ Students will use the Affinity Diagram and the Lotus Diagram.

- The Affinity Diagram is a tool to generate, organize, and consolidate information gathered through Brainstorming, and is used in many portions of the PDSA cycle.

- The Lotus Diagram is a tool to expand thinking around a single topic or theme and is used at any portion of the PDSA cycle to generate additional thoughts.

## Lesson Overview

☐ The students will learn about the attributes that make a family.

☐ The students will learn about the Affinity Diagram by grouping different pictures into categories based on their characteristics.

☐ The students will create a Lotus Diagram including the people that make up their family.

## Lesson Objectives

☐ The students will learn how to classify things into categories.

☐ The students will learn what makes a family.

☐ The students will use the Lotus Diagram and Affinity Diagram quality tools.

## Pre-Lesson Activities

☐ Cut out pictures from magazines. The pictures will be of things that are living that would belong in one of the predetermined categories (plants, animals, humans).

☐ Make a large poster of the categories (see worksheet 144).

☐ Collect books about families to read to the class (see resources).

☐ Obtain copies of the worksheets that go with the lesson.

## Materials Needed

☐ Pictures of living plants, animals, and humans.

☐ Tape.

☐ Chart paper.

☐ Copies of Lotus Diagram.

## Lesson Delivery/Procedure

☐ The teacher will give each student a picture of a plant, animal, or human.

☐ The teacher will show the students the chart paper with a picture at the top.

☐ The teacher will review the Affinity Diagram tool with students.

- [ ] One at a time, the teacher will ask students to share their picture and tell where they think the picture should go (in what column—worksheet 144).

- [ ] The student will place the picture in the correct column.

- [ ] Once every student has gone, the teacher will ask the students a question, "What do all the pictures in column one have in common?"

- [ ] The teacher will try to get the students to name the category "plants."

- [ ] When the students have named the category, the teacher should write the name at the top of the category.

- [ ] The teacher should repeat the question two more times until all the columns are named.

- [ ] At this point, the teacher will ask the class, "What makes a family?"

- [ ] The teacher will then read a book to the students about families (see Supporting Resources).

## Guided Practice

- [ ] The teacher will ask the students, "What makes a human family?"

- [ ] The teacher will review the Lotus Diagram tool with students.

- [ ] The teacher will model what makes their family on a large Lotus Diagram (see worksheet 145).

- [ ] The teacher will have students create their own family Lotus Diagram. Students can either draw pictures of their family members in each box, or write their names.

## Assessment

- [ ] Informally, the teacher can assess whether the students know what makes a family through discussion.

- [ ] The teacher can formally assess a students' understanding by looking at their Lotus Diagram.

## Post-Lesson/Follow-Up Activities/Extensions

- [ ] The teacher can invite the students to share their family Lotus Diagrams with the class.

- [ ] The teacher can engage the students in an activity to explain how grandparents, aunts, and uncles are related and in the family.

- [ ] The teacher can read several more books about families.

## Supporting Resources

- [ ] *City Stories Series* published by Rigby

- [ ] Worksheets 144 and 145

# Quality Across the Curriculum

# SOCIAL STUDIES

## 2–3

### LESSONS

Medieval Feast. . . . . . . . . . . 203

Waste Awareness . . . . . . . . . 207

Landforms . . . . . . . . . . . . . 211

Washington D.C. . . . . . . . . . 215

Our City PDSA: Part A. . . . . . 219

Our City PDSA: Part B. . . . . . 223

Our City PDSA: Part C. . . . . . 227

Our City PDSA: Part D. . . . . . 231

Our City PDSA: Part E. . . . . . 235

# Medieval Feast

Apply the skills of historical analysis and interpretation. Describe how people in different times and places viewed the world in different ways. Identify how customs and traditions from around the world influence the local community.

**Estimated Time:** Two 60-minute sessions     **Worksheets:** 146, 147, and 148

## Quality Tool/PDSA Linkage

☐ Students will use Force-Field Analysis, Nominal Group Technique, Systematic/Tree Diagram, and Flowchart.

- Force-Field Analysis is a tool used to evaluate the forces driving and restraining a desired change and is used during the plan portion of the PDSA cycle to generate the most comprehensive plan possible to test the improvement theory.

- Nominal Group Technique/Light Voting is a structured group process (ranked voting) used to make decisions during any portion of the PDSA cycle.

- The Systematic/Tree Diagram is a tool to guide a group in planning for a broad goal by determining and assigning the different levels of action needed to accomplish the goal and is used in the plan portion of the PDSA cycle.

- The Flowchart is a drawing of any process used to document the process flow during the plan portion of the PDSA cycle.

## Lesson Overview

☐ This is a lesson designed as a final activity for a unit of study on Medieval times.

☐ The students will use what they have learned in the unit to plan a Medieval feast.

☐ The students will use a Force-Field Analysis, Nominal Group Technique/Light Voting, Systematic/Tree Diagram, and Flowchart in the planning of the feast.

## Lesson Objectives

☐ The students will understand and use the Force-Field Analysis, Nominal Group Technique/Light Voting, Systematic/Tree Diagram, and Flowchart quality tools.

☐ The students will use the Force-Field Analysis to identify driving and restraining forces for initiating a feast.

☐ As a whole group, students will create a Tree Diagram to outline various student committee jobs.

☐ The students working on committees will create a Flowchart to help them develop a step-by-step process for their committee to complete the assigned task.

## Pre-Lesson Activities

☐ The students should have some basic information about the Middle Ages prior to lesson delivery.

☐ Gather books or other student materials that contain information on the Middle Ages.

☐ Obtain copies of worksheets that go with the lesson.

☐ Obtain all materials needed for the lesson.

## Materials Needed

☐ Chart paper.

☐ Post-It notes.

☐ Reference materials.

☐ Markers.

## Lesson Delivery/Procedure

☐ The teacher will review the Force-Field Analysis tool with students.

☐ The students will gather as a class to complete a Force-Field Analysis (worksheet 146).

☐ The students will answer the question, "How can we have a successful Medieval feast?"

| Driving Forces | Restraining Forces |
| --- | --- |
|  |  |
|  |  |
|  |  |
|  |  |

☐ The teacher will ask students to identify driving forces (things that will help the feast to be successful) and restraining forces (things that will hinder a successful feast).

☐ The teacher will review the Nominal Group Technique tool with students.

☐ The teacher will facilitate the class using the Nominal Group Technique/Light Voting to help prioritize the three top driving forces and the three top restraining forces.

☐ The students will use the information generated from the Force-Field Analysis to develop an Action Plan for planning the feast.

☐ Once the Force-Field Analysis is complete (worksheet 146), three committees will be developed for the feast. (These should come out of the Action Plan developed by the students.)

  • Some examples could be:
    – Games
    – Food
    – Decorations

☐ The teacher will review the Systematic Diagram tool with students.

☐ The class as a whole group will use a Systematic/Tree Diagram (worksheet 148) to plan out specific jobs for each student committee.

☐ The student committees will meet together and use the Systematic/Tree Diagram as a resource to determine individual student jobs.

☐ The teacher will review the Flowchart tool with students.

☐ Once the Systematic Diagram is complete, the individual students will develop a Flowchart to complete their task. Students will discuss ideas on the following:
  • Committee purpose
  • Desired outcomes
  • Process
    – Students will develop a process Flowchart
      ○ Teacher will direct students to focus on major steps
      ○ The Flowchart will be drafted on chart paper
    – The teacher should remind students that the Flowchart is a working tool and is meant to be revised and changed as necessary.

A very simplistic example of the Flowchart would be:

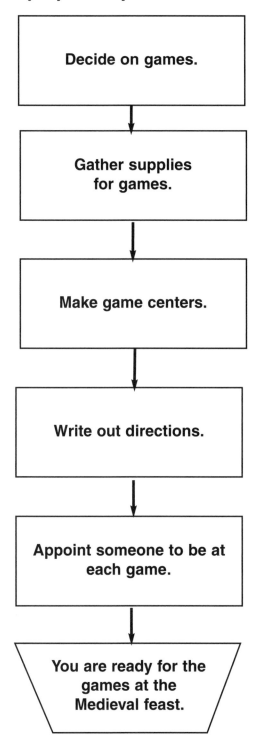

## Guided Practice

- ☐ Each committee will use the Force-Field Action Plan to implement their part of the feast (worksheet 146).

- ☐ Each committee will use the Systematic/Tree Diagram to assign jobs (worksheet 148).

- ☐ Each student on the committee will utilize the Flowchart as a tool to plan his or her part of the feast (worksheet 147).

## Assessment

☐ The students will use the Force-Field Analysis, Nominal Group Technique, Systematic/Tree Diagram, and Flowchart in a way to plan a successful feast.

☐ The students will meet in small groups with the teacher to determine understanding of the quality tools used in this lesson. Each group will present their tool and how it was used in this process.

☐ The students will evaluate each committee's Flowchart to ensure the chart accurately represents the process.

## Post-Lesson/Follow-Up Activities/Extensions

☐ Apply the knowledge learned about Flowcharts, Systematic/Tree Diagram, and Force-Field Analysis to other areas of schoolwork.

☐ Conduct the Medieval Feast from the plan created.

## Supporting Resources

☐ Medieval Games: *www.tarahill.com/instruct.html*

☐ Medieval Foods: *www.godecookery.com/begrec/begrec.htm*

☐ *A Medieval Feast* by Aliki

☐ *Medieval Life* by Andrew Langley

☐ *Knights and Castles: 50 Hands-on Activities to Experience the Middle Ages* by Avery Hart

☐ *The Time Traveler: Books of Knights and Castles* by Judy Hindley

☐ Worksheets 146, 147, and 148

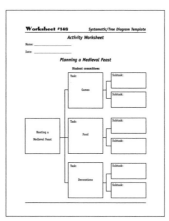

# Waste Awareness

Explain how human activity affects the environment.

**Estimated Time:** Two Social Science class periods. **Worksheets:** 149 and 150
Five lunch periods.

## Quality Tool/PDSA Linkage

- ☐ Students will use a Check Sheet.

  - • The Check Sheet/Matrix is a tool to collect and organize data in the plan portion of the PDSA cycle.

## Lesson Overview

- ☐ This is a hands-on lesson designed to enrich students' awareness of the amount of food that is thrown away at their school each day while learning about the Check Sheet.

## Lesson Objectives

- ☐ The students will see how much food is thrown away at their school each day by planning and conducting an investigation using appropriate instruments and measures to collect, record, and report data.

- ☐ The students will learn how to analyze the collected measurement data.

- ☐ The students will use a Check Sheet to determine the strength and accuracy of their predictions and comparison with other days' waste and interview information.

- ☐ The students will understand the importance of process, accuracy, and group commitment.

## Pre-Lesson Activities

- ☐ Obtain copies of the worksheets that go with the lesson.

- ☐ Obtain all materials needed for the lesson.

- ☐ Alert the school cafeteria about the activity the students will participating in.

## Materials Needed

- ☐ Plastic disposable gloves for handling food.

- ☐ Check Sheets (worksheets 149 and 150).

- ☐ Two trash containers, one for food and the second for other materials.

- ☐ Several half-gallon or gallon milk containers to collect leftover milk.

- ☐ Pencil or pen.

- ☐ Graph paper or plain paper for appropriate recording of data.

- ☐ Large graph paper on an easel or overhead transparency of graph paper to use as a tool for student demonstration.

- ☐ Markers.

- ☐ Scale.

- ☐ Audio tape recorder, camera, and videotape recorder (optional).

## Lesson Delivery/Procedure

- ☐ After the teaching of appropriate measurement taking skills, the teacher will elicit students to predict how many pounds of food and gallons of milk are thrown away each day.
- ☐ The teacher will review the Check Sheet tool with students.
- ☐ Then teacher will demonstrate how the students will be collecting data for the next week using the Check Sheet worksheets.
- ☐ The teacher will lead a discussion that will help predict what foods students will throw away and for what reasons.

## Guided Practice

- ☐ Each day of the week, a group of five to seven students will be assigned to collect milk and food waste from 40 students during lunch.
- ☐ The students will ask for the leftover milk from students in the lunchroom.
- ☐ They will pour the wasted milk into half-gallon or gallon containers.
- ☐ The students will use a Check Sheet (worksheet 149) to tally the number of containers filled and the sizes of the containers.
- ☐ Using a scale, the students will ask others to separate all the leftover food from their tray and place it in a separate container. The weight of the empty container will be subtracted from the full container to determine how many pounds of food were thrown away. Students will record the number of pounds on their Check Sheet (worksheet 150).
- ☐ To determine what foods are thrown away, students will look at the day's menu and write the names of foods served that day on the Check Sheet. Extra spaces will be used to record the contents of bag lunches. Students will stand by the trash containers and observe which foods are thrown away while making tally marks.
- ☐ To learn why people don't eat their food, students will interview students and tape record or write down their comments.
- ☐ The students will interview cafeteria workers. They will ask whether any foods are thrown away in the kitchen and what happens to leftovers. They will ask what guidelines and requirements the cafeteria must follow when planning and preparing meals.
- ☐ The students will also ask the custodial staff if they can tell them if the results on the day of their survey were typical.

## Assessment

- ☐ The students will look at the relationship between the types of waste and the amount and draw conclusions.
- ☐ The students will participate in a discussion about what can be done to cut down on food waste.
- ☐ The students will summarize their findings by reporting out and sharing their findings with their group.
- ☐ The teacher will evaluate student work, discussion, and findings to gauge level of understanding.

## Post-Lesson/Follow-Up Activities/Extensions

- ☐ The students may monitor the amount of waste that is thrown away in their own homes.
- ☐ The students may create posters or commercials to be read during morning announcements to report their findings and make others aware of the amount of waste produced during lunches.
- ☐ The students can create a Pareto Diagram from the results on their Check Sheet and share their findings with the cafeteria staff, food service director, or members of the administration.

- [ ] If possible, students can brainstorm ideas to reduce the waste and try their methods in the school cafeteria. More data could then be collected and compared with the original data to see if improvements have been made.

## Supporting Resources

- [ ] School Waste Reduction Web site—*www.ciwmb.ca.gov/Schools/WasteReduce/*
- [ ] Environmental Explorer's Club Web site—*www.epa.gov/kids/*
- [ ] Worksheets 149 and 150

**Worksheet #149**     *Check Sheet Template*

*Activity Worksheet*

Name: _____

Date: _____

Record the amount of waste each day for one week.

Group #_____

| Day of the week | Gallons of milk | Pounds of food |
|---|---|---|
| Monday | | |
| Tuesday | | |
| Wednesday | | |
| Thursday | | |
| Friday | | |
| Totals | | |

**Worksheet #150**     *Check Sheet Template*

*Activity Worksheet*

Name: _____

Date: _____

Group #_____

| Type of food | Whole serving | ___ or more of a serving | Less than ___ of a serving |
|---|---|---|---|
| Example: Pizza | | | |
| | | | |
| | | | |
| | | | |
| | | | |

# Landforms

Locate, describe, and explain places, regions, and features on the earth.

**Estimated Time:** 45 minutes          **Worksheets:** 151 and 152

## Quality Tool/PDSA Linkage

- ☐ Students will use the Lotus Diagram and Check Sheet.

  - • The Lotus Diagram is a tool to expand thinking around a single topic or theme and is used at any portion of the PDSA cycle to generate additional thoughts.

  - • The Check Sheet/Matrix is a tool to collect and organize data in the plan portion of the PDSA cycle.

## Lesson Overview

- ☐ This lesson is designed to help students sort information about the different landforms in the United States.

- ☐ The students will learn what landforms are and why they are important to the country.

- ☐ The students and the teacher will use the Lotus Diagram to sort the different landforms for further study.

## Lesson Objectives

- ☐ The students will learn the different landforms of the United States.

- ☐ The students will learn how to sort information according to specific characteristics of landforms.

- ☐ The students will further expand their knowledge by looking in reference books and Internet sources.

- ☐ The students will understand the importance of different landforms in the United States.

- ☐ The students will understand and use the Lotus Diagram and Check Sheet quality tools.

## Pre-Lesson Activities

- ☐ Obtain copies of the worksheets that go with the lesson.

- ☐ Obtain all materials needed for the lesson.

- ☐ Brainstorm with students about what the word "landform" means to them.

## Materials Needed

- ☐ Marker for appropriate recording of observations.

- ☐ Plain paper for appropriate recording of observations.

- ☐ Reference books, atlas, relief maps, globes, Internet sites.

- ☐ Large graph paper on an easel or overhead transparency of Lotus Diagram and Check Sheet.

- ☐ Worksheets 151 and 152.

- ☐ Map of the United States.

## Lesson Delivery/Procedure

- ☐ The class will discuss what the word "landform" means to them and will record their ideas on the overhead or on the board. (The teacher will ask if students know any examples of landforms.)

- ☐ The teacher will list some of the easier landforms to identify and ask students if they could name a specific location of some of these landforms. The teacher may ask if students have visited any landforms.

- ☐ The teacher will review the Lotus Diagram tool with students.

- ☐ After listing the landforms on the board, the teacher will demonstrate the Lotus Diagram tool (worksheet 151) by placing one of the landforms in the center of the diagram and having students discuss related characteristics.

- ☐ The teacher will identify the key steps in using the Lotus Diagram tool.

- ☐ The students should then be placed in groups to repeat the process for other landforms.

## Guided Practice

- ☐ In small cooperative student groups, students will complete the Lotus Diagram on a landform assigned by the teacher.

- ☐ The students will find characteristics of their assigned landform using relief maps, an atlas, and other reference tools.

- ☐ The students will list characteristics of landforms on their Lotus Diagram.

- ☐ The students will report out and share as a group what they learned about their landform. Each group will share their Lotus Diagram.

- ☐ The students will have an opportunity to ask questions of each group to gain more information.

- ☐ The students will hang their Lotus Diagrams around the room so comparisons can be made between the different landforms.

## Assessment

- ☐ The students will look at the relationship between the different landforms and draw conclusions.

- ☐ The teacher will review the Check Sheet tool with students.

- ☐ The students will use the Check Sheet to mark their comparisons between the landforms (see worksheet 152).

- ☐ The students will summarize their findings by reporting out and sharing their findings with another student.

- ☐ The teacher will review student work, discussion, and findings to gauge level of understanding.

## Post-Lesson/Follow-Up Activities/Extensions

- ☐ The students can interview family members and friends outside of the class to see what landforms they have visited and which they would like to visit sometime in the future.

- ☐ The students can plan a vacation to one of the landforms they have studied during this lesson.

- ☐ The students can display their Lotus Diagram notes in the hallway and make a graph for other grades to see and make their own comparisons.

- ☐ The students could take a survey to see which landform is the most popular in the class or school.

## Supporting Resources

- [ ] *Atlas of Geology and Landforms* by Cally Oldershaw
- [ ] *Natural Wonders of North America* by Catherine O'Neill Grace
- [ ] *www.enchantedlearning.com/geography/landforms/glossary.shtml*
- [ ] *www.geocities.com/monte7dco/*
- [ ] Worksheets 151 and 152

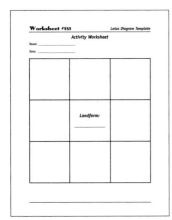

# Washington D.C.

Understand and explain basic principles of the U.S. government.

**Estimated Time:** 45 minutes          **Worksheets:** 153 and 154

## Quality Tool/PDSA Linkage

☐ Students will use the Cause-and-Effect Diagram and the Affinity Diagram.

- The Cause-and-Effect Diagram is a picture of the output of a brainstorming session that asks, "What causes . . . ," and is used to determine root causes in the plan portion of the PDSA cycle.

- The Affinity Diagram is a tool to generate, organize, and consolidate information gathered through Brainstorming, and is used in many portions of the PDSA cycle.

## Lesson Overview

☐ The students will Brainstorm and identify key locations in Washington D.C.

☐ The students will list the reasons why the locations are important to Washington D.C.

☐ The students will create a Cause-and-Effect Diagram listing what places are in Washington D.C. and how they contribute to effective government.

## Lesson Objectives

☐ The students will create a Cause-and-Effect Diagram to demonstrate how to organize different types of information.

☐ The students will share experiences they have had using data collected with their Cause-and-Effect Diagram.

☐ The students will understand and use the Cause-and-Effect Diagram and Affinity Diagram quality tools.

☐ The students will identify key places in Washington D.C. and why they are important.

## Pre-Lesson Activities

☐ The teacher will ask students if they know what a cause-and-effect relationship is and why it is important.

☐ The teacher will identify with students some uses for a Cause-and-Effect Diagram.

☐ The teacher may demonstrate several cause-and-effect relationships, which would help students start to understand this difficult concept (for example, when it rains a lot, there is usually flooding).

☐ Obtain copies of the worksheets that go with the lesson.

☐ Obtain all materials needed for the lesson.

## Materials Needed

☐ An overhead of the Cause-and-Effect Diagram (worksheet 154).

☐ Post-It notes.

☐ Two large sheets of poster paper.

☐ Pencils for students.

☐ Markers for the teacher.

## Lesson Delivery/Procedure

- ☐ The teacher will introduce or review with students the terms "cause" and "effect."
- ☐ The teacher will review the Cause-and-Effect Diagram tool with students and model how this tool is used.
- ☐ Various examples of causes and effects will be discussed in depth with the students.
- ☐ The teacher will review the Affinity Diagram tool with students and discuss its use.
- ☐ The students and the teacher will list general places and locations related to the government located in Washington D.C. and then organize these ideas by common themes using an Affinity Diagram and grouping like ideas.
- ☐ The class will make a Cause-and-Effect Diagram together on the overhead using the issues discussed as a class. Ideas generated from the Affinity Diagram can be used.
- ☐ The teacher will summarize the lesson objectives, findings, and key concepts of the lesson to remember.

## Guided Practice

- ☐ The students will discuss ideas of their own and organize them using the Affinity Diagram, which will then help them complete the Cause-and-Effect Diagram (worksheet 154).
- ☐ The students will share their ideas with the teacher before starting their own Cause-and-Effect Diagram.
- ☐ The students will complete the Cause-and-Effect Diagram on their own. The key question will be, "What structures help the government, located in Washington D.C., our nations capital, run effectively?"
- ☐ The students will share their Cause-and-Effect Diagrams in small groups to get feedback from their peers.

## Assessment

- ☐ The students will write about their understanding of the different elements of the Cause-and-Effect Diagram.
- ☐ The students will share their Cause-and-Effect Diagram to demonstrate their level of understanding and application.
- ☐ The students will review their work, discussion, and findings to gauge level of understanding of cause-and-effect relationships within Washington, D.C.

## Post-Lesson/Follow-Up Activities/Extensions

- ☐ The students can take the idea of a Cause-and-Effect Diagram home to share with their family and then generate quiz-like questions for family members to answer.
- ☐ The students can challenge themselves by developing a Cause-and-Effect Diagram for another subject area.
- ☐ The students can visit another grade with their Cause-and-Effect Diagram and teach younger or older students what they have learned.

## Supporting Resources

- ☐ *A Kid's Guide to Washington D.C.* by Richard Brown

- ☐ *Washington D.C. Guidebook for Kids* by Carol Bluestone

- ☐ *www.ameslab.gov/*

- ☐ *www.washingtondc.gov/*

- ☐ Worksheets 153 and 154

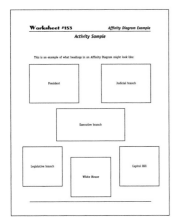

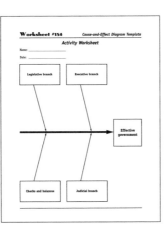

# Our City PDSA: Part A

Describe interactions of individuals, groups, and institutions in situations drawn from the local community.

**Estimated Time:** 60 minutes        **Worksheets:** 155 and 156

## PDSA Background Information

Students have been studying about different city services. After reviewing citizen complaints, students have determined that services in our city have not been up to standards. The teacher and students are utilizing the PDSA process to solve city problems. The teacher, together with the class, developed an Operational Definition to help set the stage for needed improvement. (The Operational Definition is a clear, concise, and detailed definition of measure.)

The Operational Definition stated:

- Characteristic of interest—Roles and responsibilities of each department.
- Measuring instrument—Lotus Diagram and Nominal Group Technique.
- Method of test—Record responsibilities of city departments.
- Decision criteria—Students will fill out the Lotus Diagram indicating roles and responsibilities for each city department studied.

## Quality Tool/PDSA Linkage

☐ Students will use the Lotus Diagram and Nominal Group Technique.

- The Lotus Diagram is a tool to expand thinking around a single topic or theme and is used at any portion of the PDSA cycle to generate additional thoughts.

- Nominal Group Technique/Light Voting is a structured group process (ranked voting) used to make decisions during any portion of the PDSA cycle.

## Lesson Overview

☐ This lesson will help students to identify the roles and responsibilities of each city department.

☐ The students will need to investigate the city departments with information provided by the teacher.

☐ The local city Web site can be utilized (if available). Students can also contact the City Hall for information needed.

☐ The students will use a Lotus Diagram to organize information.

☐ The students will use the Nominal Group Technique to help to identify five major roles and responsibilities of each department.

## Lesson Objectives

☐ The students will understand and use the Lotus Diagram quality tool.

☐ The students will work in small groups on various city departments, such as: fire department, police department, sanitation, and parks and recreation.

☐ The students will identify the roles and responsibilities of their assigned department using a Lotus Diagram.

☐ The students will identify the five main responsibilities of each department.

☐ The students will, as a class, share their information with all groups so everyone understands the roles and responsibilities of each city department.

## Pre-Lesson Activities

- ☐ The students should have some knowledge of how a city operates.
- ☐ Gather materials and locate Web sites about your city services.
- ☐ Obtain copies of the worksheets that go with the lesson.
- ☐ Obtain all materials needed for the lesson.

## Materials Needed

- ☐ Chart paper.
- ☐ Markers.
- ☐ Reference materials.
- ☐ Lotus Diagram for each group.

## Lesson Delivery/Procedure

- ☐ The teacher will review how to use the Lotus Diagram tool with students.
- ☐ The teacher and students will list all possible city departments to investigate.
- ☐ The students will choose a city department they wish to investigate further.
- ☐ The teacher will model some examples with each small group on how to proceed with completing the Lotus Diagram (worksheet 155).
- ☐ The students will break into their small groups and begin to use materials available and use the Lotus Diagram to organize their information.

## Guided Practice

- ☐ The students will work in small groups to investigate the city departments.
- ☐ The students will decide what will go in each box on the Lotus Diagram for the city department that they have chosen.
- ☐ The teacher will review the Nominal Group Technique tool with students.
- ☐ The students will use the Nominal Group Technique to prioritize the top five major responsibilities of each department (worksheet 156).

## Assessment

- ☐ The students will successfully use the Lotus Diagram as a way to organize research data.
- ☐ Each student group will report to the rest of the class about the job and the responsibilities of their city department.
- ☐ The students will evaluate the other groups' Lotus Diagrams focusing on the quality and organization of information.

## Post-Lesson/Follow-Up Activities/Extensions

- ☐ Students should apply the knowledge learned about Lotus Diagrams and use it in other areas of the curriculum independently.

## Supporting Resources

- [ ] Local City Web sites
- [ ] Local City Hall
- [ ] Worksheets 155 and 156

**Worksheet #155** — *Lotus Diagram Template*

Activity Worksheet

Name: _____

Date: _____

*Roles and Responsibilities of City Departments*

| | | |
|---|---|---|
| | | |
| | Roles and responsibilities of: _____ | |
| | | |

**Worksheet #156** — *Nominal Group Technique Template*

Activity Worksheet

Name: _____

Date: _____

This tool will help students to make a group decision. Using the main categories of the Lotus Diagram, list the roles and responsibilities of your department. Each team member then votes on the roles and responsibilities they consider a major responsibility of the city department they are assigned to.

| Rank order | Roles and responsibilities |
|---|---|
| | |

# Our City PDSA: Part B

Describe interactions of individuals, groups, and institutions in situations drawn from the local community.

**Estimated Time:** 60 minutes          **Worksheets:** 157, 158, and 159

## PDSA Background Information

Up to this point, students have completed the Lotus Diagram and Nominal Group Technique to study the current status of city departments as part of the plan portion of the PDSA cycle. The next step is to gather and evaluate baseline data.

## Quality Tool/PDSA Linkage

☐ Students will use the Check Sheet/Matrix and Bar Chart to gather information on each city department.

- The Check Sheet/Matrix is a tool to collect and organize data in the plan portion of the PDSA cycle.

- The Bar Chart is a graph of categorical data plotted by frequency, and is used in the plan portion of the PDSA cycle.

## Lesson Overview

☐ This lesson will help students to identify the vital statistics of each city department:
- Number of employees
- Budget
- Equipment
- Citizen complaints

☐ The local city Web site can be utilized if one is available. Students can also contact the City Hall.

☐ The students will organize their data for each department first using a Check Sheet/Matrix to gather information.

☐ The class will create a Bar Chart for each statistic identified.

☐ The students will share what they have found out with the class as a whole.

☐ The class will create a Check Sheet for each statistic identified.

## Lesson Objectives

☐ The students will understand and use the Check Sheet/Matrix and Bar Chart quality tools.

☐ The students will work in small groups on various city departments such as: fire department, police department, sanitation, and parks and recreation.

☐ The students will identify the vital statistics of their assigned department using the Check Sheet/Matrix and the Bar Chart.

☐ The students will, as a class, share their information with all groups so everyone understands how the vital statistics may impact the problem of the city.

## Pre-Lesson Activities

☐ The class should have completed the lesson Our City PDSA: Part A.

☐ The students will use the Lotus Diagrams created in the previous lesson concerning the roles and responsibilities of their department as a reference throughout this project.

☐ Gather materials and Web sites about the city.

☐ Obtain copies of the worksheets that go with the lesson.

☐ Obtain all materials needed for the lesson.

## Materials Needed

☐ Chart paper

☐ Markers

☐ Reference materials

☐ Check Sheet/Matrix and Bar Chart templates for each group (worksheets 157–159)

☐ Lotus Diagram from previous lesson

## Lesson Delivery/Procedure

☐ The teacher will call attention to the Lotus Diagram (worksheet 155), reminding the students that they can refer to the information that they have gathered previously.

☐ The teacher will review the use of the Check Sheet/Matrix and Bar Chart as data collection tools.

☐ The teacher will model some examples with each small group on how to proceed with the Check Sheet/Matrix and the Bar Chart.

☐ The students will gather in their city department groups established in the previous lessons and begin using materials available to gather pertinent data about their department.

☐ Each city department cooperative group will report their findings to the whole class.

## Guided Practice

☐ Students will work in their small groups to investigate the vital statistics of their assigned city department. Example:

• Number of employees

• Budget

• Equipment

• Citizen complaints

    – Fire Department

        ○ Equipment is outdated and slows down services received by residents.

    – Parks and Recreation Department

        ○ Parks are in disrepair and a danger to neighborhood children.

    – Sanitation Department

        ○ Sanitation workers are very poor drivers and are not careful in trash collection.

    – Police Department

        ○ When a problem is reported it takes too long for police personnel to be on the scene.

☐ The students will record their vital statistics on the group Check Sheet/Matrix (worksheet 159).

☐ The teacher will make sure students are able to gather a number of citizen complaints, since this information will be used in the following lessons. If authentic data cannot be obtained, the teacher can provide data.

☐ The students will share their group's vital statistics with the class to create a class Check Sheet/Matrix.

☐ The class will develop a Bar Chart (worksheet 158) for each vital statistic in order to compare different departments.

☐ The students will need to keep in mind the next step in the PDSA process; they will use these data to determine root cause in the next lesson.

## Assessment

- ☐ The students will use the Check Sheet/Matrix and Bar Chart to organize the vital statistics from each city department.

- ☐ Each student group will report to the rest of the class about the statistics of their department.

## Post-Lesson/Follow-Up Activities/Extensions

- ☐ Students can apply the knowledge learned about the use of the Check Sheet/Matrix and Bar Chart to other areas of their everyday lives. For example, students can use a Check Sheet to keep track of the number of minutes of homework during the week. Then a Bar Chart could be used to display the data.

## Supporting Resources

- ☐ Local city Web sites

- ☐ Contacts of the local city hall

- ☐ Worksheets 157, 158, and 159

# Our City PDSA: Part C

Describe interactions of individuals, groups, and institutions in situations drawn from the local community.

**Estimated Time:** 60 minutes          **Worksheets:** 160 and 161

## PDSA Background Information

Up to this point, students have created a Lotus Diagram and used the Nominal Group Technique to help understand the current state of each department. In addition, students used a Check Sheet/Matrix and Bar Chart to help evaluate baseline data. Next, students will use the Cause-and-Effect Diagram to determine root causes of problems identified.

## Quality Tool/PDSA Linkage

☐  Students will use a Cause-and-Effect Diagram.

• The Cause-and-Effect Diagram is a picture of the output of a brainstorming session that asks, "What causes . . . ," and is used to determine root causes in the plan portion of the PDSA cycle.

## Lesson Overview

☐  This is a lesson designed to help students to identify the cause of each city department's problems using a Cause-and-Effect Diagram.

☐  The students will utilize data collected in previous lessons and organized on the Lotus Diagram, Check Sheet/Matrix, and Bar Chart.

☐  The students will also utilize the citizen complaints that have been identified.

☐  The students will work in small groups to complete a Cause-and-Effect Diagram for each city department.

☐  The local city Web site can be utilized if one is available. Students can also contact the city hall.

☐  The students will share what they have found out with the class as a whole.

## Lesson Objectives

☐  The students will understand how to use the Cause-and-Effect Diagram to identify possible causes of the problems in each department.

☐  The students will work in small groups on various city departments such as: fire department, police department, sanitation, and parks and recreation.

## Pre-Lesson Activities

☐  The students should have completed lessons Our City PDSA: Parts A and B.

☐  The students will use the Lotus Diagrams concerning the roles and responsibilities of their department, and the Check Sheet/Matrix and Bar Chart created in prior lessons, throughout this project.

☐  Gather materials and Web sites about your city.

☐  Obtain copies of the worksheets that go with the lesson.

☐  Obtain all materials needed for the lesson.

## Materials Needed

- [ ] Chart paper.
- [ ] Markers.
- [ ] Reference materials.
- [ ] Previously prepared: Lotus Diagram, Check Sheet/Matrix, and Bar Chart for each department.

## Lesson Delivery/Procedure

- [ ] The teacher will call attention to the Lotus Diagram, Check Sheet/Matrix, and Bar Chart reminding the students that they can refer to the information that they have gathered previously.
- [ ] The teacher will review the use of the Cause-and-Effect Diagram tool with students.
- [ ] The teacher will model some examples with each small group on how to proceed with the Cause-and-Effect Diagram.
- [ ] The students will gather in their city department groups established in the previous lessons and begin using materials available to determine possible causes for the various areas contributing to the city department process.
- [ ] Each city department group will report to the whole class, demonstrating how they used the Cause-and-Effect Diagram.
- [ ] The students will then decide as a group which problem they think contributes the most to the city's problems and write an improvement theory around this (see worksheet 160).

## Guided Practice

- [ ] The students will work in their small groups to establish the possible causes of each department.
- [ ] The students will create a Cause-and-Effect Diagram for their assigned city department (worksheet 161).
- [ ] The students will need to keep in mind the next step in the PDSA process; they will use a Force-Field Analysis and Action Plan to test their improvement theory.

## Assessment

- [ ] The students will use the Cause-and-Effect Diagram to determine the cause of their city department problem.
- [ ] Each student group will share their Cause-and-Effect Diagram and their improvement theory.
- [ ] Other student groups will evaluate each group's Cause-and-Effect Diagram and the process they used to determine cause.

## Post-Lesson/Follow-Up Activities/Extensions

- [ ] The students will think about ways they can use the Cause-and-Effect Diagram in other areas of their school-work and daily life.

## Supporting Resources

- ☐ Local city Web sites
- ☐ Local city hall
- ☐ Worksheets 160 and 161

 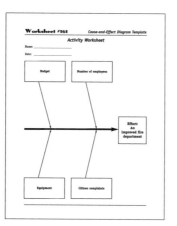

# Our City PDSA: Part D

Describe interactions of individuals, groups, and institutions in situations drawn from the local community.

**Estimated Time:** 60 minutes        **Worksheets:** 162 and 163

## PDSA Background Information

Up to this point, students have created a Lotus Diagram and used the Nominal Group Technique to help understand the current state. Students have also used a Check Sheet/Matrix and Bar Chart to help evaluate baseline data. Then, students used the Cause-and-Effect Diagram to identify root causes and come up with an improvement theory. The next step is to use a Force-Field Analysis to identify driving and restraining forces that may impede implemention of their improvement theory and to come up with an Action Plan.

## Quality Tool/PDSA Linkage

☐ Students will use a Force-Field Analysis.

• Force-Field Analysis is a tool used to evaluate the forces driving and restraining a desired change and is used during the plan portion of the PDSA cycle to generate the most comprehensive plan possible to test the improvement theory.

## Lesson Overview

☐ This lesson is designed to help students to develop an Action Plan through the use of the Force-Field Analysis to solve the problem for their city department.

☐ The students will utilize data collected in previous lessons and organized on the Lotus Diagram, Check Sheet/Matrix, Bar Chart, and Cause-and-Effect Diagram.

☐ The students will utilize the citizen complaints that have been identified.

☐ The students will work in small groups to complete a Force-Field Analysis for each city department.

☐ The students will identify driving forces (items that will push the plan forward).

☐ The students will identify restraining forces (items that will hold back the plan from succeeding).

☐ The students will share their Force-Field Analysis and their Action Plan with the class.

## Lesson Objectives

☐ The students will use an Action Plan to test the improvement theory.

☐ The students will understand how to use the Force-Field Analysis to identify driving and restraining forces that will help students to write an Action Plan to test their improvement theories.

☐ The students will work in small groups on various city departments such as: fire department, police department, sanitation, and parks and recreation.

☐ The students will share their Action Plan with the whole class.

## Pre-Lesson Activities

- [ ] The students should have completed the lessons Our City PDSA: Parts A, B, and C.
- [ ] Have students use the Lotus Diagrams concerning the roles and responsibilities of their department, the Check Sheet/Matrix, Bar Chart, and Cause-and-Effect Diagram, created in previous lessons, throughout this project.
- [ ] Gather materials and Web sites about your city.
- [ ] Obtain copies of the worksheets that go with the lesson.
- [ ] Obtain all materials needed for the lesson.

## Materials Needed

- [ ] Chart paper.
- [ ] Markers.
- [ ] Reference materials.
- [ ] Previously prepared: Lotus Diagram, Check Sheet/Matrix, Bar Chart, and Cause-amd-Effect Diagram for each department.

## Lesson Delivery/Procedure

- [ ] The teacher will call attention to the Lotus Diagram, Check Sheet/Matrix, Bar Chart, and Cause-and-Effect Diagram, reminding the students that they can refer to the information that they have gathered previously.
- [ ] The teacher will review the use of the Force-Field Analysis tool with students.
- [ ] The teacher will model some examples with each small group on how to proceed with the Force-Field Analysis (worksheet 162).
- [ ] The students will gather in their city department groups established in the previous lessons and begin identifying driving and restraining forces that will help them create the best Action Plan possible (worksheet 163).

## Guided Practice

- [ ] The students will work in their small groups to develop the Force-Field Analysis and Action Plan for their city department.
- [ ] The students will create a Force-Field Analysis for their assigned city department.
- [ ] The students will create an action plan that will be implemented in the next part of the PDSA process.
- [ ] Each city department group will report to the whole class, demonstrating how they used the Force-Field Analysis and develop an Action Plan.

## Assessment

- [ ] The students will use the Force-Field Analysis to determine an Action Plan to solve their city department problem.
- [ ] Each student cooperative group will share their Force-Field Analysis and their conclusions.

## Post-Lesson/Follow-Up Activities/Extensions

- [ ] The students will list ways they can use the Force-Field Analysis in other areas of their daily life.

## Supporting Resources

- ☐ Local city Web sites
- ☐ Local city hall
- ☐ Worksheets 162 and 163

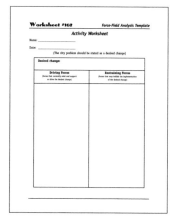

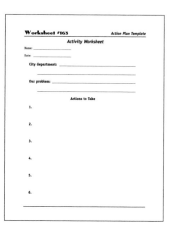

# Our City PDSA: Part E

Describe interactions of individuals, groups, and institutions in situations drawn from the local community.

**Estimated Time:** 60 minutes          **Worksheets:** 164, 165, 166, and 167

## PDSA Background Information

Up to this point, students have created a Lotus Diagram and used the Nominal Group Technique to help understand the current state. Students have also used a Check Sheet/Matrix and Bar Chart to help evaluate baseline data. Students used the Cause-and-Effect Diagram to generate root causes. They then used the Force-Field Analysis to create the best Action Plan possible. The final step in this PDSA process will be to Study the changes and Act to make the improvement standard. Note: since students cannot actually carry out the Action Plans, the teacher will need to provide sample data.

## Quality Tool/PDSA Linkage

☐ Students will use the Check Sheet/Matrix and Bar Chart to compare pre- and post-data concerning their city department. These data will show if the improvement plan that was developed was successful. Students will also use a Flowchart.

- The Check Sheet/Matrix is a tool to collect and organize data in the plan portion of the PDSA cycle.

- The Bar Chart is a graph of categorical data plotted by frequency, and is used in the plan portion of the PDSA cycle.

- The Flowchart is a drawing of any process used to document the process flow during the plan portion of the PDSA cycle.

## Lesson Overview

☐ This lesson will help students determine if their improvement plan was successful.

☐ The students will again collect data in the same areas as Lesson B. Use sample data provided by the teacher.

☐ The teacher will provide students with post-data. (This is an important step since the students will not realistically be able to implement their improvement theory and collect actual post-data.)

☐ The students will organize their data, first using a Check Sheet to gather information.

☐ The students will create a Bar Chart for each department to illustrate the statistics.

☐ The students will share what they have found out with the class as a whole.

☐ The students will decide what the data tell them:

- Should revisions be made to the improvement plan?

- Should the improvement plan be standardized?

☐ Each city group will create a Flowchart that will show the step-by-step process for standardized implementation of the improvement plan.

☐ The students will share what they have found out with the class as a whole.

## Lesson Objectives

- [ ] The students will compare pre- and post-city department data. The teacher will provide the post-data.
- [ ] The students will use a Check Sheet/Matrix and Bar Chart for this pre- and post-data comparison.
- [ ] The students will work in small groups on various city departments such as: fire department, police department, sanitation, and parks and recreation to evaluate data and determine if the improvement theory and Action Plan were successful and what revisions need to be made before the plan is standardized.
- [ ] The students in each group will develop a Flowchart for standardization of the improvement plan.

## Pre-Lesson Activities

- [ ] The students should have completed lessons Our City PDSA: Parts A, B, C, and D.
- [ ] Have students use the Lotus Diagram, Check Sheet/Matrix, Bar Chart, Cause-and-Effect Diagram, Force-Field Analysis, and Action Plan, developed in previous lessons, as a reference throughout this lesson.
- [ ] Review the student groups completed work and gather appropriate post data that students can use to create their Check Sheet/Matrix and Bar Charts.
- [ ] Gather materials and Web sites about your city.
- [ ] Obtain copies of the worksheets that go with the lesson.

## Materials Needed

- [ ] Chart paper
- [ ] Markers
- [ ] Post-data provided by the teacher

## Lesson Delivery/Procedure

- [ ] The teacher will call attention to the Lotus Diagram, Check Sheet/Matrix, Bar Chart, Cause-and-Effect Diagram, Force-Field Analysis, and Action Plans, reminding the students that they can refer to the information that they have gathered previously.
- [ ] The teacher will distribute post-data to each group since students will not realistically be able to implement their Action Plan to gather real post-data.
- [ ] The teacher will review the use of the Check Sheet/Matrix and Bar Chart as data collection tools.
- [ ] The teacher will review the use of a Flowchart and give some examples of the uses of a Flowchart.
- [ ] The students will gather in their city department groups established in the previous lessons.
- [ ] The students will use post-data (provided by the teacher) and develop a Check Sheet/Matrix and Bar Chart for each department. They should use the same process used in Lesson B (worksheets 164 and 165).

## Guided Practice

- [ ] The students will work in their small groups to evaluate pre- and post-data using the Check Sheet/Matrix and Bar Chart and determine the success or failure of the improvement plan.
- [ ] The students will come to a consensus on revisions, if needed, in the improvement plan (see Our City PDSA: Part D, worksheet 163).
- [ ] The students will develop a Flowchart to show steps for standardization of the improvement (worksheet 167).
- [ ] As a group, students will share their findings with the whole class.

## Assessment

☐ The students will use the Check Sheet/Matrix and Bar Chart as ways to organize and compare the pre- and post-data from each city department.

☐ Each student group will report to the rest of the class about the improvements made to their city department and how this will help to solve the problem of the department.

## Post-Lesson/Follow-Up Activities/Extensions

☐ Apply the knowledge learned about the use of the PDSA process along with the tools used into other areas of the students' everyday lives.

☐ Write to or visit the various city departments to share each group's suggested improvements.

## Supporting Resources

☐ Local city Web sites

☐ Local city hall

☐ Worksheets 164, 165, 166, and 167

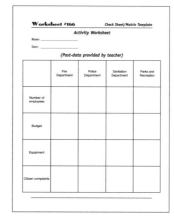

# Quality Across the Curriculum

## the

# SOCIAL STUDIES

4-5

### LESSONS

Economics. . . . . . . . . . . . . . . 241

State Project . . . . . . . . . . . . . 243

Regions . . . . . . . . . . . . . . . 247

Comparing Geographic
    Locations. . . . . . . . . . . . . 249

Branches of Government . . . . 251

Interest Groups . . . . . . . . . . . 255

Ancient Civilizations . . . . . . . 259

Civil War. . . . . . . . . . . . . . . 263

Holocaust . . . . . . . . . . . . . . 267

# Economics

Understand how different economic systems operate in the exchange, production, distribution, and consumption of goods and services.

**Estimated Time:** 45 minutes          **Worksheets:** 168 and 169

## Quality Tool/PDSA Linkage

☐ Students will use a Check Sheet and Multivoting/Nominal Group Technique.

  • The Check Sheet/Matrix is a tool to collect and organize data in the plan portion of the PDSA cycle.

  • Multivoting is a technique to assist groups in reaching consensus by conducting one or more votes during any portion of the PDSA cycle.

## Lesson Overview

☐ This is a hands-on lesson designed to enhance students' understanding of the economic system and the relationship of supply and demand.

## Lesson Objectives

☐ The students will understand and use the Check Sheet and Multivoting quality tools.

☐ The students will utilize a Check Sheet to gather data.

☐ The students will analyze that data to determine which products have a greater demand.

## Pre-Lesson Activities

☐ Introduce economic vocabulary and concepts such as supply, demand, consumers, manufacturers, and resources.

☐ Set up classrooms for groups to survey.

☐ Obtain copies of the worksheets that go with the lesson.

☐ Obtain all materials needed for the lesson.

## Materials Needed

☐ Chart paper.

☐ Black marker.

☐ Pencils (one per student).

## Lesson Delivery/Procedure

☐ The teacher will ask the students if they would like to own a bakery that specializes in making cookies.

☐ The teacher will ask the students to think about the different kinds cookies there are in the world.

☐ Through student discussion, a list will be generated of the different kinds of cookies on a sheet of chart paper.

☐ The teacher will review the Multivoting/Nominal Group Technique with students.

☐ Using Multivoting technique, the teacher will lead a discussion about the amount of time and resources it would take to make all the different kinds of cookies listed. (The teacher will try and draw students to the conclusion— it will take too much time and too many resources to make all the cookies possible.)

- ☐ The teacher will ask, "If you only had enough time and resources to make four kinds of cookies, what four cookies would you make?"
- ☐ Using tally marks, the teacher will record each student's top four cookie choices.
- ☐ Using the data generated from the students, discuss what kind of cookies your bakery should make. (During this time, it would be helpful to mention the terms "supply" and "demand.")
- ☐ The teacher will review the Check Sheet tool with students.

## Guided Practice

- ☐ Divide the students into groups of three.
- ☐ Announce that each group is now a candy company.
- ☐ Using worksheet 168, each group will need to generate a list of at least 12 different kinds of candy.
- ☐ Using the Check Sheet created from worksheet 168, the groups will survey a classroom of students, allowing each person surveyed to choose three kinds of candy they like best.

## Assessment

- ☐ Using the data provided on the Check Sheet, each student will complete worksheet 169 to draw conclusions upon the type of candy to manufacture for their candy company.
- ☐ The teacher will review the student work to assess students' understanding of the concept of supply and demand.

## Post-Lesson/Follow-Up Activities/Extensions

- ☐ The classroom will be transformed into a cookie store. Each student will be given a certain amount of classroom currency dependent upon a factor determined by the teacher. The store will have five different types of cookies dependent of the highest ranked cookies voted on earlier in the less. At the conclusion of the cookie store, check to see if the data gathered earlier indicate the kinds of cookies purchased at the cookie store.
- ☐ The teacher will create a discussion talking about the quantity and kinds of cookies that should be purchased or made if the classroom were to have another cookie store event.
- ☐ As an extension activity, the teacher could have this age group define toy store examples of items that remain expensive because the toy stores don't have enough of them, and which toys go on clearance at the toy store.

## Supporting Resources

- ☐ *Neale S. Godfrey's Ultimate Kids' Money Book* by Neale S. Godfrey
- ☐ *Feed* by M. T. Anderson
- ☐ Worksheets 168 and 169

# State Project

Understand what the government does at a state level. Understand the development of goods and services in your state. Understand your state's history. Identify environmental factors that drew settlers to the state and region. Use maps to locate, describe, and explain places, regions, and features on the earth.

**Estimated Time:** 45–60 minutes          **Worksheets:** 170 and 171

## Quality Tool/PDSA Linkage

☐ Students will use Affinity Diagram and Cause-and-Effect Diagram.

• The Affinity Diagram is a tool to generate, organize, and consolidate information gathered through Brainstorming, and is used in many portions of the PDSA cycle.

• The Cause-and-Effect Diagram is a picture of the output of a brainstorming session that asks, "What causes . . . ," and is used to determine root causes in the plan portion of the PDSA cycle.

## Lesson Overview

☐ This lesson will give students a tool to help them plan their projects.

☐ The students will use a Cause-and-Effect Diagram to describe, "What will make a successful state project?"

## Lesson Objectives

☐ The students will use the Affinity Diagram and Cause-and-Effect Diagram to lay out the specifics of the state project. (The Affinity Diagram will be constructed on chart paper.)
  • Topics
  • People
  • Materials
  • Resources

☐ The students will use the Cause-and-Effect Diagram throughout the project to help them complete the project.

## Pre-Lesson Activities

☐ Introduce the idea of the state project.

☐ Gather books, Internet sites, and other materials needed for the project.

☐ Draw the Cause-and-Effect Diagram on chart paper with labels or make an overhead transparency of worksheet 171.

☐ Obtain copies of the worksheets that go with the lesson.

## Materials Needed

☐ Chart paper.

☐ Post-It notes.

☐ Reference materials on the topic of states.

☐ Markers.

☐ Textbooks containing information about states.

☐ Access to computers (optional).

☐ Software such as PowerPoint or Hyperstudio (optional).

## Lesson Delivery/Procedure

☐ The teacher will review the Affinity Diagram tool with students.

☐ The students working in small groups will discuss and catagorize like ideas using the Affinity Diagram. Students will also use the Cause-and-Effect Diagram (worksheet 171) to develop a state project.

☐ Students will take each area individually (topic, people, materials, resources) and will discuss ideas under each category.

☐ The teacher will review the Cause-and-Effect Diagram tool with students.

☐ Once the ideas have been generated, the class will review the completed Cause-and-Effect Diagram.

☐ Each group needs to reach consensus on the topics that they will cover in the state report.

☐ The Cause-and-Effect Diagrams (worksheet 171) should be posted for students to revise and use throughout the project.

## Guided Practice

☐ The students will use the Cause-and-Effect Diagram to continue self-monitoring their progress on the state project. Students may work individually or together in cooperative groups.

## Assessment

☐ The students will use information generated from the Cause-and-Effect Diagram to self-evaluate the project.

☐ The students will summarize the uses of the Cause-and-Effect Diagram used in this lesson.

## Post-Lesson/Follow-Up Activities/Extensions

☐ Discuss with students other ways to use the Cause-and-Effect Diagram either at home or at school.

## Supporting Resources

☐ *www.50states.com*

☐ *www.ipl.org/div/kidspace/stateknow/*

☐ *www.theus50.com*

☐ *www.postcardsfrom.com/*

☐ *Fabulous Facts About the Fifty States* by Wilma S. Ross

☐ *Our National Parks* by Robin and Polly Mead

☐ *How We Named Our States* by Pauline Arnolo

☐ *Facts About the Fifty States* by Sue R. Brandt

- [ ] *State Trees* by Sue R. Brandt
- [ ] *State Birds* by Virginia Buckley
- [ ] *State Flowers* by Elaine Landaur
- [ ] *All About Our 50 States* by Margaret Roman
- [ ] Worksheets 170 and 171

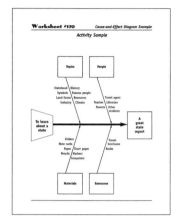
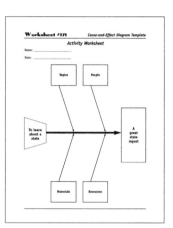

# Regions

Understand world geography and the effects of geography on society, with an emphasis on the United States.

**Estimated Time:** 30–40 minute session, Student presentations   **Worksheets:** 172 and 173

## Quality Tool/PDSA Linkage

- [ ] Students will use a Cause-and-Effect Diagram.

  - The Cause-and-Effect Diagram is a picture of the output of a brainstorming session that asks, "What causes . . . ," and is used to determine root causes in the plan portion of the PDSA cycle.

## Lesson Overview

- [ ] This is a research activity used to learn the characteristics of different states and regions.

- [ ] Utilizing the Cause-and-Effect Diagram, students will organize information about a given state to write a report.

## Lesson Objectives

- [ ] The students will be able to recognize the characteristics that make up a given state.

- [ ] The students will understand and use the Cause-and-Effect Diagram quality tool.

## Pre-Lesson Activities

- [ ] Obtain copies of the worksheets that go with the lesson.

- [ ] Obtain all materials needed for the lesson.

- [ ] Review classroom writing expectations.

- [ ] Create a poster board size Cause-and-Effect Diagram.

## Materials Needed

- [ ] Internet access.

- [ ] Encyclopedias.

- [ ] Atlas.

- [ ] State books.

- [ ] Cause-and-Effect Diagram (poster-size).

## Lesson Delivery/Procedure

- [ ] The teacher will review classroom writing and editing expectations with the class.

- [ ] The teacher will review the Cause-and-Effect Diagram tool with students.

- [ ] The teacher will display the poster-size Cause-and-Effect Diagram and explain they will be using this tool as they gather information about their chosen state.

- [ ] The teacher will use the students' home state as an example.

☐ The teacher will ask the students to aid him or her in deciding what information they would like to have in their reports. Topics could include the following from worksheet 172: state history, population, location, resources, climate, agriculture, industry, major cities, famous landmarks, important people that came from the chosen state. These topics will become the headers on the Cause-and-Effect Diagram.

☐ The teacher will then ask the students to aid him or her in locating the information necessary to fill in the topics placed on the Cause-and-Effect Diagram (worksheet 173).

☐ The teacher will then demonstrate how the diagram can now be used in writing the report using the classroom's writing and editing expectations. The teacher will place the main headings in the poster-size Cause-and-Effect Diagram.

## Guided Practice

☐ Each student will be assigned or will select a state to write his or her report on.

☐ Using the topics given in the example, each student will research and complete a Cause-and-Effect Diagram on their state.

☐ The students will then use their Cause-and-Effect Diagram to write their own state report.

## Assessment

☐ Each student will self-assess his or her assignment, checking to see if each part of the diagram has the necessary information.

☐ The teacher will evaluate the student's diagram and report to ensure that the report contains the required information.

☐ Each student will present his or her report to the class.

## Post-Lesson/Follow-Up Activities/Extensions

☐ The students will make a poster demonstrating the information gathered on their state.

## Supporting Resources

☐ *www.50states.com/*

☐ *www.ipl.org/div/kidsspace/stateknow/*

☐ *homeschooling.about.com/library/blstateunit.htm*

☐ *States and Their Symbols Series published* by School and Library Binding

☐ Worksheets 172 and 173

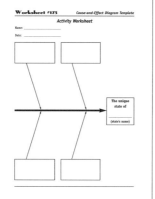

# Comparing Geographic Locations

Compare the characteristics of culture as reflected in language, literature and arts, traditions, and institutions.

**Estimated Time:** 30–40 minutes          **Worksheets:** 174 and 175

## Quality Tool/PDSA Linkage

☐ Students will use a Lotus Diagram.

 • The Lotus Diagram is a tool to expand thinking around a single topic or theme and is used at any portion of the PDSA cycle to generate additional thoughts.

## Lesson Overview

☐ This is a lesson that compares two different geographical locations using the Lotus Diagram.

☐ This is a prereading lesson for the novel *Sarah, Plain and Tall*.

☐ Utilizing a Lotus Diagram, the students will see the differences between shores of Maine and the prairie lands of Kansas.

## Lesson Objectives

☐ Students will be able to recognize the differences between two geographical locations.

☐ Students will understand and use the Lotus Diagram.

## Pre-Lesson Activities

☐ Obtain copies of the worksheets that go with the lesson.

☐ Obtain all materials needed for the lesson.

☐ Obtain resources on both the states of Maine and Kansas.

## Materials Needed

☐ Books, Web sites, and other resources on Maine and Kansas.

☐ Worksheets.

☐ U.S. map.

## Lesson Delivery/Procedure

☐ The teacher will explain that the class will be reading the book, *Sarah Plain and Tall*, a story about a woman who answers an ad to go to live with a family that has lost their mother.

☐ The teacher will then explain, as she or he shows the two locations on the map, that the main character has chosen to leave her home in Maine to be with this family in Kansas. In order for the students to understand how different these two locations are, they are going to research and use the Lotus Diagram to compare and contrast the locations.

☐ The teacher will review the Lotus Diagram tool with students and will pass out the two Lotus Diagrams to the students (worksheets 174 and 175).

☐ The teacher will have the students work in groups to search for facts on each of the locations. The information they find will be placed in the Lotus Diagrams.

## Guided Practice

- [ ] The teacher will pass out the two Lotus Diagrams (worksheets 174 and 175) to the students.

- [ ] The teacher will have the students work in groups to search for facts on each of the locations. The information students find will be placed in the diagram.

- [ ] The class will then use the completed diagrams to discuss the similarities and differences between the two locations.

## Assessment

- [ ] Each student group will self-assess to see that he or she has filled all of the boxes in on his or her diagram.

- [ ] The students will examine the commonalities and differences between the two diagrams.

- [ ] The teacher will evaluate if each student was able to complete the diagram and participate in the class discussion.

## Post-Lesson/Follow-Up Activities/Extensions

- [ ] As a homework assignment, students will write a comparison/contrast essay on the two locations.

- [ ] Read the book, *Sarah, Plain and Tall* by Patricia MacLachlan.

## Supporting Resources

- [ ] *Sarah, Plain and Tall* by Patricia MacLachlan
- [ ] *www.gslis.utexas.edu/~schapa/page.html*
- [ ] *www.netstate.com/states/geography/me_geography.htm*
- [ ] *Kansas* (America the Beautiful) by Kent Zachary
- [ ] *Maine* (America the Beautiful) by Deborah Kent
- [ ] Worksheets 174 and 175

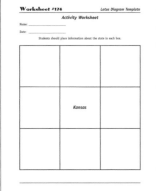

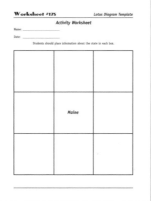

 # Branches of Government

Understand the structures and functions of the political systems of Illinois, the United States, and other nations.

**Estimated Time:** 30 minutes          **Worksheet:** 176

## Quality Tool/PDSA Linkage

☐ Students will use the Cause-and-Effect Diagram and Brainstorming.

- The Cause-and-Effect Diagram is a picture of the output of a brainstorming session that asks, "What causes . . . ," and is used to determine root causes in the plan portion of the PDSA cycle.

- The Brainstorming technique is the generation of ideas by a group and is used at any portion of the PDSA cycle when every person needs to be heard from and many ideas need to be generated.

## Lesson Overview

☐ Using the Cause-and-Effect Diagram, students will determine how the roles of the executive, legislative, and judicial branches cause the United States to have a balanced government.

## Lesson Objectives

☐ The students will understand and use a Cause-and-Effect Diagram to organize information gathered.

☐ The students will understand and use the Brainstorming quality tool to acquire data discussing the branches of government.

☐ The students will enhance their knowledge about cause-and-effect relationships of the branches of government.

## Pre-Lesson Activities

☐ The students should be set up in a cooperative group setting.

☐ Obtain copies of the worksheets that go with the lesson.

☐ Obtain all materials needed for the lesson.

☐ Create a replica of Worksheet 176 on a poster board.

☐ Teach lessons pertaining to the three branches of government (legislative, judicial, executive) prior to the implementation of this lesson.

☐ Provide a large variety of text discussing the branches of government (these sources might be picture books, newspaper articles, weekly readers, and social science textbooks).

## Materials Needed

☐ Pencils (one per group).

☐ Markers.

☐ Posterboard.

☐ Worksheet.

## Lesson Delivery/Procedure

- [ ] The teacher will review the roles of the three branches of government.

- [ ] The teacher will facilitate a discussion about the importance of the three branches of government.

- [ ] The teacher will pose the following question to the class, "What would happen if one branch were given more power than the other two?"

- [ ] The poster-board replica of worksheet 176 should be displayed to the class.

- [ ] The teacher will review the Cause-and-Effect Diagram tool with students.

- [ ] In the effect box on the Cause-and-Effect Diagram, the teacher will place the following effect: "Balance of Power in the United States Government."

- [ ] The teacher will review the Brainstorming tool with students.

- [ ] The teacher will ask the class to brainstorm how the judicial branch (in relation to the other branches) causes the United States to have a balanced government.

- [ ] The class will discuss and write down the ideas on the Cause-and-Effect Diagram under the box labeled "judicial branch" (worksheet 176).

- [ ] The teacher will pass out the worksheet and various texts discussing the branches of government to each cooperative group.

- [ ] The teacher will assign each group a portion of the Cause-and-Effect Diagram for Brainstorming. (Note: Depending upon the number of cooperative groups, some groups might work on the same section.)

## Guided Practice

- [ ] The teacher will pass out the worksheet to each cooperative group setting (worksheet 176).

- [ ] The teacher will assign each group a portion of the Cause-and-Effect Diagram for Brainstorming and encourage the groups to gather information using the sources provided. (Note: A cooperative group will be working on the section discussing executive or the legislative branch.)

- [ ] The teacher will discuss with the class the information gathered by cooperative groups and add the information to the poster-board replica of the Cause-and-Effect Diagram.

## Assessment

- [ ] The teacher will review student work (such as Cause-and-Effect Diagram), discussions, and findings to gauge the level of understanding.

- [ ] The teacher will summarize the lesson objective, findings, and key concepts of the lesson students need to remember.

## Post-Lesson/Follow-Up Activities/Extensions

- [ ] Utilizing the Cause-and-Effect Diagram, the students could write a report discussing the relationship between the branches of government.

- [ ] Students could write about what would happen if one branch were given more power than other two.

- [ ] Students could write letters to the President of the United States (1600 Pennsylvania Avenue, Washington, DC 20500).

## Supporting Resources

- ☐ *www.congressforkids.net/*
- ☐ *www.whitehouse.gov/government/*
- ☐ *www.voteutah.org/learning/government/three_branches.html*
- ☐ Worksheet 176

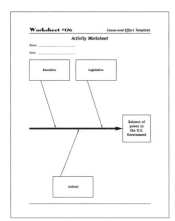

# Interest Groups

Understand the roles and influence of individuals and interest groups in the political systems of the state, the United States, and other nations.

**Estimated Time:** 55 minutes          **Worksheets:** 177 and 178

## Quality Tool/PDSA Linkage

☐ Students will use the Force-Field Analysis quality tool.

- Force-Field Analysis is a tool used to evaluate the forces driving and restraining a desired change and is used during the plan portion of the PDSA cycle to generate the most comprehensive plan possible to test the improvement theory.

## Lesson Overview

☐ Utilizing the Force-Field Analysis, students will create plans designed to increase an interest group's (parents and students) involvement in major school events.

## Lesson Objectives

☐ The students will learn how to analyze the collected data.

☐ The students will understand the role of and influences of individuals and interest groups.

☐ The students will be able to develop a plan to acquire a desired result.

☐ The students will understand and use the Force-Field Analysis quality tool.

## Pre-Lesson Activities

☐ The teacher will introduce social science concepts, such as interest groups and political systems, to students.

☐ The teacher will acquire data of the number of parents who attended the most recent school function. (For example, parent–teacher conferences, open houses, and/or school assemblies.)

☐ The teacher will acquire the data of the number of students who attended the most recent after-school function.

☐ The teacher will develop a Force-Field Analysis on a piece of poster board (a replica of worksheet 177).

☐ The teacher will develop action plan chart on a piece of poster board (a replica of worksheet 178).

☐ Obtain copies of the worksheets that go with the lesson.

☐ Obtain all materials needed for the lesson.

## Materials Needed

☐ Worksheets 177 and 178.

☐ Chart paper.

☐ Black marker.

☐ Notebook paper.

## Lesson Delivery/Procedure

- ☐ The teacher will begin a reflective dialogue about the most recent school function. The following questions might be asked:
  - Was it an enjoyable event?
  - What were some of the highlights?
  - What members of the classroom attended?
  - Whose parents attended the function?
- ☐ At this time, the teacher will present the data of the number of parents who attended the last school function.
- ☐ The teacher will pose the following question to the students, "Why is it important to have a high percentage of parental involvement in schools?"
- ☐ As students develop reasons, the teacher will jot them down on a sheet of chart paper.
- ☐ The teacher will explain the need to increase the number of parents attending school functions to achieve some of the desired results listed on the chart paper. During this explanation, the teacher will emphasize a need to create a plan to improve the number of parents attending school functions.
- ☐ The teacher will review the Force-Field Analysis tool with students.
- ☐ The teacher will present the Force-Field Analysis to students. The teacher will explain that this is a tool that will help to create a plan to increase the number of parents attending school functions.
- ☐ The teacher will ask the students, "What should we entitle our plan?" Place the name given next to the word or topic (it should be the desired change, that is, "Increasing Parental Attendance").
- ☐ The teacher will explain that driving forces are ideas, actions, and so on, that move one toward a goal and restraining forces are ideas, actions, and so on, that keep one from obtaining the goal.
- ☐ The class will discuss the current forces that are encouraging parents to attend school functions. Jot down these items under the driving forces column.
- ☐ The class will discuss the current forces that are keeping parents from attending the school functions. Jot down these items under the restraining forces column.
- ☐ Looking only at the list of driving forces, the teacher will give each student one vote to choose the most important force in that column.
- ☐ Looking only at the list of restraining forces, the teacher will give each student one vote to choose the most important force in that column.
- ☐ Using the top three choices of both the driving and restraining forces, the teacher will develop a plan of action to be implemented that would increase the number of parents attending school functions.

## Guided Practice

- ☐ The teacher will place students into cooperative groups.
- ☐ Each group of students should be given notebook paper, copies of worksheets 177 and 178, and writing utensils.
- ☐ The data discussing the number of students attending should be displayed.
- ☐ Each group should discuss the importance of students attending after-school functions on notebook paper.
- ☐ Using their Force-Field Analysis worksheet, each group will create a name for their plan of action.
- ☐ Each group should discuss the driving forces of students attending after-school events.
- ☐ Each group should discuss the restraining forces of students attending after-school events.

- Looking at only the driving forces, each student in his or her group setting should choose the most important force in that column.

- Looking at only the restraining forces, each student in his or her group setting should choose the most important force in that column.

- Using the top three or four choices of both driving and restraining forces, each cooperative group will create an action plan to increase the number of students attending after-school functions discussing time and persons responsible.

## Assessment

- Each group will be responsible for presenting the plan (worksheet 178) to the class.

- While plans are being presented, each group will be responsible for checking to see if the plan includes the most important driving and restraining forces.

- The teacher will review student work, discussions, and findings to gauge level of understanding.

- The teacher will summarize the lesson objective, findings, and key concepts of the lessons to remember.

## Post-Lesson/Follow-Up Activities/Extensions

- Implement plans for improving student and parent attendance in school events.

- Create a Force-Field Analysis to improve a predetermined interest group's voting percentage.

## Supporting Resources

- Worksheets 177 and 178

# Ancient Civilizations

Understand your state, the United States, and world social history.

**Estimated Time:** 45 minutes          **Worksheets:** 179, 180, and 181

## Quality Tool/PDSA Linkage

☐ Students will use Brainstorming and a Lotus Diagram.

- The Brainstorming technique is the generation of ideas by a group and is used at any portion of the PDSA cycle when every person needs to be heard from and many ideas need to be generated.

- The Lotus Diagram is a tool to expand thinking around a single topic or theme and is used at any portion of the PDSA cycle to generate additional thoughts.

## Lesson Overview

☐ This is an introductory lesson of the different ancient civilizations around the world.

☐ The students will be learning where different people lived and what they needed to survive (shelter, clothing, food source, and so on).

☐ The students will work in small cooperative groups to learn about the different ancient civilizations around the world.

## Lesson Objectives

☐ The students will learn about what makes a civilization.

☐ The students will learn to use the Brainstorming quality tool to identify what things are needed to survive.

☐ The students will learn that there are many different ancient civilizations to study.

☐ The students will complete a Lotus Diagram of the different ancient civilizations.

☐ The students will compile information gained about each of the civilizations on the Lotus Diagram to make a Super Lotus Diagram.

## Pre-Lesson Activities

☐ Gather all materials needed for the lesson.

☐ Obtain copies of worksheets that go with the lesson.

☐ Copy the Lotus Diagram onto an overhead transparency.

☐ Gather books about ancient civilizations.

## Materials Needed

☐ Overhead projector.

☐ Overhead transparencies.

☐ Overhead markers.

☐ Books about ancient civilizations for student use.

## Lesson Delivery/Procedure

- ☐ The teacher will inform the students that they will be studying ancient civilizations.
- ☐ The teacher will explain the rules of Brainstorming (see worksheet 179).
- ☐ The teacher will write a question on the blank overhead transparency. "What makes a civilization?" Things that the students may say are: language spoken, writing, government/social organization, buildings, rituals, dishes, shelters, clothing, source of food, and so on.
- ☐ If students are struggling with what to say, the teacher can ask the question, "What items are needed for a civilization to survive (water, good soil, supplies for shelter, and fuel source)?"
- ☐ Once the Brainstorming has subsided, the teacher will ask the students if they are familiar with any of the ancient civilizations that are commonly studied.
- ☐ The teacher will write down any of the correct civilizations and the teacher will fill in the ones the students did not say. (The western civilizations are: Aztec, Inca, Mayan. The eastern civilizations are: Greek, Roman, Egyptian, Mesopotamian, Chinese.)
- ☐ The teacher will explain that they are going to learn about each of the different civilizations.
- ☐ The teacher will ask the students what information they want to know or what information they think is important to know about each ancient civilization.
- ☐ The teacher and students will create a list of 9–10 things everyone wants to know about the ancient civilizations. These questions will be used to research each civilization.
- ☐ The teacher will then explain that to help organize their thoughts, the students will be using a Lotus Diagram.
- ☐ The teacher will demonstrate what a Lotus Diagram is on the overhead projector (see worksheet 180).
- ☐ The teacher will demonstrate the Super Lotus Diagram (see worksheet 181). The teacher will explain how the center of the Super Lotus Diagram is the same as the regular Lotus Diagram previously completed.

## Guided Practice

- ☐ The teacher will explain to the students that they will be completing a Super Lotus Diagram. Students will use information they learn and add it to the Super Lotus Diagram.
- ☐ The teacher will get the students into groups of four.
- ☐ The teacher will allow each group to choose one ancient civilization they want to know more about.
- ☐ The teacher will allow only one group to research each civilization using the corresponding Lotus Diagram.
- ☐ The students will research and read about the civilization they chose or were assigned.
- ☐ The students will write the answers to the questions in the boxes on their group's Lotus Diagram.
- ☐ The students will work on this for the rest of the class period.

## Assessment

- ☐ The teacher will informally assess whether the students are actively engaged in the research.
- ☐ The teacher will formally assess students' understanding of the different ancient civilizations by evaluating the completed Super Lotus Diagram.

## Post-Lesson/Follow-Up Activities/Extensions

- ☐ Since each group only researched one ancient civilization, each group can share their information with the entire class. Oral presentations can be given while the rest of the class completes their Super Lotus Diagram and/or students can use information shared in oral presentations to fill in the Super Lotus Diagram.

# Supporting Resources

☐ Worksheets 179, 180, and 181

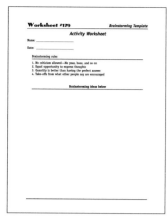

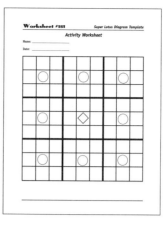

# Civil War

Understand the state, the United States, and world social history.

**Estimated Time:** 45 minutes          **Worksheets:** 182, 183, and 184

## Quality Tool/PDSA Linkage

- ☐ Students will use a Cause-and-Effect Diagram and a Relations Diagram.
  - • The Cause-and-Effect Diagram is a picture of the output of a brainstorming session that asks, "What causes . . . ," and is used to determine root causes in the plan portion of the PDSA cycle.
  - • The Relations Diagram is a picture of the cause and effect relationships between elements of the problem and is used to determine root cause in the plan portion of the PDSA cycle.

## Lesson Overview

- ☐ In this lesson, students will be learning about the Civil War.
- ☐ The students will be shown different reasons that people believe started the Civil War.
- ☐ The students will be looking at these reasons and discusses causes of the Civil War.

## Lesson Objectives

- ☐ The students will learn to disseminate information about the Civil War.
- ☐ The students will work in cooperative groups to share ideas relating to the Civil War.
- ☐ The students will learn about the Cause-and-Effect Diagram and Relations Diagram quality tools.
- ☐ The students will review research strategies and techniques.
- ☐ The students will formulate questions to accompany learning about the Civil War.

## Pre-Lesson Activities

- ☐ The teacher will obtain copies of a Cause-and-Effect Diagram for each student.
- ☐ The teacher will write the prompting questions onto chart paper.
- ☐ The teacher will make an overhead transparency of the Cause-and-Effect Diagram.
- ☐ The teacher will collect resource books and Internet sites about the Civil War.
- ☐ Obtain copies of the worksheets that go with the lesson.
- ☐ Obtain all materials needed for the lesson.

## Materials Needed

- ☐ Overhead projector.
- ☐ Transparency films.
- ☐ Chart paper.
- ☐ Markers.
- ☐ Civil War resource books.
- ☐ Overhead markers.

## Lesson Delivery/Procedure

- ☐ The teacher will begin by telling the students that they will be studying the Civil War.
- ☐ The teacher will ask the students to share ideas as to why the Civil War started.
- ☐ The teacher will write these ideas on an overhead transparency film or chart paper.
- ☐ The teacher will review the Cause-and-Effect Diagram tool.
- ☐ The teacher will give hints to guide students in the discussion. The students' ideas will be used to devise five headings on the Cause-and-Effect Diagram. (See worksheet 182 for suggested headings.)
- ☐ The teacher will help students decide on what the three to five categories should be.
- ☐ The teacher will randomly divide the class into five groups of students.
- ☐ The teacher will hand out a blank Cause-and-Effect Diagram (worksheet 182) to each group.
- ☐ The students will fill in the category headings on the Cause-and-Effect Diagram. (The teacher can model this at the same time to demonstrate where to place the categories.)
- ☐ Each student group will write under each heading the possible reasons why a war would break out.
- ☐ On the overhead projector, the teacher will place questions to assist the students in their thinking. (See worksheet 183 for prompting questions.)
- ☐ The teacher will give the groups five or six minutes to discuss reasons for each heading. (Adjust time as needed.)
- ☐ After time is up, the teacher will have each group report back to the whole class the reasons they wrote under each category.
- ☐ The teacher will write each groups' responses under the correct headings on an overhead.
- ☐ The students will listen to other groups' responses so items are not repeated.
- ☐ The teacher guides discussion about what probably happened first, second, third, and so on.

## Guided Practice

- ☐ The students will investigate further by looking in books, on the Internet, and in pamphlets to find out more about the areas identified on the Cause-and-Effect Diagram.
- ☐ The students will think of other things they might want to find out about the Civil War.
- ☐ The students will write down a list of questions the class posed during the day's activity about the Civil War.

## Assessment

- ☐ The teacher will informally assess students' understanding of the lesson by their level of involvement during class and small group discussions.
- ☐ The teacher can formally assess students by looking at the group's Cause-and-Effect Diagram.
- ☐ The teacher can formally assess students by giving them a small quiz where they state what the three to five causes of the Civil War were thought to be.

## Post-Lesson/Follow-Up Activities/Extensions

- ☐ The teacher and students can create a Relations Diagram to explore what the root cause of the Civil War was (see worksheet 184). The teacher should review the Relations Diagram tool with students.
- ☐ The teacher could ask "How would our country look today if the south had won?"
- ☐ The teacher could ask "Is there slavery today in the world?"

# Supporting Resources

- ☐ *www.civil-war.net*

- ☐ *www.civilwar.com*

- ☐ Worksheets 182, 183, and 184

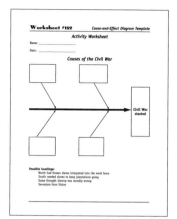

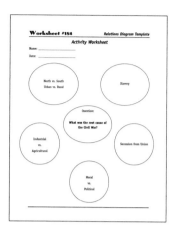

# Holocaust

Understand the state, the United States, and world history.

**Estimated Time:** 45–60 minutes          **Worksheets:** 185 and 186

## Quality Tool/PDSA Linkage

☐  Students will use Brainstorming, Nominal Group Technique, Force-Field Analysis, and a Radar Chart.

- The Brainstorming technique is the generation of ideas by a group and is used at any portion of the PDSA cycle when every person needs to be heard from and many ideas need to be generated.

- Nominal Group Technique/Light Voting is a structured group process (ranked voting) used to make decisions during any portion of the PDSA cycle.

- Force-Field Analysis is a tool used to evaluate the forces driving and restraining a desired change and is used during the plan portion of the PDSA cycle to generate the most comprehensive plan possible to test the improvement theory.

- The Radar Chart is a graph with multiple scales to report self-assessed knowledge or competence, often over time and is used during both the plan and study portions of the PDSA cycle.

## Lesson Overview

☐  In this lesson, the students will be learning about the Holocaust.

☐  The students will work in cooperative groups to Brainstorm basic rights every human being should have.

☐  The students will vote, using Nominal Group Technique, to select the top human rights everyone should have.

☐  The students, in small groups, will investigate whether people during the Holocaust had those rights identified in the Nominal Group Technique activity.

☐  The students will then learn how to use a Force-Field Analysis for problem solving.

☐  The students will use the Radar Chart to self-assess their involvement during the cooperative group activity.

## Lesson Objectives

☐  The students will learn the types of living conditions people in the Holocaust were faced with.

☐  The students will practice working together in cooperative learning groups.

☐  The students will review their research skills when looking for conditions exposed to during the Holocaust.

☐  The students will learn about the Brainstorming, Nominal Group Technique, Force-Field Analysis, and Radar Chart quality tools.

## Pre-Lesson Activities

☐  Gather books and resources about the Holocaust.

☐  Make a large Force-Field Analysis on chart paper.

☐  Obtain copies of the worksheets that go with the lesson.

☐  Obtain all materials needed for the lesson.

## Materials Needed

- ☐ Chart paper.
- ☐ Markers.
- ☐ Books on the Holocaust.
- ☐ Internet access.
- ☐ Paper.

## Lesson Delivery/Procedure

- ☐ The teacher will explain how to conduct a Brainstorming session. (Select a recorder of ideas, then generate ideas, recorder records the ideas, organize the results, and select a reporter. The rules of Brainstorming are: no criticism allowed, equal opportunity to express ideas, quantity over quality, and build off of each others ideas.)
- ☐ The teacher will ask each cooperative group to Brainstorm basic rights that ALL human beings should have for everyday living. (Examples are: clean water to drink, warm clothes to wear in cold weather, and so on.)

## Guided Practice

- ☐ The teacher will review the Brainstorming tool with students.
- ☐ In cooperative groups, the students should brainstorm basic rights every human being should have in their everyday living.
- ☐ After about five minutes of brainstorming, the teacher should ask for the students' attention.
- ☐ Students should have a reporter for their group to report out ideas from their Brainstorming session.
- ☐ The teacher should ask one group at a time to report out an idea that they had about everyone's basic rights as humans.
- ☐ The teacher will record what the students say onto a large poster-size chart paper.
- ☐ The students will listen to what everyone is saying in the sharing session so that an idea is not repeated.
- ☐ The teacher will review the Nominal Group Technique tool with students.
- ☐ Once all the ideas that were generated in the Brainstorming session are shared, the teacher will educate the students on how to use the Nominal Group Technique to choose the class' choice for top rights everyone should have.
- ☐ The teacher will explain to the students that each person will vote on the top three rights they think everyone should have. The teacher will explain that they will write a *three* next to their top choice, a *two* to their second choice, and a *one* to their third choice.
- ☐ The teacher will ask each group to come up one at a time to write their number next to their top three choices.
- ☐ Once everyone has had the opportunity to vote, the teacher will add up the numbers next to the human rights chosen by the students.
- ☐ The teacher will report out what the class thinks are the top three human rights everyone should have.
- ☐ The teacher will now assign each group a human right from the top ones identified.
- ☐ The students are responsible for researching the assigned human right within the context of the Holocaust. Did the people in the concentration camps and villages have that human right? What kinds of conditions were they exposed to? How did the people live?

## Assessment

- ☐ The teacher will informally assess students' level of understanding during class discussion and Brainstorming.
- ☐ The teacher will informally assess students' ability to use resources to seek out answers to their questions.
- ☐ The students and the teacher will assess the students' involvement in cooperative groups.

- [ ] The teacher will review the Radar Chart tool with students.

- [ ] The students will use a Radar Chart (worksheet 185) to assess their success with the assignment and cooperative group activity.

- [ ] The students will compile all the researched information into paragraphs to be assessed by the teacher.

## Post-Lesson/Follow-Up Activities/Extensions

- [ ] Complete the Force-Field Analysis (worksheet 186) with students about the Holocaust. Make sure to review the Force-Field Analysis tool with students.

- [ ] Continue to study the Holocaust: where it took place, how it started, who was responsible, and so on.

## Supporting Resources

- [ ] *fcit.coedu.usf.edu/holocaust/*

- [ ] *shamash.org/holocaust/*

- [ ] Worksheets 185 and 186

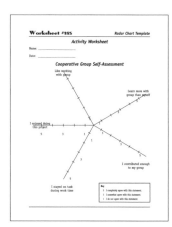
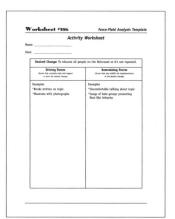

# Quality Across the Curriculum

# LANGUAGE ARTS

## K-1

### LESSONS

Story Sequence . . . . . . . . . . . 273

Homographs . . . . . . . . . . . . . 275

Fairy Tale Elements . . . . . . . . 277

Prewriting Strategy . . . . . . . . 281

Writing PDSA: Part A . . . . . . . 285

Writing PDSA: Part B . . . . . . . 289

Writing PDSA: Part C . . . . . . . 293

Writing PDSA: Part D . . . . . . . 297

Writing PDSA: Part E . . . . . . . 301

# Story Sequence

Summarize content of reading material using text organization
(for example, story, sequence).

**Estimated Time:** 45 minutes          **Worksheets:** 187, 188, 189, 190, 191, 192, and 193

## Quality Tool/PDSA Linkage

- ☐ Students will use a Flowchart.
  - The Flowchart is a drawing of any process used to document the process flow during the plan portion of the PDSA cycle.

## Lesson Objectives

- ☐ The students will recall the events of the story.
- ☐ The students will identify key elements of the story.
- ☐ The students will sequence the events of the story in correct order.
- ☐ The students will be introduced to the Flowchart quality tool.

## Pre-Lesson Activities

- ☐ Obtain copies of the worksheets that go with the lesson.
- ☐ Obtain all materials needed for the lesson.
- ☐ Review vocabulary and concepts such as introduction, beginning/setting, end, main characters, problem, solution, and conclusion.

## Materials Needed

- ☐ Crayons for students to draw their given element of the story.
- ☐ Chart paper for display of the Flowchart.
- ☐ Chart pens for drawing the Flowchart.
- ☐ Tape to post students' drawings in correct position next to the Flowchart.
- ☐ Story book (if possible, four to five copies).
- ☐ Post-It notes for use in moving story events on the Flowchart.

## Lesson Delivery/Procedure

- ☐ After teaching the story elements, the teacher will read a story book to the class.
- ☐ The teacher will ask the class, "What happened in the story?"
- ☐ Ideas shared by students will be recorded on a Post-It note.
- ☐ The teacher will explain that they will be using the Flowchart to show the order of the story.
- ☐ The teacher will ask the class to put the events in order using the Flowchart.
- ☐ The teacher will also place missing elements on the Flowchart.
- ☐ The teacher will summarize the lesson objectives, findings, and key concepts of the lesson to remember.

## Guided Practice

- ☐ The students are given worksheets (187–193) that go with this lesson and are assigned different story events to illustrate.

- ☐ The teacher will review the Flowchart tool with students and the students will complete worksheets 188–193.
- ☐ Once the student's drawing is completed, it will be checked by the teacher and the student will explain where the picture belongs on the Flowchart (worksheet 187).
- ☐ After all pictures are displayed, students may take turns using a pointer and summarize the story in the correct sequence.

## Assessment

- ☐ The teacher will observe students' responses during classroom discussion.
- ☐ The teacher will review the students' picture and picture placement to gauge level of understanding.
- ☐ The teacher will listen and review the students summarizing of the story to gauge level of understanding.

## Post-Lesson/Follow-Up Activities/Extensions

- ☐ Have the students make puppets and scenery to retell the story using the Flowchart.
- ☐ Display each story Flowchart around the classroom and let students retell their favorite stories to visitors (using the Flowcharts).
- ☐ Allow students to retell the story in order to others during center time.
- ☐ As the students become more familiar with the Flowchart, have them use the chart when reading their own stories.

## Supporting Resources

- ☐ Sequencing game for use in a center: pbskids.org/arthur/games/storyscramble/scramble.html
- ☐ Worksheets 187–193

# Homographs

Apply word analysis and vocabulary skills to comprehend selections.

**Estimated Time:** 45 minutes          **Worksheets:** 194 and 195

## Quality Tool/PDSA Linkage

☐ Students will use a Check Sheet/Matrix and Brainstorming.

  • The Check Sheet/Matrix is a tool to collect and organize data in the plan portion of the PDSA cycle.

  • The Brainstorming technique is the generation of ideas by a group and is used at any portion of the PDSA cycle when every person needs to be heard from and many ideas need to be generated.

## Lesson Overview

☐ This is a hands-on lesson designed to help students organize homographs to increase reading comprehension.

☐ The students will understand that when they come across a word while reading, it may have more than one pronunciation for the same spelling, and it may have more than one meaning for the same spelling.

## Lesson Objectives

☐ The students will comprehend and identify homographs.

☐ The students will Brainstorm several homographs.

☐ The students will comprehend at least two meanings of each homograph.

☐ The students will understand and use a Check Sheet.

## Pre-Lesson Activities

☐ Obtain copies of the worksheets that go with the lesson.

☐ Obtain all materials needed for the lesson.

## Materials Needed

☐ A blank worksheet for each student.

☐ Examples of several homographs; see Web sites for many examples.

## Lesson Delivery/Procedure

☐ The teacher will say and write this sentence on the board, "I saw a saw."

☐ The students will notice "saw" in the sentence two times.

☐ The teacher will guide students to the realization that even though we say the word the same way, it has more than one meaning.

☐ The teacher will introduce and define the term "homograph."

☐ The teacher will review the Brainstorming tool with students.

☐ The students will brainstorm other words that are homographs.

## Guided Practice

- [ ] The students will be allowed to talk in cooperative groups or pairs about many words that are homographs. If students are having difficulty, the teacher could suggest a few and allow students to discover how they have multiple meanings. Use worksheet 195 for this activity.

- [ ] The students will report to the group the homographs that they came up with.

- [ ] The teacher will review the Check Sheet tool with students.

- [ ] The teacher will place homographs on the Check Sheet with their meanings. See example in worksheet 194.

## Assessment

- [ ] The students will define two common homographs, and use them correctly.

- [ ] The students will complete the Check Sheet accurately to demonstrate understanding.

## Post-Lesson/Follow-Up Activities/Extensions

- [ ] Small groups of students could make their own Check Sheet of homographs.

- [ ] Keep a list of homographs to be added to by students as they come across homographs in their reading and speaking.

- [ ] Go on a homograph search (in books or objects found in their environment).

- [ ] Write funny sentences using homographs.

- [ ] Read *Fruit Trees Produce Produce* aloud.

- [ ] Add new homographs to the Check Sheet.

## Supporting Resources

- [ ] *www.marlodge.supanet.com/wordlist/homogrph.html*

- [ ] *The Dove Dove: Funny Homograph Riddles* by Marvin Terban

- [ ] *Fruit Trees Produce Produce* by Carey Molter

- [ ] Worksheets 194 and 195

# Fairy Tale Elements

Understand how literary elements and techniques are used to convey meaning.

**Estimated Time:** 30–45 minutes          **Worksheet::**    196

## Quality Tool/PDSA Linkage

- ☐ Students will use the Gallery Walk.

  - The Gallery Walk is a communication/consensus tool to allow everyone to provide input in a structured manner and is used at various portions of the PDSA cycle to create a written record of the group's thoughts.

## Lesson Overview

- ☐ In this lesson, students will use the Gallery Walk quality tool to identify and illustrate story elements of fairy tales.

- ☐ This lesson is designed to increase a student's auditory comprehension using the Gallery Walk quality tool to compare and contrast fairy tales read aloud.

- ☐ The teacher introduces common elements of fairy tales that can be identified and used to make comparisons across reading selections. (For the purposes of this lesson, the common elements are setting (place), good or evil characters, problem, solution/ending, and lesson learned.)

- ☐ After the teacher reads fairy tales aloud, students will use a Gallery Walk to illustrate and label the common story elements of at least six tales on enlarged charts posted or placed on surfaces around the classroom.

## Lesson Objectives

- ☐ The students will improve their listening comprehension.

- ☐ The students will identify important story elements of fairy tales.

- ☐ The students will make comparisons across reading selections.

- ☐ The students will understand and use the Gallery Walk quality tool.

## Pre-Lesson Activities

- ☐ Obtain a variety of fairy tales to read aloud to students from the classroom, school, or public libraries—one to two stories daily.

- ☐ As the teacher reads these tales aloud, discuss the comon elements of fairy tales.

- ☐ Acquire assistance from intermediate students (for example, reading buddies) or adult volunteers to facilitate and supervise each station on the Gallery Walk.

- ☐ Predetermine group size (suggested six groups of four to five students).

- ☐ Create poster-size charts—one for each story element—as shown on worksheet 196. Label the charts with your selected fairy tales.

- ☐ Obtain copies of the worksheets that go with the lesson.

- ☐ Obtain all materials needed for the lesson.

## Materials Needed

- [ ] Variety of fairy tales to read each day (at lease six prior to this lesson).
- [ ] Poster-size chart paper for each story element (see worksheet 196 for example).
- [ ] Markers and/or crayons for labeling and illustrating.

## Lesson Delivery/Procedure

- [ ] The teacher will review the story elements most commonly found in fairy tales. For the purpose of this lesson, the following elements should be emphasized and clearly defined: setting (place), good characters, evil characters, problem of the story, solution/end of the story, and lesson learned.
- [ ] The teacher will explain to the students that they will be taking a "Gallery Walk" to illustrate and label a fairy tale's story elements. The teacher will explain how this tool works.
- [ ] The teacher will assign one fairy tale to a group of four to five students.
- [ ] Direct the students' attention to the posted charts placed around the classroom.
- [ ] Explain that each group will rotate to all of the charts to label and illustrate the elements specific to their fairy tale. The book can be carried with them for reference and to promote recall.
- [ ] For example, Group #1 has the fairy tale "Cinderella." They will begin with the poster entitled "setting"; match their story title to insure they're labeling the correct square on the chart; and label and draw the primary setting(s) of the story; that is, Cinderella's stepmother's house and/or the castle ballroom. After a designated amount of time, this group will then walk to the next chart entitled "good characters" and label and draw Cinderella and the Fairy Godmother, and so on.
- [ ] Each student will contribute to the chart drawings. Students can refer to the book illustrations, if desired, to guide their drawings.
- [ ] Intermediate-age students or adult volunteers should be stationed at each chart to dictate responses, help the students look back into the text to identify story elements, and monitor the group work.
- [ ] The groups will continue this process until each group has visited each poster and added labels/illustrations for all story elements.
- [ ] Following all group rotations, use the posted charts to facilitate discussion of the story elements from each fairy tale.

## Guided Practice

- [ ] Student groups can become "experts" at each station or posted chart. For example, using the "Settings" poster, one group can describe the settings from all of the fairy tales. Another group can describe all of the evil characters, and so on.
- [ ] Students are encouraged to read and retell other fairy tales during independent reading times.
- [ ] After listening to additional fairy tales read, students can complete story maps on their own or with a partner.

## Assessment

- [ ] The students will demonstrate (listening) comprehension of fairy tales read aloud by correctly illustrating and labeling the required story elements.
- [ ] The students will identify the correct story elements and illustrate/label them on the Gallery Walk charts.
- [ ] Students will demonstrate understanding of at least one story element by comparing and contrasting this element for all fairy tales charted.

## Post-Lesson/Follow-Up Activities/Extensions

☐ The students can read or have someone read fairy tales at home.

☐ Give a related homework assignment, such as to listen to a fairy tale at home and identify the story elements.

☐ Identify common story elements in other genres, such as mysteries or biographies.

☐ Chart story elements from other genres using a similar format.

☐ Read "fractured" fairy tales and compare to original versions.

☐ Make similar comparisons between "Cinderella-type" stories. (Example, *Cinderella*, the original version; *The Rough-Faced Girl* by Rafe Martin; *The Persian Cinderella* by Shirley Climo; and *Ashpet—An Appalachian Tale* retold by Joanne Compton.)

## Supporting Resources

☐ Library Call Number for fairy tales—398.2

☐ *Grimm's Fairy Tales—www.nationalgeographic.com/grimm/*

☐ *Myths, Folk Tales, and Fairy Tales—www.teacher.scholastic.com/writewit/mff/index.htm*

☐ Worksheet 196

# Prewriting Strategy

Compose well-organized and coherent writing for specific purposes and audiences.

**Estimated Time:** 30 minutes          **Worksheet:** 197

## Quality Tool/PDSA Linkage

- ☐ Students will use a Lotus Diagram.

  - • The Lotus Diagram is a tool to expand thinking around a single topic or theme and is used at any portion of the PDSA cycle to generate additional thoughts.

## Lesson Overview

- ☐ In this lesson, students will learn about the Lotus Diagram quality tool.

- ☐ This is a prewriting strategy to generate and organize ideas to use in a personal experience story.

- ☐ First, the teacher reviews the purpose and structure of a personal experience story.

- ☐ Then, using a Lotus Diagram, the students will list (or illustrate) eight details about one of their own personal experiences.

## Lesson Objectives

- ☐ The students will learn or review the meaning of a personal experience story, such as a story about the author's own experiences. Personal experience stories have a beginning, middle, and end.

- ☐ The students will review the importance of prewriting strategies to generate and organize ideas.

- ☐ The students will understand how effective prewriting strategies will help them focus on their topic when writing.

- ☐ The students will learn how to use a Lotus Diagram to generate and organize these writing ideas.

## Pre-Lesson Activities

- ☐ Obtain copies of the worksheets that go with the lesson.

- ☐ Obtain all materials needed for the lesson.

## Materials Needed

- ☐ One Lotus Diagram template/worksheet for each student (worksheet 197).

- ☐ Pencil.

- ☐ Large chart paper on an easel for whole-class Brainstorming of personal experience story ideas.

## Lesson Delivery/Procedure

- [ ] The teacher will tell the students that personal experience stories are not made up, but something that has actually happened to the author. If possible, read examples of personal experience stories written by former students.

- [ ] The teacher will explain that one reason to write a personal experience story is to record an event or memory.

- [ ] The teacher will ask students to search their memories for ideas that can be turned into stories.

- [ ] As the students identify memories, the teacher will list these story ideas on large graph paper.

- [ ] The teacher will review the Lotus Diagram tool with students.

- [ ] The teacher can give memory prompts, such as, "I remember a time when . . . I took a vacation; visited a relative; received a special gift; or learned something new."

- [ ] The teacher will model the use of the Lotus Diagram to provide details (support and elaboration) to a story idea. Example: "I remember a time when . . . I went to Texas for a vacation."

- [ ] Students are given the Lotus Diagram template (worksheet 197). Students then write (or dictate) one experience in the middle rectangle. (Students can refer to the ideas listed on the chart paper from the brainstorming session.)

- [ ] The teacher will emphasize that the story ideas they select must be something they care or know a lot about.

- [ ] The students then write or dictate eight details about their experience.

- [ ] Students will use their Lotus Diagram to write personal experience stories.

## Guided Practice

- [ ] Select students to orally retell a personal experience using their Lotus Diagram (worksheet 197). (The teacher ensures the oral retellings have a beginning, middle, and end.)

- [ ] The students can create their own Lotus Diagrams in lieu of using a template. Using a blank piece of paper, students can fold it in thirds lengthwise. Next, it should be "fan folded" into thirds again. When the paper is opened, it will have nine small rectangles or squares.

## Assessment

- [ ] The students will demonstrate understanding of the prewriting strategy by producing a readable and usable Lotus Diagram (as age-appropriate by writing, dictating, illustrating, or using pictures).

- [ ] The students will use their Lotus Diagram to write, dictate, or recite a personal experience.

## Post-Lesson/Follow-Up Activities/Extensions

- [ ] The students may take a Lotus Diagram template home and generate additional topic ideas with family members.

- [ ] The students can be given a Writing Frame to better organize their ideas for a personal experience story that has a beginning, middle, and end.

- [ ] The students can share their personal experience stories with their classmates in an "Author's Chair."

- [ ] The students can ask friends and relatives to tell them stories and listen carefully for the beginning, middle, and end of the stories.

- [ ] The students can find Web sites that publish stories from children to read examples of personal experience stories and/or submit their own stories.

## Supporting Resources

☐   Web site that publishes student work—*www.kidpub.org/kidpub/*

☐   Worksheet 197

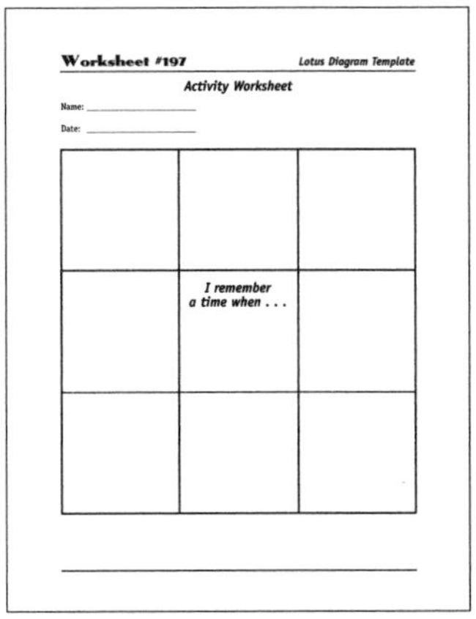

**Worksheet #197**      *Lotus Diagram Template*

**Activity Worksheet**

Name: _____

Date: _____

|  |  |  |
|---|---|---|
|  |  |  |
|  | *I remember a time when . . .* |  |
|  |  |  |

# Writing PDSA: Part A

Write to communicate for a variety of purposes.

**Estimated Time:** Once per quarter or regularly throughout the PDSA cycle; 30-minute sessions

**Worksheets:** 198 and 199

## PDSA Background Information

**Process name:** Kindergarten-First Grade Writing Skills (Note: The primary focus of this improvement process is on writing skills aligned with first grade learning standards. Modifications can be easily made throughout the plan for younger and older students.)

**Opportunity:** Writing is an area in need of improvement in many school improvement plans. Early elementary teachers want to help develop writers that love to write, as well as teach the students skills needed to evaluate their own writing. Students can build on their strengths in later grades become better writers and potentially score well on standardized writing tests.

**Importance to process:** Learning and using the quality tools to improve writing through the PDSA cycle can help students take responsibility for their own learning and improvement. Teachers will also feel confident they are building a good foundation for students in the area of writing.

**Project statement:** It is believed that students are their own most important evaluators. Teachers will do the following to develop effective writers: provide a risk-free, child-centered writing environment; teach skills and offer the tools needed to produce effective writing pieces; provide a variety of (age-appropriate) writing opportunities to build writing fluency and to learn the different genres of writing; train students to evaluate their own and their classmates' writing; and send their writing to a broader audience.

## Quality Tool/PDSA Linkage

☐ Students will use a Scatter Diagram as a Learning/Enthusiasm Matrix.

 • The Scatter Diagram is a tool used to show the relationship between two factors in the plan portion of the PDSA cycle.

## Lesson Overview

☐ This is a procedure designed for the teacher and students to assess student learning of the writing process and the students' enthusiasm level for writing activities.

☐ The assessment will be conducted once per quarter throughout one school year to measure any change in student feelings about writing and help students self-assess learning and understanding of what stage of writing they think they are in.

☐ The students will keep an individual Scatter Diagram (worksheet 198) and the teacher will keep a whole-class Scatter Diagram (worksheet 199) to be updated, interpreted, and discussed once per quarter.

## Lesson Objectives

☐ The students will be able to express their feelings about the writing activities/lessons conducted each quarter.

☐ The students will be able to assess their own confidence levels in the area of writing.

☐ The students and teacher will be able to gauge the whole-class enthusiasm level for writing tasks, and become more aware of the students' self-assessment of writing progress.

☐ The students will understand and use the Scatter Diagram.

## Pre-Lesson Activities

- [ ] Conduct a preassessment of whole-class learning/enthusiasm levels at the beginning of the school year (prior to direct instruction of the writing process).
- [ ] Obtain copies of the worksheets that go with the lesson.
- [ ] Create a poster board size of whole-class Scatter Diagram.
- [ ] Obtain all other materials needed for the lesson.

## Materials Needed

- [ ] Enlarge one Scatter Diagram for display of whole-class data (one per quarter).
- [ ] Markers for teacher use.
- [ ] Large colored (sticker) dots—four colors (suggested colors—red, green, blue, and yellow, as these colors are most readily available).
- [ ] Small colored (sticker) dots—same colors as large dots.
- [ ] Narrow markers for student use (colors must be the same as sticker dots).

## Lesson Delivery/Procedure

- [ ] The teacher will explain the purpose for a Scatter Diagram in the area of writing and will distribute worksheet 198 to each student.
- [ ] The teacher will explain the Scatter Diagram keys and how the tool works.
- [ ] The students will affix one small dot (of designated color) on individual Scatter Diagrams at the appropriate axis for Learning and Enthusiasm levels. (For example, "What type of writer I think I am"—Level 4; "How much I like writing"—Level 3—one dot is affixed where these two levels intersect.)
- [ ] Students will keep individual Scatter Diagrams in their student data folder.
- [ ] Students will then affix one large red dot in the same place on the enlarged Scatter Diagram (worksheet 199) to show whole-class data. (No names are necessary.)
- [ ] The teacher and students will interpret the data on the whole-class Scatter Diagram. "Where do most of the dots lie? Do you see any patterns?"
- [ ] The teacher and students will discuss the feelings shown on the whole-class Scatter Diagram. "How can we improve feelings for writing?" "How can we feel more confident about the writing process?"
- [ ] The teacher will than transfer the whole-class data to a (smaller) blank Scatter Diagram for comparison each quarter.

## Guided Practice

- [ ] The teacher will provide age-appropriate, direct instruction of the writing process on a regular basis.
- [ ] The teacher will provide a variety of writing tasks throughout each quarter to try to pique the varied interests of each student.
- [ ] With assistance as needed, the students will complete their individual Scatter Diagrams at the beginning of each quarter. (Change the color of the small dots each quarter.)
- [ ] The class will complete the whole-class Scatter Diagram at the beginning of each quarter. (Remember to change the color of the large dots and ensure they are the same color as the small dots.)
- [ ] The teacher and students will compare each quarter's Scatter Diagram and discuss.
- [ ] The teacher and students will conduct comparative studies of the Scatter Diagram after completion each quarter.

## Assessment

- ☐ The students will self-assess their enthusiasm for writing once per quarter by placing their dots accordingly on the individual Scatter Diagrams.

- ☐ Self-reflection should include reasons for any negative feelings toward writing tasks. Feelings can be shared verbally, if desired.

- ☐ The students will self-assess his or her confidence levels in the area of writing by completing the Scatter Diagram once per quarter.

- ☐ Once per quarter, the teacher and students will assess the enthusiasm and confidence levels of the entire class in the area of writing through discussion and interpretation of the whole-class Scatter Diagram.

## Post-Lesson/Follow-Up Activities/Extensions

- ☐ The students will keep a learning log of writing activities and their feelings about each task. This log will help students give an accurate assessment of their confidence/enthusiasm levels each quarter on the Scatter Diagrams.

- ☐ The students will keep individual Scatter Diagrams in other content areas: reading, math, science, and so on.

## Supporting Resources

- ☐ Worksheets 198 and 199

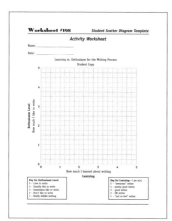
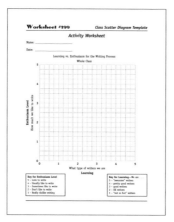

# Writing PDSA: Part B

Write to communicate for a variety of purposes.

**Estimated Time:** 20 minutes initially, then again after a predetermined time (post-assessment)

**Worksheets:** 200, 201, 202, and 203

## PDSA Background Information

Up to this point, the class has determined that there is a need for improvement in the writing area. The students first completed a Scatter Diagram to show the relationship between student attitudes and confidence levels. The teacher will continue to assess performance within this next lesson by using the Check Sheet and Pareto Diagram quality tools.

## Quality Tool/PDSA Linkage

☐ The teachers will use the Check Sheet and Pareto Diagram.

- The Check Sheet/Matrix is a tool to collect and organize data in the plan portion of the PDSA cycle.

- The Pareto Diagram is a bar chart that ranks categorical data from largest to smallest to find the "significant few" in the plan portion of the PDSA cycle.

## Lesson Overview

☐ This is a simple procedure designed for teachers to conduct a pre- and post-assessment of early writing skills and to develop a baseline of current student performance.

☐ Utilizing a Check Sheet, teachers will determine the number of students at each writing stage.

☐ Utilizing a Pareto Diagram, teachers will have a visual representation of the number of students at each writing stage in order of its frequency.

☐ Teachers will determine class and personal writing goals, as appropriate.

## Lesson Objectives

☐ The students will be introduced to the early stages of writing.

☐ The students will understand the Check Sheet quality tool.

☐ The students will understand how to interpret the Pareto Diagram (with teacher assistance), and to set personal and class writing goals accordingly.

☐ The students will learn how these two tools fit into the class PDSA plan for writing improvement.

## Pre-Lesson Activities

☐ Complete writing PDSA: Part A.

☐ Obtain four to five (informal) writing samples from each student within the first two to four weeks of the school term.

☐ Obtain copies of the worksheets that go with the lesson.

☐ Add student names to the blank Check Sheet.

☐ Enlarge the Pareto Diagram to poster size.

## Materials Needed

- ☐ Blank Check Sheet and Pareto Diagram.
- ☐ Enlarged Pareto Diagram.
- ☐ Easel or means to post enlarged Pareto Diagram.
- ☐ Markers.

## Lesson Delivery/Procedure

- ☐ Within the first two to four weeks of the school year, the teacher will assign informal writing activities in order to collect a portfolio sample for each student.
- ☐ The teacher will review each child's collection of writing samples to determine his or her primary stage of writing.
- ☐ The teacher will review the Check Sheet tool with students.
- ☐ The teacher will use the student-labeled Check Sheet (worksheet 201) to tally each student's stage in the writing process.
- ☐ The teacher will review the Pareto Diagram tool with students.
- ☐ The teacher will transfer the data from the Check Sheet to the blank Pareto Diagram (worksheet 203).
- ☐ The teacher will enlarge the completed Pareto Diagram and it will be displayed and explained to students.
- ☐ The teacher will share the completed Pareto Diagram of the whole-class results. Discussion and analysis of the Pareto Diagram should occur.
- ☐ The students and teacher will determine whole-class goals to improve writing skills. The teacher may ask "By the end of the school year, in which stage should most of us be if we work together to improve our writing?"
- ☐ If appropriate, students will determine personal goals for writing improvement based on their individualized results (developed during a student/teacher conference).

## Guided Practice

- ☐ The students will be shown samples of student writing pieces that reflect the varied writing levels from the Check Sheet.
- ☐ The teacher will again explain how these two tools fit into the class PDSA plan for writing improvement.
- ☐ The teacher will display the Pareto Diagram.

## Assessment

- ☐ With teacher assistance, students will self-assess their collection of writing samples and determine where on the Check Sheet an "X" should be placed.
- ☐ The students will use their understanding of the writing stages to monitor their own progress and set goals on how to progress to the next stage.

## Post-Lesson/Follow-Up Activities/Extensions

- ☐ When ready, the students will keep their own "Stages of Writing" Check Sheet in their student data folders.

## Supporting Resources

☐ *www.inkspot.com/* (Bulletin board for posting writing-related questions and for locating peer-critique partners)

☐ *Aunt Isabel Tells a Good One* by Kate Duke

☐ Worksheets 200, 201, 202, and 203

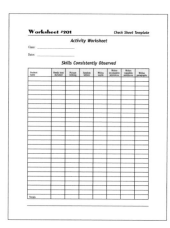

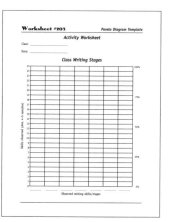

# Writing PDSA: Part C

Write to communicate for a variety of purposes.

**Estimated Time:** 20–30 minutes          **Worksheet:** 204

## PDSA Background Information

Up to this point, students have completed a Scatter Diagram to show the relationship between student attitude and how they think they are as writers. The teacher has obtained four to five writing samples from each student and used both a Check Sheet and Pareto Diagram to determine the number of students at each writing stage. In this next lesson, the teacher and students will use a Cause-and-Effect Diagram to help determine next steps to improve their writing skills. It will also help ensure that the classroom environment is conducive to writing improvement.

## Quality Tool/PDSA Linkage

☐ Students will use the Cause-and-Effect Diagram.

- The Cause-and-Effect Diagram is a picture of the output of a brainstorming session that asks, "What causes . . . ," and is used to determine root causes in the plan portion of the PDSA cycle.

## Lesson Overview

☐ This is a process the teacher and students will use to identify factors needed to help students improve their writing and to produce effective writing pieces.

☐ Using a Cause-and-Effect Diagram, teachers and students will discuss possible causes as they relate to factors affecting writing improvement. Examples of factors include people (teacher, student, parents), classroom environment, materials, and procedures.

## Lesson Objectives

☐ The students will become more aware of a classroom environment conducive to writing improvement.

☐ The students will recognize the materials needed to write well.

☐ The students will learn and understand procedures to follow in order to write more effectively.

☐ The students will understand the Cause-and-Effect Diagram quality tool.

## Pre-Lesson Activities

☐ Obtain copies of worksheets that go with the lesson.

☐ Complete writing PDSA: Part B.

☐ Create a poster board– or chart paper–sized Cause-and-Effect Diagram (could also photocopy Cause-and Effect Diagram to overhead projector sheet).

## Materials Needed

☐ Cause-and-Effect Diagram—enlarged or photocopied for overhead projector use

☐ Markers

## Lesson Delivery/Procedure

- ☐ The teacher will review the Cause-and-Effect Diagram with students.
- ☐ The teacher will display the Cause-and-Effect Diagram (worksheet 204) and will explain that the goal will be to determine and list factors that help students improve their writing skills and produce effective writing pieces.
- ☐ The following factors are listed on the Diagram: procedures, materials, environment, parents, teacher, and students. (The teacher will ensure that students understand the definition of each of these terms as they relate to writing improvement.)
- ☐ The teacher questions students by asking, "What can help you improve your writing skills this year?"
- ☐ By directing the students' attention to each factor given on the Cause-and-Effect Diagram (worksheet 204), the teacher will promote discussion and list student responses on the diagram.
- ☐ The following *examples* may help promote and focus class discussion:
  - Procedures—Work quietly during writing times; raise your hand if you need assistance; follow the writing process directions or Flowchart (specific to each class)
  - Materials—Sharpened pencils; writing journals and/or notebook paper; eraser; Word Wall
  - Environment—Quiet workers; helpful classmates; print-rich environment; rubrics in child-friendly terms; writing frameworks for early writers; handwriting desk strips
  - Students—Know about your topic; write using own "voice"; ask for help if needed; use best handwriting; sound out words; use Word Wall; proofread work; write willingly; respond to suggestions for improvement
  - Teachers—Encourage us; help us; give us positive suggestions for improvement; read "quality" writing pieces as examples; provide direct instruction in writing process; teach us how to proofread; keep the classroom quiet
  - Parents—Encourage us to write at home; help us with our writing homework; buy us new pencils or paper if we need it
- ☐ Discussion will continue until all responses are recorded on the whole-class Cause-and-Effect Diagram (worksheet 204).

## Guided Practice

- ☐ The teacher will display the Cause-and-Effect Diagram for daily use.
- ☐ The students will refer to the Cause-and-Effect Diagram to see if adequate materials are on hand before writing.
- ☐ Students may role-play a "conducive" and "nonconducive" classroom environment (for example, noisy versus quiet classroom during writing times).
- ☐ Students will write for a variety of purposes, such as, write a letter, make a list, write a personal narrative. (Emphasize that to become better writers, students must write often.)

## Assessment

- ☐ The students will tell at least one way that their parents can help them improve their writing skills.
- ☐ The students will exhibit behaviors listed under "procedures" (worksheet 204) during writing times.

## Post-Lesson/Follow-Up Activities/Extensions

- ☐ The students (and parents) will create a Cause-and-Effect Diagram for home use to promote continuous writing improvement and/or to complete homework assignments in an environment conducive to learning.
- ☐ The students and teacher will use the Cause-and-Effect Diagram to identify possible causes of other classroom problems or to analyze a process, such as "A Perfect Scientific Experiment."
- ☐ The students and teacher can try using a "negative" or "reverse" Cause-and-Effect Diagram, that is, "A Poorly Written Writing Piece" selected by the teacher as a nonexample.

## Supporting Resources

☐ Worksheet 204

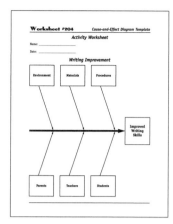

# Writing PDSA: Part D

Write to communicate for a variety of purposes.

**Estimated Time:** 30 minutes        **Worksheets:** 205

## PDSA Background Information

Up to this point the students have completed a Scatter Diagram, and the teacher used both a Check Sheet and Pareto Diagram to gather baseline data. A Cause-and-Effect Diagram was used to determine the root causes and, in particular, to determine what students need to consistently progress in writing, as well as to ensure a classroom environment that is conducive to writing improvement. The class then developed an improvement theory—"If all stakeholders work collaboratively to provide students with the necessary skills, knowledge, and positive attitude, then even the youngest students will write effectively and learn to evaluate their own writing." Using the baseline data from the previous three lessons, the teacher and students will now develop an Action Plan, that is, the "road map" to carrying out the improvement theory.

## Quality Tool/PDSA Linkage

- ☐ Teachers and students will use the WWW Chart/Action Plan.

  - The WWW Chart/Action Plan is a description of the actions necessary to make a desired change and is used in the plan portion of the PDSA cycle when preparing to test the improvement theory.

## Lesson Overview

- ☐ This is a process designed to help teachers develop an Action Plan to test the improvement theory.

- ☐ The Action Plan will be used to identify the different tasks/responsibilities, identify people within the process (teacher/student/parent or guardian), and to define a general time frame for task completion.

- ☐ Data for the Action Plan can be found in the two previous activities, that is, Pareto Diagram (worksheet 203) and Cause-and-Effect Diagram (worksheet 204).

## Lesson Objectives

- ☐ The students will recognize and begin to take responsibility for some of these continuous improvement processes.

- ☐ The students will understand and help develop the Action Plan.

## Pre-Lesson Activities

- ☐ Complete writing PDSA: Part C.

- ☐ Review the WWW Chart/Action Plan with students.

- ☐ Create own or modify sample Action Plan (worksheet 207).

- ☐ Identify the tasks involved by referring to the previously completed Pareto Diagram (worksheet 205) and Cause-and-Effect Diagram (worksheet 206).

- ☐ Identify stakeholders that will be involved in the process. (Recommended stakeholders: teacher, students, parent or guardian.)

- ☐ Enlarge the Action Plan chart (worksheet 205).

- ☐ Obtain copies of the worksheet that goes with the lesson.

- ☐ Obtain all other materials.

## Materials Needed

- ☐ Enlarged Action Plan Chart (worksheet 205).
- ☐ Whole-Class Pareto Diagram and Cause-and-Effect Diagram (previously developed worksheets 205 and 206).
- ☐ Markers.

## Lesson Delivery/Procedure

- ☐ The teacher and students will complete the Action Plan together (worksheet 205).
- ☐ Referring to the two previously developed diagrams, list responsibilities or tasks, those responsible for the tasks, and estimated times for task completion. It is recommended that quarterly tasks are completed throughout the school year.
- ☐ Determine the primary tasks to accomplish. (It is suggested that the teacher assists in developing the Action Plan.)
- ☐ The teacher will list all responses from students.
- ☐ **Suggested teacher responsibilities:** Establish a classroom environment conducive to learning; provide direct instruction in writing (spacing of words; letter-sound correspondence; appropriate use of end marks or capital letters, complete sentences; and so on); provide feedback on writing pieces in a timely manner; communicate progress to parents; review and enrich writing lessons as needed; regularly add words to the Word Wall.

  **Suggested student responsibilities:** Come prepared to write (paper, sharpened pencil); keep a positive attitude toward writing process; listen attentively during writing mini-lessons; respond to suggestions; ask for help when needed; complete writing tasks in a timely manner; use the Word Wall.

  **If needed, suggested parent responsibilities:** Accept and encourage spelling approximations; provide writing experiences at home; supply child with paper, pencils, as needed; communicate with teacher about writing progress.
- ☐ Pictures or symbols can be added to the Action Plan (worksheet 205) to promote (student) understanding of each step.
- ☐ Post the Action Plan in a prominent place in the classroom to refer to on a regular basis.

## Guided Practice

- ☐ The teacher and students refer to the Action Plan often to monitor progress in task completion, and to set goals/lessons for the unaccomplished tasks. Highlight the goals met.

## Assessment

- ☐ The students will verbally contribute to the Action Plan by suggesting at least one responsibility for each stakeholder involved.

## Post-Lesson/Follow-Up Activities/Extensions

- ☐ The students and the teacher will refer to the chart frequently to ensure progress is made on the Action Plan.
- ☐ Personal writing goals can be listed and kept in student data folders. These goals could be reviewed regularly and modified if necessary.
- ☐ New goals are established and regularly assessed as progress in writing is made.

# Supporting Resources

☐ Worksheet 205

**Worksheet #205**                    *Action Plan Template*

*Activity Worksheet*

Name: _____

Date: _____

*Writing Improvement*

| Who | What | How | When |
|-----|------|-----|------|
|     |      |     |      |
|     |      |     |      |
|     |      |     |      |
|     |      |     |      |
|     |      |     |      |
|     |      |     |      |
|     |      |     |      |

# Writing PDSA: Part E

Write to communicate for a variety of purposes.

**Estimated Time:** 30 minutes      **Worksheets:** 206

## PDSA Background Information

Up to this point, the class used baseline data from the first three lessons (writing PDSA Parts A–C) to develop an Action Plan. The Action Plan is the "road map" to carrying out the improvement theory. The final step of the PDSA cycle is to standardize improvements. Students will further commit to this process by developing a Flowchart that outlines what they need to do to get ready for writing during each regularly scheduled writing time.

## Quality Tool/PDSA Linkage

☐ The students will use a Flowchart quality tool.

- The Flowchart is a drawing of any process used to document the process flow during any part of the PDSA cycle.

## Lesson Overview

☐ Once the Action Plan is developed, the teacher and students will work together to create a Flowchart for student use.

☐ This Flowchart will analyze the sequence of the work required and to ensure continuous improvement.

☐ The main components of the Flowchart will be taken from the (previously developed) "Student Responsibilities" section of the Action Plan.

☐ This Flowchart will be posted in a prominent place in the classroom so that students can refer to it frequently as a review of necessary steps to get ready to write.

## Lesson Objectives

☐ The students will help develop a Flowchart that will produce a visual "picture" of the process they should follow when getting ready to write.

☐ The students will learn how to analyze the flow of work in the process of preparing for in-class writing times.

☐ The students will demonstrate understanding of the Flowchart quality tool.

## Pre-Lesson Activities

☐ Complete writing PDSA: Part D.

☐ Review the Flowchart provided (worksheet 206) for suggested components.

☐ Review Flowchart symbols.

☐ Obtain chart paper for Flowchart (to be developed together).

☐ Display previously written Action Plan chart for reference.

☐ Obtain copies of the worksheet that goes with the lesson.

☐ Obtain all other materials.

## Materials Needed

- ☐ Enlarged Action Plan Chart.
- ☐ Chart paper for Flowchart development and final product.
- ☐ Large size Post-It notes.
- ☐ Markers.

## Lesson Delivery/Procedure

- ☐ The teacher will display the Action Plan (from worksheet 205) and explain that the class will now use the data from the student section to develop a Flowchart that will provide a visual picture of the process.
- ☐ The teacher will review the Flowchart tool with students.
- ☐ The teacher will set the purpose by explaining to the students that referring to the Flowchart before beginning in-class writing sessions will help them consistently become prepared for writing.
- ☐ The teacher will explain how preparedness can promote writing improvement.
- ☐ The teacher will explain and clarify the symbols used in a Flowchart.
- ☐ The teacher will, on chart paper, begin the Flowchart by writing primary tasks on Post-It notes. (It is recommended that you write each step on Post-It notes so they can then be rearranged as needed before the final draft is written. This will also ensure correct sequence in the process.)
- ☐ The teacher will gain student input for each step. Frequently refer to the Action Plan for suggested tasks.
- ☐ The teacher will ensure accuracy and sequence of the process by rearranging the Post-It notes until the correct sequence is established.
- ☐ The teacher (with help from the students) will rewrite the final Flowchart on another piece of chart paper.
- ☐ Pictures can be added to the Flowchart for additional visual cues to promote (student) understanding of each step in the process. (For example, a picture of a student raising his or her hand when help is needed.)
- ☐ Post the Flowchart in a prominent place in the classroom and refer to it regularly.

## Guided Practice

- ☐ The students will frequently refer to the Flowchart to ensure preparedness for writing sessions.
- ☐ The teacher will refer students to the Flowchart as needed if a step in the process is regularly missed.
- ☐ The teacher will monitor use of the Flowchart and note any changes or modifications that need to be made before standardizing improvements. These notes can be written directly on the Flowchart until a new one can be created.

## Assessment

- ☐ The students will contribute at least three of the steps to the creation of the Flowchart.
- ☐ The students will be able to explain one step in the process and how it will help them become better writers.
- ☐ The students will be able to explain how preparedness for writing sessions can promote writing improvement.
- ☐ The students will use at least one step of the Flowchart to set a personal goal to improve writing skills. For example, "I will raise my hand if I need help."

## Post-Lesson/Follow-Up Activities/Extensions

- ☐ The students and the teacher will create Flowcharts for other purposes, for example, morning procedures.
- ☐ The students and the teacher will create Flowcharts in other content areas, for example, the steps of the long-division process.

- [ ] After implementing and testing the improvement theory for a predetermined amount of time, data should be collected by readminstering Parts A and B (of the Writing Improvement PDSA) to determine if improvements have been made, that is, to study and compare the results. This can be done at the end of each grading term or quarter.

- [ ] Ways to make improvements standard (act):
  - Create a new Flowchart to represent the improved changes to the process.
  - Students share writing pieces with a broader audience.
  - Showcase students successes (effective writing pieces) on a "Quality Work Bulletin Board" or in a section of student data folders designated for quality work.
  - Develop a list of modifications to the PDSA process for younger and older students.
  - Create and display Flowcharts for each writing genre to provide structure for early writers.
  - Develop individual improvement plans for writing.
  - Develop a schoolwide PDSA in the area of writing.
  - Develop or find student-friendly rubrics for each grade level.

- [ ] Ways to continue improvement (act):
  - Display PDSA process on public bulletin board.
  - Publish recommendations for all.
  - Create data gathering plan to ensure the new system continues to work effectively.

## Supporting Resources

- [ ] Worksheet 206

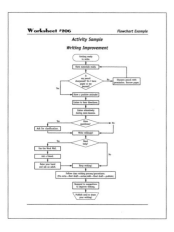

# LANGUAGE ARTS

2-3

## LESSONS

Making Connections. . . . . . . 307

Word Choice . . . . . . . . . . . . 309

Fiction/Nonfiction. . . . . . . . 313

Summarizing Nonfiction . . . . 315

Writing Improvement. . . . . . 317

Prediction. . . . . . . . . . . . . . 321

Following Directions . . . . . . 323

Context Clues . . . . . . . . . . . 325

Commonly Misspelled Words. . 327

# Making Connections

Establish purposes for reading, make predictions, connect important ideas and link to previous experiences and knowledge.

**Estimated Time:** 45 minutes          **Worksheets:** 207 and 208

## Quality Tool/PDSA Linkage

☐ Students will use Brainstorming and the Relations Diagram.

- The Brainstorming technique is the generation of ideas by a group and is used at any portion of the PDSA cycle when every person needs to be heard from and many ideas need to be generated.

- The Relations Diagram is a picture of the cause and effect relationships between elements of the problem and is used to determine root cause in the plan portion of the PDSA cycle.

## Lesson Overview

☐ The students will listen to the teacher read *Sarah, Plain and Tall*.

☐ The students and the teacher will discuss how the characters' relationships influence each other.

☐ The class will use the Brainstorming technique to make a Relations Diagram.

## Lesson Objectives

☐ The students will learn or review how to brainstorm ideas about certain subject matter.

☐ The students will create a Relations Diagram using the story content.

☐ The students will share experiences they have had in making real-life connections with stories they have read.

## Pre-Lesson Activities

☐ Read aloud the story of *Sarah, Plain and Tall* to the class over the course of one week.

☐ Review how to Brainstorm with students.

☐ Obtain copies of the worksheets that go with the lesson.

☐ Obtain all materials needed for the lesson.

## Materials Needed

☐ A copy of the Relations Diagram.

☐ Post-It notes.

☐ Large sheet of paper to put the Post-It notes on.

☐ Large sheet of paper to write categories on for discussion.

☐ Pencils for students.

☐ Markers for the teacher.

☐ *Sarah, Plain and Tall* by Patricia MacLachan.

## Lesson Delivery/Procedure

☐ The teacher will review the Brainstorming tool with students.

☐ After the teacher has finished reading the book, the class will brainstorm important characteristics of each character and how they may have been related to each other or to a real-life example of the student.

☐ The students and the teacher will brainstorm elements of the story and how those elements might be related to real-life situations. See example on worksheet 207.

☐ The teacher will review the Relations Diagram tool with students.

☐ The class will make a Relations Diagram (worksheet 208) together on the overhead using the elements discussed as a class.

☐ The students will summarize the lesson objective, findings, and key concepts of the lesson to remember when using the Relations Diagram.

## Guided Practice

☐ The class will work together to complete the Relations Diagram (worksheet 208) over the material in *Sarah, Plain and Tall*.

## Assessment

☐ The students will complete notes of a Relations Diagram over *Sarah, Plain and Tall* material.

☐ The teacher will review student work, discussion, and findings to gauge level of understanding.

## Post-Lesson/Follow-Up Activities/Extensions

☐ The students can take the idea of a Relations Diagram home to share with parents and have them try to make a real-life connection with a piece of literature they have read themselves. This will also promote the importance of reading in the home.

☐ The students can challenge themselves by developing a Relations Diagram on their own for another subject area.

☐ The students can visit another grade with their Relations Diagram and teach younger or older students what they have learned about *Sarah, Plain and Tall* and what real-life connections can be made to literature.

## Supporting Resources

☐ *Sarah, Plain and Tall* by Patricia MacLachan

☐ Worksheets 207 and 208

# Word Choice

Write to communicate for a variety of purposes.

**Estimated Time:** Day 1: 60 minutes          **Worksheets:** 209, 210, and 211
Day 2: 60 minutes
Bar Chart graphing will be ongoing

## Quality Tool/PDSA Linkage

☐ Students will use Brainstorming, Nominal Group Technique, Tree Diagram, and Bar Chart.

- The Brainstorming technique is the generation of ideas by a group and is used at any portion of the PDSA cycle when every person needs to be heard from and many ideas need to be generated.

- Nominal Group Technique/Light Voting is a structured group process (ranked voting) used to make decisions during any portion of the PDSA cycle.

- The Systematic/Tree Diagram is a tool to guide a group in planning for a broad goal by determining and assigning the different levels of action needed to accomplish the goal and is used in the plan portion of the PDSA cycle.

- The Bar Chart is a graph of categorical data plotted by frequency, and is used in the plan portion of the PDSA cycle.

## Lesson Overview

☐ This lesson will encourage students to use new and interesting vocabulary in their writing.

☐ The students will use the quality tools: Brainstorming, Nominal Group Technique, Tree Diagram, and Bar Chart.

☐ The students will set a goal and chart their progress.

## Lesson Objectives

☐ The students will understand and use the quality tools: Brainstorming, Nominal Group Technique, Tree Diagram, and Bar Chart.

☐ The students will expand their writing pieces by incorporating targeted words into their writing.

☐ The students will set a goal, revise, and re-evaluate word usage from the data collected.

## Pre-Lesson Activities

☐ The students should have some knowledge of the writing process.

☐ The students should have some experience with various parts of speech.

☐ Gather children's literature that will help students to choose new and interesting words in which to focus on in their writing.

☐ Obtain copies of the worksheets that go with the lesson.

☐ Obtain all materials needed for the lesson.

## Materials Needed

☐ Chart paper.

☐ Children's literature.

☐ Post-It notes.

☐ Markers.

## Lesson Delivery/Procedure

- [ ] In groups of four, students will work with a piece of children's literature selected by the teacher.
- [ ] The teacher will review the Brainstorming tool with students.
- [ ] After reading the book, students will brainstorm interesting words that they have found (worksheet 209).
- [ ] The teacher will review the Nominal Group Technique with students.
- [ ] The students will use the Nominal Group Technique to select 10 to 15 target words that they will incorporate in future writing pieces (worksheet 209).
- [ ] Each student within the group will choose three words from worksheet 209 to further analyze using the Tree Diagram.
- [ ] The teacher will review the Tree Diagram tool with students.
- [ ] The students will share their Tree Diagram (worksheet 210) with other members of the group so that all students have a clear understanding of the meaning of the words.
- [ ] The teacher will review the Bar Chart tool with students.
- [ ] The students will create a Bar Chart (worksheet 211) to collect data on the usage of targeted words in their writing.
- [ ] The students will set a goal for the number of targeted words they will use in each writing piece.
- [ ] The students will revise, re-evaluate, and reflect on their use of targeted words in writing.

## Guided Practice

- [ ] The students will complete their Tree Diagram (worksheet 210) for three of the targeted words.
- [ ] The students will receive copies of other students' Tree Diagrams as they work through this process.
- [ ] The students will chart word usage on the Bar Graph (worksheet 211) and set individual goals.

## Assessment

- [ ] The students will use Brainstorming, Nominal Group Technique, Tree Diagram, and Bar Chart to improve types of vocabulary used in writing. This will be demonstrated and charted in future writing assignments.
- [ ] The students and teacher will meet in small groups to help students refine their target list.
- [ ] Students will be provided with guidelines for completing the Tree Diagram to demonstrate understanding of the concepts of vocabulary developments.
- [ ] The teacher will conference with each student throughout this process in order to gauge student progress.

## Post-Lesson/Follow-Up Activities/Extensions

- [ ] The students will continue to use this process to make their writing more interesting.
- [ ] Tree Diagrams can be used as a homework assignment.

## Supporting Resources

- ☐ *Book, Lessons, Ideas* published by Great Source Education Group
  - • Includes bibliography of children's literature related to word choice and vocabulary development
- ☐ *Seeing with New Ideas* published by Northwest Regional Education Laboratory
- ☐ *Brining Words to Life* by Isabel L. Beck
- ☐ *6 + 1 Traits of Writing* by Ruth Culhan
- ☐ Worksheets 209, 210, and 211

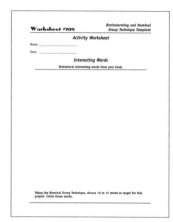

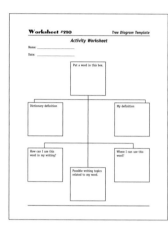

# Fiction/Nonfiction

Classify literary works as fiction or nonfiction.

**Estimated Time:** 45 minutes     **Worksheets:** 212, 213, and 214

## Quality Tool/PDSA Linkage

- ☐ Students will use a Lotus Diagram.

  - • The Lotus Diagram is a tool to expand thinking around a single topic or theme and is used at any portion of the PDSA cycle to generate additional thoughts.

## Lesson Overview

- ☐ This is a class participation lesson designed to enrich students' knowledge of the difference between fiction and nonfiction literature.

- ☐ Following a review of the definitions of fiction and nonfiction, the students will list titles of books that would be either fiction or nonfiction and place them on the correct Lotus Diagram.

- ☐ The students will then keep a record of books they have heard of or read as fiction or nonfiction.

## Lesson Objectives

- ☐ The students will learn the characteristics of fiction and nonfiction literature.

- ☐ The students will further expand their literature selection by being aware of books that are fiction and nonfiction.

- ☐ The students will use the Lotus Diagram to record cited examples to prove that a given book is fiction or nonfiction.

## Pre-Lesson Activities

- ☐ Obtain copies of the worksheets that go with the lesson.

- ☐ Make a transparency of each of the worksheets for class discussion.

- ☐ Obtain all materials needed for the lesson.

- ☐ Review the attributes of fiction and nonfiction literature.

## Materials Needed

- ☐ Teacher overhead of Lotus Diagram for fiction and nonfiction.

- ☐ Pencil or pen for appropriate recording of data.

- ☐ Examples of both fiction and nonfiction literature (at least one example of each type of literature).

- ☐ A copy of worksheets 212–214 for each student for independent recording of book titles.

## Lesson Delivery/Procedure

- ☐ After teaching the appropriate attributes of fiction and nonfiction literature, the teacher will show the class a familiar fiction selection.

- ☐ The teacher will review the Lotus Diagram tool with students.

- ☐ The class will work together to cite reasons why the selection is considered fiction. The reasons will be recorded on the Lotus Diagram. Repeat this process for a nonfiction book.

## Guided Practice

- ☐ Each student will be given two Lotus Diagrams (worksheets 212 and 213), one for fiction literature and one for nonfiction literature.

- ☐ The students may use the classroom or school library to look for titles of both fiction and nonfiction books. Students will record the titles on worksheet 214.

- ☐ The students will select a fiction and nonfiction book and cite reasons why the books are fiction or nonfiction on the appropriate Lotus Diagrams.

## Assessment

- ☐ The students will explain to other students why they put the cited examples on the Lotus Diagrams.

- ☐ The students will give feedback to their classmates if they do not agree with the cited examples.

- ☐ The teacher will review student work, discussion, and findings to gauge level of understanding.

## Post-Lesson/Follow-Up Activities/Extensions

- ☐ The students may create book covers of books they read and classify them as fiction or nonfiction by attaching them to a classroom bulletin board under the correct heading.

- ☐ The students may keep a list where they write down the titles to both fiction and nonfiction books they have read.

- ☐ The students may expand their Lotus Diagram to include the categories of fiction (for example, mysteries, animal stories, fairy tales) and nonfiction (for example, biographies, science, historical narratives) and then find examples of each in the expanded Lotus Diagram.

## Supporting Resources

- ☐ Educate the Children Web site—*www.educate.org.uk/teacher_zone/classroom/literacy/text_4.htm*

- ☐ Worksheets 212, 213, and 214

# Summarizing Nonfiction

Compose well-organized and coherent writing for specific purposes and audiences.

**Estimated Time:** Two 45-minute sessions     **Worksheets:** 215, 216, and 217

## Quality Tool/PDSA Linkage

☐ Students will use a Lotus Diagram and an Affinity Diagram.

- The Lotus Diagram is a tool to expand thinking around a single topic or theme and is used at any portion of the PDSA cycle to generate additional thoughts.

- The Affinity Diagram is a tool to generate, organize, and consolidate information gathered through Brainstorming, and is used in many portions of the PDSA cycle.

## Lesson Overview

☐ This lesson is designed to help students summarize nonfiction.

☐ This method of summarizing nonfiction allows for greater support when writing nonfiction essays.

☐ This lesson can be used following a social studies, science, or any other nonfiction lesson.

## Lesson Objectives

☐ The students will summarize nonfiction using the five-paragraph essay format.

☐ The students will understand and use the Lotus Diagram quality tool.

☐ The students will understand and use the Affinity Diagram quality tool.

## Pre-Lesson Activities

☐ Obtain copies of the worksheets that go with the lesson.

☐ Obtain all materials needed for the lesson.

## Materials Needed

☐ A blank worksheet for each student.

☐ Chart paper.

☐ Post-It notes.

☐ A nonfiction book or text for each student or one copy of a nonfiction book to be read aloud.

## Lesson Delivery/Procedure

☐ The teacher will preview text or a book to be read in order to build background knowledge with students.

☐ The students will read the book/text or the teacher will read aloud.

☐ Having finished the book/text, students will write everything they remember about the text on Post-It notes. One idea per Post-It.

## Guided Practice

- ☐ The students will bring their Post-It notes to designated area (chart paper works well).

- ☐ The teacher will guide students to sort Post-It notes by category. For example, if the topic is "whales," categories may include: "kinds," "size," "what/how they eat," and so on.

- ☐ The teacher will review the Affinity Diagram tool with students. Using the ideas generated, the students will complete the Affinity Diagram (worksheet 215).

- ☐ Having sorted the Post-Its, students will take one category or topic and fill out a Lotus Diagram (worksheet 217) about that area, for example "habitat." The teacher will review the Lotus Diagram tool.

- ☐ The students will write a five-paragraph essay about the topic (opening paragraph, three supporting paragraphs, closing paragraph).

## Assessment

- ☐ The Affinity Diagram will be assessed for a variety of answers and correct sorting/grouping.

- ☐ The Lotus Diagram (worksheet 217) will be assessed for specific examples and accuracy.

- ☐ The five-paragraph essay will be assessed for sufficiency of support and elaboration.

## Post-Lesson/Follow-Up Activities/Extensions

- ☐ Make a visual aid to go along with topic, that is, a diorama, poster, or PowerPoint presentation.

- ☐ The students research a related topic and use this method in small groups to write a collaborative essay and present to class.

## Supporting Resources

- ☐ Worksheets 215, 216, and 217

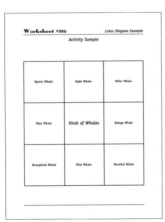
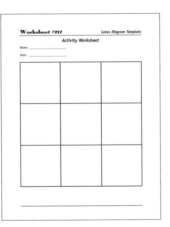

# Writing Improvement

Compose well-organized and coherent writing for specific purposes and audiences.

**Estimated Time:** 20-30 minutes      **Worksheets:** 218 and 219

## Quality Tool/PDSA Linkage

☐ Students will use the Cause-and-Effect Diagram.

- The Cause-and-Effect Diagram is a picture of the output of a brainstorming session that asks, "What causes . . . ," and is used to determine root causes in the plan portion of the PDSA cycle.

## Lesson Overview

☐ This is a process the teacher and students will use to identify factors needed to help students improve their writing and produce effective writing pieces.

☐ Utilizing a Cause-and-Effect Diagram, teachers and students will discuss possible causes as they relate to factors that can effect writing improvement, for example, people (teacher, student, parents), classroom environment, materials, and procedures.

## Lesson Objectives

☐ The students will become more aware of a classroom environment conducive to writing improvement.

☐ The students will identify the materials needed to write well.

☐ The students will learn and understand procedures to follow in order to write effective pieces.

☐ The students will understand and use the Cause-and-Effect Diagram quality tool.

## Pre-Lesson Activities

☐ Obtain copies of the worksheets that go with the lesson.

☐ Obtain all materials needed for the lesson.

☐ Create a poster-board– or chart paper–sized Cause-and-Effect Diagram (could also photocopy Cause-and-Effect Diagram [worksheet 218] to overhead projector sheet).

## Materials Needed

☐ Cause-and-Effect Diagram—enlarged or photocopied for overhead projector use.

☐ Markers.

## Lesson Delivery/Procedure

☐ The teacher will review the Cause-and-Effect Diagram tool with students.

☐ The teacher will display the Cause-and-Effect Diagram (worksheet 218) and explain that the goal will be to determine and list the many factors that help students improve their writing skills and produce effective writing pieces.

☐ The following factors are listed on the diagram: procedures, materials, environment, parents, teacher, and students. (The teacher will ensure that students understand the definition of each of these terms as they relate to writing improvement.)

☐ The teacher will question students by asking, "What can help you improve your writing skills this year?"

☐ By directing the students' attention to each factor given on the Cause-and-Effect Diagram (worksheet 218), the teacher will promote discussion and list student responses on the diagram.

☐ The following examples may help promote and focus class discussion:
  • Procedures—Work quietly during writing times; raise your hand if you need assistance; follow the "writing process" specific to each class/grade level (See sample Flowchart—worksheet 219)
  • Materials—Sharpened pencils; writing journals and/or notebook paper; eraser; Word Wall
  • Environment—Quiet workers; helpful classmates; print-rich environment; rubrics in child-friendly terms; writing frameworks for early writers; handwriting desk strips
  • Students—Know about your topic; write using own "voice;" ask for help if needed; use best handwriting; sound out words; use Word Wall; proofread work; write willingly; respond to suggestions for improvement
  • Teachers—Encourage us; help us; give us positive suggestions for improvement; read "good" writing pieces as examples; provide direct instruction in writing process; teach us how to proofread; keep the classroom quiet
  • Parents—Encourage us to write at home; help us with our writing homework; buy us new pencils or paper if we need it

Discussion will continue until all responses are recorded.

## Guided Practice

☐ The teacher will display the Cause-and-Effect Diagram (worksheet 218) for daily use.

☐ The students will refer to the Cause-and-Effect Diagram to see if adequate materials are on hand before writing.

☐ Students may role-play a "conducive" and "nonconducive" classroom environment (for example, noisy versus quiet classroom during writing times).

☐ Students will write for a variety of purposes, that is, write a letter, make a list, write a personal narrative. (Emphasize that to become better writers, students must write often.)

## Assessment

☐ The students will self-assess whether they are creating or disrupting a "conducive" classroom environment during writing activities.

☐ The students will become more aware of and be able to verbalize the factors that contribute to continuous writing improvement.

## Post-Lesson/Follow-Up Activities/Extensions

☐ The students and parents will create a Cause-and-Effect Diagram for home use to promote continuous writing improvement.

☐ The students and the teacher will use the Cause-and-Effect Diagram to identify possible causes of other classroom problems or to analyze a process such as "A Perfect Scientific Experiment."

☐ The students and the teacher can try using a "negative" Cause-and-Effect Diagram, for example, place "A Perfectly Disastrous Writing Piece" in the "effect" box of the Cause-and-Effect Diagram as a nonexample.

# Supporting Resources

☐ Worksheets 218 and 219

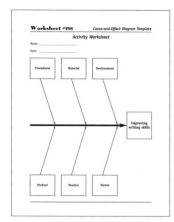

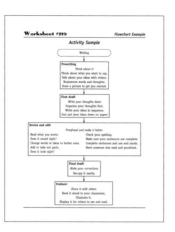

# Prediction

Apply reading strategies to improve understanding and fluency.

**Estimated Time:** 30–40 minutes          **Worksheets:** 220, 221, and 222

## Quality Tool/PDSA Linkage

☐ Students will use a Lotus Diagram.

- The Lotus Diagram is a tool to expand thinking around a single topic or theme and is used at any portion of the PDSA cycle to generate additional thoughts.

## Lesson Overview

☐ This is a hands-on lesson designed for students to demonstrate and apply knowledge of the prediction strategy.

☐ This lesson uses the Lotus Diagram quality tool to help students share ideas about their predictions.

## Lesson Objectives

☐ The students will be able to predict story elements using clues such as pictures and limited story information.

☐ The students will understand and use the Lotus Diagram quality tool.

## Pre-Lesson Activities

☐ Obtain copies of the worksheets that go with the lesson.

☐ Obtain age-appropriate books, block out text with paper and paperclips (one per group).

☐ Review prediction reading strategies with the students.

## Materials Needed

☐ Worksheets 220, 221, and 222.

☐ Age-appropriate books (one per group).

## Lesson Delivery/Procedure

☐ The teacher will review how students should use the information given (prior knowledge, pictures, and cover) to determine what will happen in the story.

☐ The teacher will explain that good readers predict in order to become active rather than passive participants in their learning.

☐ The teacher will divide the class into groups of four.

☐ The teacher will pass out a book and worksheets 220–222 to each group.

☐ The teacher will instruct the group to look through their book and answer the questions on worksheet 220.

☐ The teacher will review the Lotus Diagram with students.

☐ The teacher will ask the students to choose one general prediction they made about the material they are reading.

☐ The students will place the chosen prediction in the center of the Lotus Diagram (worksheet 222) and then place clues, additional thoughts, and so on, about the reading material in the surrounding squares.

☐ The students will then share what they have developed on their Lotus Diagram with the class.

## Guided Practice

- [ ] The groups will switch books and again answer the questions on worksheet 220.
- [ ] This process will continue until each group has seen every book.
- [ ] The teacher will have the students return to their original book.
- [ ] The teacher will begin revealing some of the content for each book to the class.
- [ ] The group will then answer the questions on worksheet 221, given the information about each book.
- [ ] The teacher will continue with this exercise until all the books have been read through to the end.

## Assessment

- [ ] Each group will self-assess their beginning and ending predictions, comparing worksheets 220 and 221.
- [ ] Using the Lotus Diagram (worksheet 222), each group will explain the clues, additional thoughts, and so on, they found in the reading material.
- [ ] The teacher will check to see if each group provided reasons for arriving at their prediction and conclusions.
- [ ] The teacher will check to see if each group gave predictions that made sense according to information given in the story.
- [ ] The teacher will check to see if each group revised their predictions after more of the story was revealed.

## Post-Lesson/Follow-Up Activities/Extensions

- [ ] The students may use the worksheets with other books or stories online.
- [ ] A Lotus Diagram can be completed not only at the beginning but at the end of the story to compare pre- and post- ideas.

## Supporting Resources

- [ ] *www.acs.ucalgary.ca/~dkbrown/stories.html*
- [ ] *www.ipl.org/div/kidspace/browse/rzn0000/*
- [ ] Worksheets 220, 221, and 222

# Following Directions

Students will communicate ideas in writing to accomplish a variety of purposes.

**Estimated Time:** 60 minutes          **Worksheets:** 223, 224, and 225

## Quality Tool/PDSA Linkage

☐ Students will use a Flowchart and Force-Field Analysis.

• The Flowchart is a drawing of any process used to document the process flow during the plan portion of the PDSA cycle.

• Force-Field Analysis is a tool used to evaluate the forces driving and restraining a desired change and is used during the plan portion of the PDSA cycle to generate the most comprehensive plan possible to test the improvement theory.

## Lesson Overview

☐ This is a hands-on lesson designed to help students visualize the correct steps in a process.

☐ Students will examine reasons why following a plan is easy and what challenges they face while following a plan.

## Lesson Objectives

☐ The students will break a process down into simple steps.

☐ The students will analyze the driving and restraining forces for following the process.

☐ The students will understand and use a Flowchart.

☐ The students will understand and use a Force-Field Analysis.

## Pre-Lesson Activities

☐ Obtain copies of the worksheets that go with the lesson.

☐ Obtain all materials needed for the lesson.

☐ Create or obtain a poster or overhead of the symbols used when creating the Flowchart.

☐ Create the beginning of a blank Flowchart and Force-Field Analysis on the overhead or on poster board.

## Materials Needed

☐ A list of symbols for the Flowchart.

☐ *The Story of Noodles* by Ying Chang Compestine.

☐ Pudding mix and ingredients for student groups.

## Lesson Delivery/Procedure

☐ The teacher will read *The Story of Noodles* aloud. In this story two brothers "botch" a recipe that they have been asked to make for a cooking contest by their mother because they did not follow the directions properly.

☐ The teacher will review the Flowchart tool with students. Use worksheet 223 as an example.

- [ ] After listening to the story, the class will create a Flowchart that lists step by step the recipe the brothers followed.
- [ ] The teacher will review the Force-Field Analysis tool with students. Use worksheet 224 as an example.
- [ ] The class will create a Force-Field Analysis that lists the driving forces and restraining forces for following directions to make pudding.

## Guided Practice

- [ ] The teacher will give each group of students a box of pudding.
- [ ] The students will list the key steps for making the pudding using a Flowchart (the teacher will guide the process).
- [ ] The students will then create a Force-Field Analysis (worksheet 225) for their group's ability to follow the steps in the process of making pudding (the teacher will guide the process). This tool will help the students identify reasons to follow the Flowchart procedure they developed.

## Assessment

- [ ] The students will use the proper symbols in the Flowchart.
- [ ] The students will list steps accurately.
- [ ] The teacher will assess each student's Force-Field Analysis for content and demonstration of understanding.

## Post-Lesson/Follow-Up Activities/Extensions

- [ ] Read aloud the sequel *The Story of Chopsticks* by Ying Chang Compestine.
- [ ] As a homework assignment, students will be asked to create a Flowchart for one thing they do at home (get ready to go to school, get ready for bed, making Kool-Aid).

## Supporting Resources

- [ ] *familyfun.go.com/recipes/kids/*
- [ ] *web.tampabay.rr.com/tshoaf/hhs/cookie.htm*
- [ ] *The Duchess Bakes a Cake* by Virginia Kahl
- [ ] *The Runaway Rice Cake* by Ying Chang Compestine
- [ ] *The Story of Noodles* by Ying Chang Compestine
- [ ] *The Story of Chopsticks* by Ying Chang Compestine
- [ ] Worksheets 223, 224, and 225

# Context Clues

Continuously check and clarify for understanding.

**Estimated Time:** 45 minutes          **Worksheet:** 226

## Quality Tool/PDSA Linkage

- ☐ Students will use the Lotus Diagram.

  - • The Lotus Diagram is a tool to expand thinking around a single topic or theme and is used at any portion of the PDSA cycle to generate additional thoughts.

## Lesson Overview

- ☐ The students will listen to a basal story or a section of a chapter book.

- ☐ The students and the teacher will discuss the main idea of the story.

- ☐ The class will make a Lotus Diagram based on the main idea identified.

## Lesson Objectives

- ☐ The students will learn or review how to draw out important details from a story.

- ☐ The students will create a Lotus Diagram from the story material.

- ☐ The students will share experiences they have had in making the Lotus Diagram and what they have learned from the experience.

## Pre-Lesson Activities

- ☐ The teacher will review how to pick out details from the story or chapter. The teacher will also review what is important to think about when remembering important details.

- ☐ Obtain copies of the worksheets that go with the lesson.

- ☐ Obtain all materials needed for the lesson.

## Materials Needed

- ☐ A copy of the Lotus Diagram (see worksheet 226).

- ☐ Pencils for students.

- ☐ Markers for teacher use.

## Lesson Delivery/Procedure

- ☐ The teacher or class will read aloud the basal story or a selection of a chapter book.

- ☐ After the teacher has finished reading the book or chapter, the class will discuss important details of the book.

- ☐ The teacher will introduce or review with students the use of the Lotus Diagram.

- ☐ The students and the teacher will discuss elements of the story and how those elements might be related to the given topic on the Lotus Diagram.

- ☐ The class will make a Lotus Diagram (worksheet 226) together on the overhead or board using the elements discussed as a class.

## Guided Practice

- ☐ The class will put the title of the book or chapter in the center of the Lotus Diagram (worksheet 226).
- ☐ The students will then list elements of the story or chapter, which will then help them complete the Lotus Diagram. All ideas will be shared with the class.
- ☐ The class will work together to complete the Lotus Diagram over the material in the chosen book or chapter.

## Assessment

- ☐ The students will make notes of their understanding of the different elements of the Lotus Diagram.
- ☐ The teacher will review student work, discussion, and findings to gauge level of understanding.
- ☐ The students will recall the lesson objectives, findings, and key concepts of the lesson to remember.

## Post-Lesson/Follow-Up Activities/Extensions

- ☐ The students can take the idea of a Lotus Diagram home to share with parents and have them try to identify details for something they are working on. This will also promote the idea of thinking things out in a more complete manner.
- ☐ The students can challenge themselves by developing a Lotus Diagram on their own for another subject area.
- ☐ The students can visit another grade with their Lotus Diagram and teach younger or older students what they have learned about with that book or chapter.

## Supporting Resources

- ☐ *Inferencing: Using Context Clues to Infer Meaning* (Basic Skills Series) by Karen Clemens Warrick and Linda Hohag
- ☐ Worksheet 226

# Commonly Misspelled Words

Estimate measurements and determine acceptable levels of accuracy. Measure and compare quantities using appropriate units, instruments, and methods.

**Estimated Time:** Done once every week    **Worksheets:** 227, 228, and 229

## Quality Tool/PDSA Linkage

☐ Students will use a Run Chart, Flowchart, and Cause-and-Effect Diagram.

- The Run Chart graphically reports system performance over time and is used to compare performance before and after changes in both the plan and study portions of the PDSA cycle.

- The Flowchart is a drawing of any process used to document the process flow during the plan portion of the PDSA cycle.

- The Cause-and-Effect Diagram is a picture of the output of a brainstorming session that asks "What causes . . . ," and is used to determine root causes in the plan portion of the PDSA cycle.

## Lesson Overview

☐ This is a lesson that can be used repeatedly over an extended period of time. Conducting this activity once a week for an entire grading period will provide insightful data on how well students are able to spell common words that they use every day in their writing.

☐ The teacher will place frequently misspelled words from students' writing in a jar. The teacher will randomly select words out of a jar. Students will try to spell the selected words. Once the teacher checks the words, the students will record their data on a Run Chart.

☐ The class will also keep a large Run Chart and graph of the class's total misspelled words each week.

## Lesson Objectives

☐ The students will learn how to record their misspelled word scores on an individual Run Chart.

☐ The students will learn how to plot their scores on an individual line graph.

☐ The students will reflect on their strengths and areas of needed improvement in their spelling of common words by doing the Cause-and-Effect Diagram.

☐ The students will understand the importance of keeping data and determining its relevance.

☐ The students will practice their computation by adding up their team's misspelled words for a class Run Chart.

☐ The students will understand and use the Run Chart, Flowchart, and Cause-and-Effect Diagram.

## Pre-Lesson Activities

☐ Obtain materials needed for this lesson.

☐ Obtain copies of the worksheets that go with the lesson.

☐ Make a large Run Chart and graph for the class totals.

☐ Identify a place for the students to keep their Run Charts and graphs.

☐ Copy two lists of the 100 misspelled words for the grade level taught to each student (one for home and one for school).

☐ Review how to make a line graph and how to plot a data point on a line graph.

## Materials Needed

- ☐ Markers.
- ☐ Chart paper.
- ☐ Folders.
- ☐ Jar.
- ☐ Sticks to write the 100 words on.

## Lesson Delivery/Procedure

- ☐ The teacher will review the Cause-and-Effect Diagram tool with students.
- ☐ The teacher and students will complete the Cause-and-Effect Diagram together to identify the reasons the students are not mastering the sight words. (See cause-and-effect worksheet 229.)
- ☐ The teacher will explain to the students that there are repeated misspellings of common words that students should already know how to spell. The teacher will ask, "How can we reduce the number of misspellings?"
- ☐ The teacher will try to get the students to understand the importance of practicing these words.
- ☐ The teacher will inform students that there is a tool that can keep track of performance over time.
- ☐ The teacher will ask the students to get out a piece of paper to practice spelling words. The teacher will give them 10 words chosen randomly out of the jar. Students will try to spell the words and then the students will switch papers and correct them.
- ☐ Once papers have been graded, the teacher will ask the students to add up their group's total misspelled words.
- ☐ The teacher will have students report the total errors on each paper to the group. The teacher will write those numbers on the board as they are being read. Once complete, the students will add up the numbers.
- ☐ The teacher will review the Run Chart tool with students.
- ☐ When the total number of words misspelled has been recorded, the teacher will then show students how to keep track and graph errors each week using the Run Chart (worksheet 227).
- ☐ The teacher will explain how each student will keep track of his or her own misspelled words the same way on their papers.
- ☐ The teacher will review the Flowchart tool with students.
- ☐ At this time, the teacher should show the students the Flowchart example (worksheet 228) to complete this activity. The teacher should enlarge the Flowchart for the wall as well as give a copy to each student. The students can refer to it on days when the tests are given.
- ☐ The teacher will give students two copies of the 100 most misspelled words for their grade. (High-frequency word lists can be used.) The teacher will ask students to place the list in the folder and take one home to practice.
- ☐ The teacher will have the students practice their words every day for five to 10 minutes with a partner or individually.

## Guided Practice

- ☐ After a short period of time, the teacher will conduct a spelling test covering the distributed word list.
- ☐ The teacher will randomly chose 10–20 words out of the jar. (The teacher will always want to use the same number of words from the jar each week.)
- ☐ When the spelling test is complete, the teacher will have the students switch papers for grading purposes. The teacher will *slowly* spell each of the words so students can correct the papers.
- ☐ When the students have completed checking the papers, the teacher will have the students return the papers to the teacher, and prepare to graph the recorded errors.

- ☐ The teacher will have students record the date of the test and the number of words they missed on the Run Chart.
- ☐ The students will plot a dot on the line (Run Chart) showing the number of words they missed.
- ☐ The teacher will assist the class in adding up all the misspelled words for their group and recording it on the board.
- ☐ Once every group has placed their numbers on the board, each group will add up the total number of words the class missed that day and record that information on the class Run Chart.

## Assessment

- ☐ The teacher and students will look at the Run Chart to reflect on how well they are doing each time they take the commonly misspelled words quiz.
- ☐ The teacher will reflect on how well the class is doing. They will use this information to guide further word study lessons.

## Post-Lesson/Follow-Up Activities/Extensions

- ☐ The students will set measurable goals according to improvements they see need to occur.
- ☐ The students will also write how they will achieve these goals to improve their score.
- ☐ The teacher will allow for time to practice these words.
- ☐ The teacher can play word games using these words throughout the week to practice.

## Supporting Resources

- ☐ *Month-by-Month Phonics for Upper Grades* by Patricia Cunningham and Dorothy Hall
- ☐ Worksheets 227, 228, and 229

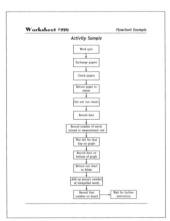

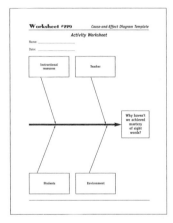

# Quality Across the Curriculum

# LANGUAGE ARTS

4–5

## LESSONS

Fact and Opinion . . . . . . . . . 333

Sequencing . . . . . . . . . . . . . 335

Cause and Effect . . . . . . . . . 337

Homophones . . . . . . . . . . . . 339

Vocabulary Development . . . . 341

Fluency Rate . . . . . . . . . . . . 345

Character Analysis . . . . . . . . 349

Questioning Strategy . . . . . . 353

Responding to Fiction . . . . . . 357

# Fact and Opinion

Summarize and make generalizations from content and relate to purpose of material.

**Estimated Time:** 45 minutes          **Worksheet:** 230

## Quality Tool/PDSA Linkage

☐ Students will use a Flowchart.

  • The Flowchart is a drawing of any process used to document the process flow during the plan portion of the PDSA cycle.

## Lesson Overview

☐ The students will learn how to take a piece of information and determine if it is a fact or an opinion.

## Lesson Objectives

☐ The students will understand what facts and opinions are and why it is important to determine the differences between the two.

☐ The students will make a Flowchart to help determine the differences between facts and opinions.

## Pre-Lesson Activities

☐ Obtain copies of the worksheet that goes with the lesson.

☐ Obtain all materials needed for the lesson.

## Materials Needed

☐ A copy of a Flowchart.

☐ Pencils for students.

☐ Markers for teacher use.

## Lesson Delivery/Procedure

☐ The teacher (or class) will read aloud a piece of nonfiction literature.

☐ The teacher will review how to determine if a piece of information is a fact or if it is an opinion.

☐ After the teacher has finished reading the book or piece of information, the class will list important details and elements from the nonfiction piece.

☐ The teacher will introduce or review with students the use of the Flowchart and how to construct it.

☐ Working together, the class will make a Flowchart on the overhead or board using the events and elements discussed in class.

## Guided Practice

☐ The class will review the definitions of fact and opinion.

☐ The students will then list important elements from the nonfiction piece of literature.

☐ The teacher will summarize the lesson objectives, findings, and key concepts of the lesson to remember when working with a Flowchart.

## Assessment

☐ The class will work together to complete the Flowchart (example on worksheet 230) that defines the events that occured for the material in the chosen book or chapter.

☐ The teacher will review student work, discussion, and findings to gauge student's level of understanding.

## Post-Lesson/Follow-Up Activities/Extensions

☐ The students can take the idea of a Flowchart home to share with parents and have them try to list details for something they are working on. (This will also promote the idea of thinking things through when needing to make a decision.)

☐ The students can challenge themselves by developing a Flowchart to help them draw a picture of a process they need to follow.

☐ The students can visit another grade with their Flowchart and teach younger or older students what they have learned in following a process.

## Supporting Resources

☐ *Fact and Opinion* by McGraw-Hill Children's Publishing

☐ Worksheet 230

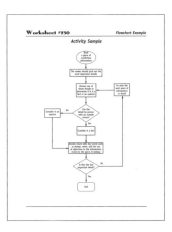

# Sequencing

Apply reading strategies to improve understanding and fluency.

**Estimated Time:** 45 minutes          **Worksheets:** 231 and 232

## Quality Tool/PDSA Linkage

☐ Students will use Brainstorming and a Flowchart.

- The Brainstorming technique is the generation of ideas by a group and is used at any portion of the PDSA cycle when every person needs to be heard from and many ideas need to be generated.

- The Flowchart is a drawing of any process used to document the process flow during the plan portion of the PDSA cycle.

## Lesson Overview

☐ The students will Brainstorm ideas of a particular event.

☐ The students will put ideas into sequential order.

☐ The students will act out their Flowchart to the class to see if they may have missed any crucial steps.

## Lesson Objectives

☐ The students will learn or review how to Brainstorm ideas about a certain subject matter.

☐ The students will create a Flowchart to demonstrate how to complete a particular activity.

## Pre-Lesson Activities

☐ The teacher will ask students if they know what a Flowchart is or why one is important.

☐ The teacher will Brainstorm with students some uses for a Flowchart.

☐ The teacher may share an experience when they needed to do something in a particular order and why a Flowchart may have helped during that situation.

## Materials Needed

☐ An overhead of a blank Flowchart.

☐ Post-It notes.

☐ Large sheet of paper to put the Post-It notes on.

☐ Large sheet of paper to write categories on for discussion.

☐ Pencils for students.

☐ Markers for the teacher.

## Lesson Delivery/Procedure

☐ The teacher will introduce or review with students the concept of the Flowchart.

☐ The teacher will share examples of when a Flowchart may be used. (For example, when a process has multiple steps to be followed like performing long division.)

☐ The teacher will review the Brainstorming tool with students.

☐ The students and the teacher will Brainstorm other ways a Flowchart could be used and will select one to practice as a group. Students should place one idea on each Post-It note.

- ☐ All student ideas should be displayed on a poster.
- ☐ The teacher will assist the class in making a Flowchart together on the overhead using the selected topic from the brainstorm agreed upon by the class. (See worksheet 232 as an example.)
- ☐ After practicing the Flowchart with the whole class, students will brainstorm possible ways of their own that they could use a Flowchart.
- ☐ The students will share their ideas with the teacher before starting their own Flowchart (worksheet 231).

## Guided Practice

- ☐ The students will complete their Flowchart on their own (or with assistance from the teacher as needed).
- ☐ The students will share their Flowcharts in small groups to get feedback from their peers.
- ☐ Peers will assess themselves on whether any crucial part of the Flowchart or sequential process was left out.

## Assessment

- ☐ The teacher will make notes of students' understanding of the different elements of the Flowchart.
- ☐ If possible, students will act out their Flowcharts exactly as they have them listed to demonstrate their level of understanding and application.
- ☐ The teacher and student will review student work, discussion, and findings to gauge level of understanding of Flowcharts.

## Post-Lesson/Follow-Up Activities/Extensions

- ☐ Students will take the information learned from the lesson and apply it to a selection of literature.
- ☐ The students can take the idea of a Flowchart home to share with parents and other family members, encouraging those members to work on creating their own Flowchart.
- ☐ The students can challenge themselves by developing a Flowchart for a difficult issue such as recycling or changing the oil in a car. The idea would be to have them make a Flowchart for something the students don't come into daily contact with.
- ☐ The students can visit another grade with their Flowchart and see if that grade can complete the activity that has been described.

## Supporting Resources

- ☐ *Short Story: Sequencing* by Jo Evans
- ☐ *Picture Sequencing* by Vicky Shiotsu
- ☐ Worksheets 231 and 232

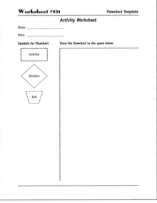

# Cause and Effect

Identify structure such as description, cause-and-effect, and compare and contrast.

**Estimated Time:** 45 minutes          **Worksheets:** 233 and 234

## Quality Tool/PDSA Linkage

☐ Students will use a Cause-and-Effect Diagram.

- The Cause-and-Effect Diagram is a picture of the output of a brainstorming session that asks, "What causes . . . ," and is used to determine root causes in the plan portion of the PDSA cycle.

## Lesson Overview

☐ The students will learn how to determine if something is a cause or an effect of a given issue.

## Lesson Objectives

☐ The students will review what are causes and what are effects of a given situation.

☐ The students will separate the two (causes and effects) into correct categories.

☐ The teacher and the class will make a Cause-and-Effect Diagram.

☐ The students will use and understand the Cause-and-Effect Diagram quality tool.

## Pre-Lesson Activities

☐ Review with the class how to determine if a piece of information is a cause or an effect.

☐ Obtain copies of the worksheets that go with the lesson.

☐ Obtain all materials needed for the lesson.

## Materials Needed

☐ A copy of a blank Cause-and-Effect Diagram (see worksheet 234).

☐ Pencils for students.

☐ Markers for teacher use.

☐ A copy of a grade-appropriate book that contains a cause and effect situation.

☐ Book: *Three Little Pigs*.

## Lesson Delivery/Procedure

☐ The teacher will read the *Three Little Pigs*.

☐ The students and the teacher will discuss which of the details may be a cause and which may be an effect.

☐ The teacher will introduce or review with students the use of the Cause-and-Effect Diagram.

☐ The class will make a Cause-and-Effect Diagram together on the overhead or board using the discussion from the *Three Little Pigs* story. Use worksheet 233 as a guide.

☐ After completing the Cause-and-Effect Diagram with the class, the teacher will read another book or piece of literature that has a cause and effect situation.

- [ ] The class will list causes and effects from the new piece of literature.
- [ ] The students will summarize how to create a Cause-and-Effect Diagram.

## Guided Practice

- [ ] The class will work together to complete the Cause-and-Effect Diagram for the material in the chosen piece of literature (use worksheet 234).

## Assessment

- [ ] The teacher will make notes of students' understanding of the different elements of the Cause-and-Effect Diagram.
- [ ] The teacher will review student work, discussion, and findings to gauge level of understanding with students during individual conferences.

## Post-Lesson/Follow-Up Activities/Extensions

- [ ] The students can take the idea of a Cause-and-Effect Diagram home to share with parents and friends and then have them try to list causes and effects of something they are trying to analyze themselves. This will also promote the idea of thinking things through when needing to make a decision.
- [ ] The students can challenge themselves by developing a Cause-and-Effect Diagram to help them solve a problem if one should arise.
- [ ] The students can visit another grade with their Cause-and-Effect Diagram and teach younger or older students how to use the tool to separate causes and effects.
- [ ] The teacher may want to use the water cycle as an example of an event that has many causes and effects.

## Supporting Resources

- [ ] Piece of literature that has many issues of cause and effect
- [ ] *Cause and Effect: Intermediate Reading Practice* by Patricia Ackert
- [ ] *Three Little Pigs* by Patricia Seibert
- [ ] Worksheets 233 and 234

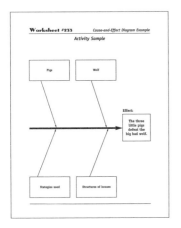
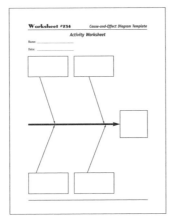

# Homophones

Students will read and comprehend unfamiliar words using root words, synonyms, homophones, antonyms, word origins, and derivations.

**Estimated Time:** 40 minutes          **Worksheets:** 235, 236, and 237

## Quality Tool/PDSA Linkage

☐ Students will use the Gallery Walk.

• The Gallery Walk is a communication/consensus tool to allow everyone to provide input in a structured manner and is used at various portions of the PDSA cycle to create a written record of the group's thoughts.

## Lesson Overview

☐ This is a hands-on lesson designed for students to demonstrate and apply knowledge of homophones.

☐ Utilizing the Gallery Walk quality tool, students will be able to visualize and help add to a collage of pictures for each set of homophones.

## Lesson Objectives

☐ The students will be familiar with many sets of homophones.

☐ The students will see how phonemes can be spelled in a variety of ways.

☐ The students will understand and use the Gallery Walk quality tool.

## Pre-Lesson Activities

☐ Obtain copies of the worksheets that go with the lesson.

☐ Obtain all materials needed for the lesson.

## Materials Needed

☐ Large piece of poster board for each group.

☐ Crayons.

☐ Markers.

☐ Dictionaries.

☐ Glue.

## Lesson Delivery/Procedure

☐ The teacher will review homophones as words that sound the same, but are spelled differently and have different meanings.

☐ The teacher will have students pair up within their seating arrangements, and will allow them five minutes to come up with sets of homophones. If students are having trouble, the teacher may use the examples from worksheet 235.

☐ The teacher will ask the class for homophone sets and write them on the board.

☐ The teacher will assign a set of homophones to each group.

☐ The teacher will direct each group to look up the words they were assigned and write the definitions on worksheets 236 and 237.

- ☐ The teacher will then have the students glue worksheet 236 to one side of the poster and worksheet 237 to the other side.
- ☐ The students will then be asked to draw a picture of each of the words and write a sentence using the word.
- ☐ The teacher will review the Gallery Walk tool with students.

## Guided Practice

- ☐ The teacher will assign a set of homophones to each group.
- ☐ The teacher will direct each group to look up the words they were assigned and write the definitions on worksheets 236 and 237.
- ☐ The teacher will then have the students glue worksheet 236 to one side of the poster and worksheet 237 to the other side.
- ☐ The students will then be asked to draw a picture of each of the words and write a sentence using the word and place it on the correct side of the poster.
- ☐ The students will then choose one member of their group to stay with the poster as the others rotate to another table.
- ☐ The student from the original group will explain the poster to the new group, and the new group will add a new sentence to each side of the poster using the correct word.
- ☐ The class will continue this process until each group has visited each poster and added sentences.

## Assessment

- ☐ Each student will review their assignment, checking to see if their original poster has correct sentences written for each of their words.
- ☐ The teacher will select students to verbally explain one of the posters.
- ☐ The teacher will check to see if the correct information is included on each poster.

## Post-Lesson/Follow-Up Activities/Extensions

- ☐ The posters will be displayed in the classroom for use in future writing assignments.

## Supporting Resources

- ☐ *www.mumstudents.org/~jdavy/homophone.html*
- ☐ *Harry Is Not Hairy (Homophones)* by Pam Scheunemann
- ☐ Worksheets 235, 236, and 237

# Vocabulary Development

Read well with understanding.

**Estimated Time:** Two 45-minute sessions     **Worksheets:** 238 and 239
(5–10 min. review daily)

## Quality Tool/PDSA Linkage

☐ Students will use Brainstorming and an Affinity Diagram.

- The Brainstorming technique is the generation of ideas by a group and is used at any portion of the PDSA cycle when every person needs to be heard from and many ideas need to be generated.

- The Affinity Diagram is a tool to generate, organize, and consolidate information gathered through Brainstorming, and is used in many portions of the PDSA cycle.

## Lesson Overview

☐ This is a two-part lesson designed to teach and review vocabulary words that are taken out of a guided reading book or other curriculum materials.

☐ Following a Brainstorming session with the students (focused on the meaning of the words the teacher has chosen), students will use the definitions and descriptions that they gave to make an Affinity Diagram.

## Lesson Objectives

☐ The students will identify words that they do not know the meaning of from their guided reading, science, social studies, or math books.

☐ The students will discover how to learn the meaning of those words by Brainstorming ideas and using the text to help them generate contextual clues.

☐ The students will master the vocabulary words with constant review and usage of the words.

☐ The students will understand and use the Brainstorming and Affinity Diagram quality tools.

## Pre-Lesson Activities

☐ Obtain copies of the worksheets that go with the lesson.

☐ Gather vocabulary words from a reading source. (Choose one currently being used by the teacher or student. It could be a guided reading book, science book, math book, or social studies book.)

☐ Review with the students the procedure they should follow for listing unknown words from their reading source.

☐ Gather all materials that are needed for the lesson and have them ready.

## Materials Needed

☐ Chart paper.

☐ Markers.

☐ Index cards or computer with printer.

☐ Reading source.

☐ List of possible vocabulary words.

## Lesson Delivery/Procedure

- ☐ Either in small groups or as a whole class, the teacher will pull the students together to give directions for the activity.
- ☐ The teacher will ask the students to read a small section identified from their reading source.
- ☐ While they are reading, students need to identify words that they do not know the meaning of. The teacher will explain that the words can be ones that they can pronounce, but do not know the meaning of, or words that they cannot pronounce.
- ☐ The teacher will give the students time to read their selection.
- ☐ The teacher will review the Brainstorming tool with students.
- ☐ After students have completed this task, the teacher will ask for the words that they identified. The teacher will want to use between five and eight words from the students' lists.
- ☐ The teacher will take each word and have the students reread the sentence in which the word is used. Then, the teacher will have the students try to explain what the word means. Students can use synonyms, short definitions, and associations to come up with the definition. Incorrect definitions can de addressed at this time, too. The teacher will ask prompting questions or have the students look up the incorrectly Brainstormed meanings of words in a dictionary.
- ☐ The teacher will write down what the students say on the chart paper for that word.
- ☐ The teacher and students will repeat the above process for each word given.
- ☐ When the teacher and students have completed Brainstorming the meaning of each word, the teacher will have the students reread the selection from their reading source, this time with the knowledge of the meaning of the word.
- ☐ The teacher will review the Affinity Diagram tool with students.
- ☐ After the Brainstorming activity, the teacher needs to type up students' definitions, vocabulary words, and associations into a scrambled order. The typed sheet will be used to make an Affinity Diagram (worksheet 238) the next day.

## Guided Practice

- ☐ In the follow-up session, (in small groups) students will need to cut up all the typed definitions and words that the teacher supplies and put them into categories.
- ☐ The vocabulary word will be the header of the group. All the definitions and associations should be grouped below the vocabulary words.
- ☐ The students will look at the relationship between the vocabulary words and their definitions and associations.
- ☐ The students will share their experience with a small group of peers to check their work.

## Assessment

- ☐ The teacher will observe their level of understanding of the words by the Affinity Diagram (worksheet 238) that they created.
- ☐ The teacher will review the vocabulary words and make sure that all lesson objectives were met.
- ☐ The teacher will check the student's word choice and created definitions to see if the students gained the correct meaning from context.

## Post-Lesson/Follow-Up Activities/Extensions

☐ Periodically check for further usage of the vocabulary words. Use the words in your everyday conversations.

☐ Challenge the students to use the words in a writing activity in which you engage them.

☐ Ask the students to try to come up with a list of antonyms for each of the words.

☐ Using the words from this lesson, have the students use a T-chart to review the words and their meanings (see worksheet 239).

## Supporting Resources

☐ *www.onelook.com/*

☐ *www.wordfocus.com/*

☐ Worksheets 238 and 239

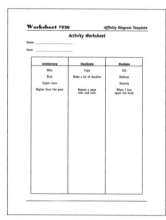

# Fluency Rate

Read age-appropriate material aloud with fluency and accuracy.

**Estimated Time:** 30 minutes first time, then 20–30 minutes per month

**Worksheets:** 240 and 241

## Quality Tool/PDSA Linkage

- ☐ Students will use a Run Chart.

  - • The Run/Control Chart graphically reports system performance over time and is used to compare performance before and after changes in both the Plan and Study portions of the PDSA cycle.

## Lesson Overview

- ☐ The students will be read a selected piece of literature once a month.

- ☐ The students keep track of how many words they read while also keeping track of mistakes that occurred while reading the piece.

- ☐ A Run Chart will organize each student's results to show growth in fluency rate.

## Lesson Objectives

- ☐ The students will learn the importance of reading automatically with speed and expression, for better reading comprehension.

- ☐ The students will learn how to keep track of mistakes their partner incurs while reading a selected piece of literature.

- ☐ The students will record data on a Run Chart to track performance over time.

## Pre-Lesson Activities

- ☐ Select a grade-appropriate piece of literature for the students to read.
- ☐ Obtain copies of the literature for each student.
- ☐ Obtain copies of the worksheets that go with the lesson.
- ☐ Obtain all materials needed for the lesson.

## Materials Needed

- ☐ Piece of literature to read.
- ☐ Pencil.
- ☐ Timer.
- ☐ Run Chart for each student.
- ☐ Folder to keep Run Charts in.
- ☐ Clipboard (optional).

## Lesson Delivery/Procedure

- [ ] The teacher will read a piece of literature slowly with a few mistakes to demonstrate what reading without fluency is.
- [ ] The teacher will read the same piece of literature again, this time reading it with expression, automaticity, and speed.
- [ ] The teacher will ask the students which one they preferred listening to.
- [ ] The teacher will ask the students why they liked the second reading and why it was better.
- [ ] The teacher will explain to the students that the second time he or she read the piece of literature, she or he read fluently.
- [ ] The teacher will review the Run Chart tool with students.
- [ ] The teacher will explain to the students that they will keep track of how well they read with fluency using a Run Chart.
- [ ] The teacher will tell the students that once a month (or a predetermined amount of time), students will partner up and read to each other. While one partner is reading, the other will keep track of time and mistakes made.
- [ ] The teacher will demonstrate how to keep track of mistakes while reading using the Run Chart (worksheet 240).
- [ ] The teacher will ask for a volunteer to read a piece of literature with the teacher.
- [ ] The teacher will ask the student to record every time the teacher makes a mistake by putting an 'X' above the word.
- [ ] This demonstration should be done with an overhead projector where the words are copied and on the overhead for ALL students to see while the teacher is reading.
- [ ] The student sets the timer for one minute while the teacher reads the passage.
- [ ] As the teacher reads, the student needs to mark on the overhead every time the teacher makes a mistake.
- [ ] When the timer goes off, the teacher and students will look at the overhead to view the passage.
- [ ] The teacher and students will discuss the mistakes that were made, count them, and put the total number of mistakes at the top of the selection.
- [ ] The teacher will then take the total amount of mistakes and subract them by the total amount of possible mistakes to get the number correctly read in one minute. Then the teacher will explain how to put the total onto a Run Chart (see worksheet 240).

## Guided Practice

- [ ] The teacher will put the students into pairs. (Preferably, with partners they are comfortable with.)
- [ ] The teacher will give each student a copy of the literature.
- [ ] The students will practice timing and recording errors onto the papers.
- [ ] The teacher will walk around and help as needed.
- [ ] Once the students have practiced several times, the teacher can hand out the Run Chart (see worksheet 240).
- [ ] Partners will take turns reading the selection and timing each other. Partners will record errors made while reading. Students will total up the mistakes and subtract them from possible mistakes to be made and record their number correctly read in one minute on the Run Chart.

## Assessment

- [ ] The teacher will conference with each child using the Run Charts to discuss progress.
- [ ] The teacher can use the Run Chart data to formally assess each child's progress over time.
- [ ] The student will self-assess their progress over time by analyzing their Run Chart.

## Post-Lesson/Follow-Up Activities/Extensions

☐ The teacher will encourage students to read a piece of literature several times, as research shows that reading text more than once improves fluency and comprehension.

☐ The teacher can have the students' time and record errors made after a child reads a piece of literature (first reading, second reading, third reading, and so on, of the same piece). If the students record the data for this, they will see that with repetition, they will improve their fluency rate and comprehension (see worksheet 241).

## Supporting Resources

☐ *Building Fluency: Lessons and Strategies for Reading Success* By Wily Blevins

☐ Worksheets 240 and 241

# Character Analysis

Understand how literary elements and techniques are used to convey meaning.

**Estimated Time:** 50 minutes     **Worksheets:** 242 and 243

## Quality Tool/PDSA Linkage

- ☐ Students will use a Plus/Delta Chart.

  - The Plus/Delta Chart is a tool to record feedback about the current state or a recent experience and is used anytime feedback is needed in the PDSA cycle.

## Lesson Overview

- ☐ Using the Plus/Delta Chart, students will analyze the characteristics and descriptions of characters of fictional and nonfictional material to create interesting characters in their own narrative writing.

## Lesson Objectives

- ☐ Students will utilize the Plus/Delta Chart as a tool to analyze text to enhance narrative writing aptitude.

## Pre-Lesson Activities

- ☐ Obtain copies of the worksheets that go with the lesson.
- ☐ Lessons discussing narrative writing and character description should be performed before implementing this lesson.
- ☐ Reading aloud with rich character descriptions should be conducted before utilizing this lesson.
- ☐ Obtain the book *The Stranger* written by Chris Van Allsburg.
- ☐ Obtain all materials needed for the lesson.
- ☐ Each student should obtain a sample of a student's narrative writing.

## Materials Needed

- ☐ Pencils (for each student).
- ☐ Worksheets 242 and 243.
- ☐ *The Stranger* by Chris Van Allsburg.

## Lesson Delivery/Procedure

- ☐ The teacher will review the key features of narrative writing.
- ☐ The teacher will facilitate a discussion about the importance of good or rich character development and/or description. (During this time, the teacher might ask: Why is it important for the author to describe his or her characters well? How does good character development and description help a story?)
- ☐ The teacher will review the Plus/Delta Chart tool with students.
- ☐ The teacher will pass out worksheet 242 (Plus/Delta Chart).

☐ The teacher will give directions on how to use the Plus/Delta Chart. [The following announcement might be made: I'm going to read the story *The Stranger* by Chris Van Allsburg to the class. As I read the story, I want you to think like a writer. Ask yourself the following questions: What are some the techniques or things done to make the character, the stranger, interesting and alive? What are some things or techniques that could have been used to add richness or spice to the character development of the stranger? (These questions could be written on the board.) If, while I'm reading, you find answers to those questions, use the Plus/Delta Chart to record your thoughts. In the plus section of the chart, place your ideas of things or techniques that were done to make the character interesting and alive. In the delta section, place your ideas of things or techniques that could have been done to add more spice and/or richness to the character. After I finish reading the story, we will discuss character description and/or development as a class.]

## Guided Practice

☐ The teacher will read *The Stranger* out loud to the class while students will record ideas on their Plus/Delta Charts (worksheet 242).

☐ The class will discuss the pluses found in the text. During this discussion, the good techniques that the author used to describe the characters in the story will be highlighted.

☐ The teacher will place the pluses discussed on the poster-board replica of the Plus/Delta Chart.

☐ The class will discuss the deltas found. During this discussion, the class will emphasize the techniques utilized by the author that they will want to improve upon when describing their own characters.

☐ The teacher will place the deltas discussed on the poster-board replica of the Plus/Delta Chart.

☐ The teacher will ask each student to find one plus item that he or she would like to try to use (or check to see if it exists) in his or her writing sample.

☐ The student will write the item he or she would like to use on the bottom of the Plus/Delta Chart.

☐ The teacher will ask each student to find one delta item that he or she would like to use (or check to see if it exists) in his or her writing sample.

☐ The student will write the item he or she would like to use on the bottom of the Plus/Delta Chart.

## Assessment

☐ The students will analyze their narrative samples checking to see if the items they would like to use are discussed in their Plus/Delta Chart are present. (Special note: if a student finds both of his or her plus and delta items present in their writing, he or she should be encouraged to find an item that is not pre-existing in their writing sample.)

☐ The students will revise their narrative writing samples to exhibit the ideas highlighted.

☐ The students will complete the reflective form (worksheet 243).

☐ The teacher will conference with each student about the writing sample and the ideas he or she wished to utilize in his or her writing.

## Post-Lesson/Follow-Up Activities/Extensions

☐ The students can utilize another idea captured on the Plus/Delta Chart to enhance their narrative writing.

☐ The students can peer-edit utilizing the Plus/Delta Chart.

## Supporting Resources

- ☐ *Craft Lessons: Teaching Writing K–8* by Ralph Fletcher and Joann Portalupi
- ☐ *The Stranger* by Chris Van Allsburg
- ☐ Worksheets 242 and 243

# Questioning Strategy

Comprehend a broad range of reading materials.

**Estimated Time:** 50 minutes          **Worksheets:** 244, 245, and 246

## Quality Tool/PDSA Linkage

☐ Students will use the Check Sheet, Bar Chart, and Plus/Delta Chart.

- The Check Sheet/Matrix is a tool to collect and organize data in the plan portion of the PDSA cycle.

- The Bar Chart is a graph of categorical data plotted by frequency, and is used in the plan portion of the PDSA cycle.

- The Plus/Delta Chart is a tool to record feedback about the current state or a recent experience and is used anytime feedback is needed in the PDSA cycle.

## Lesson Overview

☐ Using a Check Sheet/Matrix, students will record the number of explicit and implicit questions generated about the elements of a story.

☐ Using a Bar Chart, students will make decisions to improve their learning from the picture of data drawn.

☐ Using a Plus/Delta Chart, students will evaluate their own work.

## Lesson Objectives

☐ The students will use the Check Sheet to gather data.

☐ The students will use a Bar Chart to organize the data collected.

☐ The students will use a Plus/Delta Chart to evaluate their work.

☐ The students will analyze data to make decisions about their learning.

☐ The students will use the questioning strategy to enhance comprehension of text.

☐ The students will be introduced to explicit and implicit types of questions.

## Pre-Lesson Activities

☐ Obtain copies of the worksheets that go with the lesson.

☐ Lessons discussing the comprehension strategy of questioning and prediction should be conducted.

☐ Introduce the elements of a story such as setting, plot, and characters.

☐ Obtain all materials needed for this lesson.

## Materials Needed

☐ Pencils (for each student).

☐ 24-pack of crayons (for each student).

☐ Post-It notes.

☐ A class set of narrative fiction or nonfiction material (that could be read by students in 15 to 20 minutes).

## Lesson Delivery/Procedure

- ☐ The teacher will introduce the text to the class, aiding the students in making predictions about the text and building anticipation for the reading of the material.

- ☐ The teacher will review the elements of a story.

- ☐ The teacher will review the comprehension strategy of questioning.

- ☐ The teacher will pass out the reading material to each student.

- ☐ The teacher will pass out at least ten Post-It notes to each student.

- ☐ The teacher will instruct the student to read the text, stopping to ask at least ten questions about the story elements on the Post-It notes. (The teacher might model how to ask a question about a story element.)

- ☐ Upon completion of the task, the teacher will introduce implicit and explicit questioning. (It might help to introduce explicit as something easily seen and implicit as something hidden that needs clues to aid you in finding it.)

- ☐ The teacher will model how to tell the difference between an implicit and explicit question using student examples created. (The teacher might need to make up questions if there are limited numbers of any type of question.)

## Guided Practice

- ☐ The teacher will pass out the worksheets to each student (worksheets 244–246).

- ☐ The teacher will review the Check Sheet tool with students.

- ☐ The students will record the data discussing the questions asked on their Check Sheet (worksheet 244). (During this time, the teacher will walk around the room to monitor progress.)

- ☐ The teacher will review the Bar Chart tool with students.

- ☐ Using the Check Sheet, students will create a Bar Chart (worksheet 245) of the data recorded.

- ☐ The teacher will review the Plus/Delta tool with students.

## Assessment

- ☐ Using the Bar Chart, the students will look to see their areas of strengths and areas to improve. (For example: A student might be great at asking explicit questions about the setting.)

- ☐ Students will complete a Plus/Delta Chart worksheet discussing their strengths and areas to improve.

- ☐ The teacher may determine guided reading groups based upon the information provided by Bar Charts.

## Post-Lesson/Follow-Up Activities/Extensions

- ☐ Independently, students will strive to work on their areas to improve with the use of the questioning strategy during independent reading time.

- ☐ The Plus/Delta Chart could be utilized to help students and teachers develop plans to help students' use of the questioning strategy.

## Supporting Resources

- [ ] *Strategies That Work* by Stephanie Harvey and Anne Goudvis

- [ ] *Guiding Readers and Writers* (Grades 3-6: Teaching Comprehension, Genre, and Content Literacy) by Irene C. Fountas and Gay Su Pinnell

- [ ] *www.geocities.com/whitt2_1999/chapter_5_534.html*

- [ ] Worksheets 244, 245, and 246

# Responding to Fiction

Estimate measurements and determine acceptable levels of accuracy. Measure and compare quantities using appropriate units, instruments, and methods.

**Estimated Time:** 45 minutes          **Worksheets:** 247 and 248

## Quality Tool/PDSA Linkage

☐ Students will use the Plus/Delta Chart.

• The Plus/Delta Chart is a tool to record feedback about the current state or a recent experience and is used anytime feedback is needed in the PDSA cycle.

## Lesson Overview

☐ This is a lesson geared to enhance students' use of strategies to increase comprehension while reading fiction material.

## Lesson Objectives

☐ The students will utilize reading strategies (prediction and questioning) to enhance comprehension of fiction material.

☐ The students will learn to respond to fiction using a Plus/Delta Chart as an evaluative tool.

## Pre-Lesson Activities

☐ Create a poster-board replica of worksheet 248.

☐ A lesson discussing prediction and questioning strategies should be performed before implementing this lesson.

☐ The teacher should preview the reading material observing any new vocabulary words and concepts that will be introduced to the students when the reading material is presented to the students.

☐ Obtain copies of the worksheets that go with the lesson.

☐ Obtain all materials needed for the lesson.

## Materials Needed

☐ A class set of fiction material (that could be read by students in 15 to 20 minutes).

☐ Copies of worksheet 247.

## Lesson Delivery/Procedure

☐ The teacher will introduce the fiction material to the class. (Hint: During this time, the teacher will strive to make a connection with the text and the students and build up anticipation for the reading of the material.)

☐ The teacher will pass out copies of the reading material to each student.

☐ The teacher will preview the text with the students pointing out new vocabulary words and concepts.

☐ The teacher will review the Plus/Delta tool with students.

☐ After previewing the text, the teacher will pass out worksheet 247.

## Guided Practice

- ☐ Using worksheet 247, each student will create at least two predictions about the fiction material.
- ☐ Students will read the fiction material (independently, with a partner, and/or with the teacher).
- ☐ As the students read, they will pause at least twice to ask a question about the fiction material.
- ☐ When students complete reading the material, they will discuss the confirmation or contradiction of predictions using worksheet 247.
- ☐ Working with a partner, students will discuss the questions posed during the reading of the material.

## Assessment

- ☐ As a class, the students will assess the fiction material using the Plus/Delta Chart (worksheet 248). (Students will place the things that they enjoyed in the plus section and things that they wish to improve upon or change in the delta section.)

## Post-Lesson/Follow-Up Activities/Extensions

- ☐ Using the Plus/Delta Chart, students can analyze the personality of the main character.
- ☐ Using the Plus/Delta Chart, students can analyze the author's writing style to later create a fictional story of their own.
- ☐ Using the Plus/Delta Chart, students could respond to the text independently.

## Supporting Resources

- ☐ *Strategies That Work* by Stephanie Harvey and Anne Goudvis
- ☐ *Reading Comprehension, Tools for Tackling Text* by Trisha Callella
- ☐ Worksheets 247 and 248

# Quality Across the Curriculum

# APPENDIX

## QUALITY TOOLS

Affinity Diagram . . . 361

Bar Chart . . . . . . . . 362

Brainstorming . . . . . 363

Cause-and-Effect
   Diagram. . . . . . . . 364

Check Sheet/
   Matrix . . . . . . . . . 365

Flowchart . . . . . . . . 366

Force-Field
   Analysis. . . . . . . . 367

Gallery Walk . . . . . . 368

Lotus Diagram . . . . . 369

Multivoting/
   Light Voting. . . . . 370

Nominal Group
   Technique/
   Light Voting. . . . . 371

Operational
   Definition . . . . . . 372

Pareto Diagram . . . . 373

Plus/Delta Chart . . . 374

Radar Chart. . . . . . . 375

Relations Diagram . . 376

Run/Control Charts . 377

Scatter Diagram. . . . 378

Systematic Diagram/
   Tree Diagram . . . . 379

WWW Chart/
   Action Plan . . . . . 380

# Affinity Diagram

## Description

A tool to generate, organize, and consolidate information gathered through Brainstorming.

## Utility

Affinity Diagrams help to give a sense of the ideas that a group has concerning a given issue, provides an anonymous, nonjudgmental format for gathering group input. They give the group a sense of how serious a concern is because of the number of thoughts written on the issue. They also focuses on how the group is similar in thought.

## Construction

1. The leader states the problem or issue to be addressed.

2. Brainstorm and record all ideas, one per slip of paper, silently. (Use index cards or Post-Its.)

3. Post the ideas on a board or arrange on a table.

4. Have the entire group move the cards into piles by like ideas or common themes.

5. Name each group with a header that summarizes the content.

6. List all ideas under the categories or tape up ideas under headers to create the diagram.

7. Discuss the piles. Look at frequency of recurring themes, ask questions as needed and address next steps.

**Worksheet #129**  *Affinity Diagram Template*

*Activity Worksheet*

Name: _____

Date: _____

*Abraham Lincoln*

| Abe's Childhood | Abraham's family | Moving |
|---|---|---|
| | | |
| Jobs before presidency | When Abraham Lincoln was president | How Abe died |

# Bar Chart

## Definition

A a graph of categorical data on a horizontal axis, with frequency plotted, using bars, on the vertical axis.

## Utility

Bar Charts are used to show comparisons of frequency of related factors (categories of data) and allow the user to make conclusions about the data.

## Construction

1. Determine the categories of interest within the data.

2. Specify the time to collect the data and prepare Operational Definitions and Check Sheets if they do not already exist.

3. Collect the data and organize them on a frequency chart.

4. Plot the data on the graph, scaling the vertical axis by frequency of occurrence, and placing the categories in equal-width bars across the horizontal axis.

5. Interpret the chart.

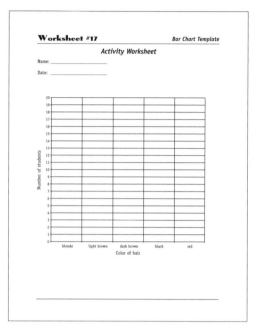

# Brainstorming

## Definition

The open, uninhibited generation of ideas by a group.

## Utility

Our purpose in Brainstorming is to generate a wide variety of ideas, to ensure that everyone on the team becomes involved, to assure that nothing is overlooked, and to provide an atmosphere in which creativity can flourish, and we can break out of conventional thought. Any time group input is required. Problem selection, identifying cause and effect, group consensus efforts, and many others are good examples of the use of Brainstorming.

## Construction

1. Facilitator announces and records the question or topic to Brainstorm.

2. Facilitator provides rules if none have been determined previously.

   Rules—No criticism (verbal or nonverbal); take turns—each person should have equal, ample opportunity to express ideas; quantity is important—the more the better; Piggyback, hitch-hike, or reverse ideas if you like.

3. Members of the group take turns generating ideas. The facilitator makes sure this happens. Members have the right to pass at any point if they have no ideas. Each person may give one idea per person per turn.

4. Facilitator records the ideas as closely as possible to what was said and verifies the idea with contributor.

Twists:

- If your group is reluctant to participate because of pressure (real or perceived) within the group, consider asking participants to record ideas on like slips of paper and submit to the facilitator, who will then record all ideas, separating ideas from personalities. (Also called Silent Brainstorming or Brain writing.)

- If you have people who pass more than they participate, perhaps they need more time to think before they speak. Consider giving Brainstorm topics out in advance of the team meeting so they can "prepare."

- Always give groups feedback on what was done with the material they generated during Brainstorming, or you may find that participation diminishes.

> **Worksheet #179**  *Brainstorming Template*
>
> *Activity Worksheet*
>
> Name: _____
>
> Date: _____
>
> Brainstorming rules
> 1. No criticism allowed—No yeas, boos, and so on
> 2. Equal opportunity to express thoughts
> 3. Quantity is better than having the perfect answer
> 4. Take-offs from what other people say are encouraged
>
> **Brainstorming ideas below**

# Cause-and-Effect Diagram

## Definition

Also known as a Fishbone or Ishikawa Diagram, a Cause-and-Effect Diagram is a picture of many system elements (causes) that may contribute to a problem (effect). It is organized output from a Brainstorming session concerning "what causes . . . ?"

## Utility

A Cause-and-Effect Diagram is useful whenever root causes of a problem need to be identified to find effective solutions. It allows a group to organize many ideas around a central theme of effect. Cause-and-Effect Diagrams help teams locate both special and common causes of variation.

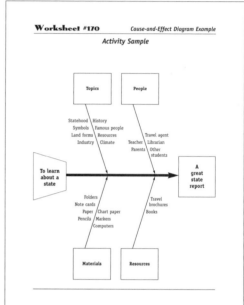

## Construction

1. Name the problem or effect the team will be analyzing.

2. Record the statement for all to see.

3. Draw and label the main bones by category. Typical categories may be people, methodology, curriculum, materials, assessment, and others.

4. Ask the team to Brainstorm likely causes (follow rules for Brainstorming).

5. Record all ideas on the chart under the logical category or categories, if a cause fits under more than one category.

6. Ask the team, through consensus, to identify the most likely (root) causes, or work through a Relations Diagram.

# Check Sheet/Matrix

## Definition

A tool to collect and organize data in a way that makes both collection and interpretation clear and understandable.

## Utility

Check Sheets and matrices are useful when specifics in the data collection need to be reported. The block format makes the collection easier, and the clear categories make understanding and interpretation more clear.

## Construction

1. Determine the data to be collected and reported. (Based upon the information or measurement that is important to you.)

2. Identify categories within the measurement that are of interest to you. (Example: Types of errors, types of assignments, students, and so on)

3. Construct the Check Sheet/Matrix in a format that is useful to you.

4. Test the Check Sheet/Matrix.

5. Collect the data.

**Worksheet #105**          *Check Sheet Template*

*Activity Worksheet*

Name: _____

Date: _____

Keep track of the times you use a renewable and nonrenewable resource. Place a tally in either the renewable or nonrenewable box depending upon the resource used.

| Resource used | Renewable resource | Nonrenewable resource |
|---|---|---|
| | | |
| | | |
| | | |
| | | |
| | | |
| | | |
| | | |
| | | |
| | | |
| | | |
| | | |

# Flowchart

## Definition

A drawing of any process, using standard symbols, that includes tasks, decisions, paper-work, and others in the sequence in which they occur.

## Utility

A Flowchart provides a common understanding of the process as it currently operates or as it is projected to operate. It defines the system the team will study. The Flowchart can be studied to look for ways to streamline, simplify, error-proof, and redesign the system. It also can be useful in system design to show how a system will work.

## Construction

1. Define the boundaries to the process. (Where does it start? Where does it stop?)

2. Observe the process in operation; ask people how work is done or should be done, and note the order in which steps occur.

3. List the major steps in the process (tasks and decisions).

4. Using the symbols, draw the Flowchart (or piece it together using Post-Its and easel paper).

5. Study your Flowchart.

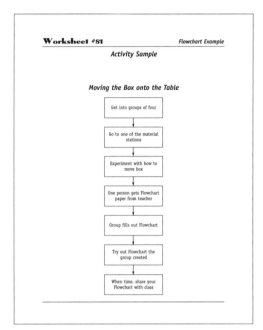

# Force-Field Analysis

## Definition

A tool to assess the likelihood of accomplishing a change. The tool defines driving forces, or any resources, attitudes, experience, and so on, that will support the change, and restraining forces as any resources, attitudes, or experiences that will cause the change to be stopped or delayed. Set up in a two-column format (driving and restraining), with the desired change listed across the top of the page, the tool relies heavily on group input through some form of Brainstorming.

## Utility

Force-Field Analysis should be used whenever a change needs to be initiated as part of our process improvement. It is useful in that it not only provides a complete picture of what will be working for you and what will be working against you, but also because the group can move closer to consensus on the change by discussing the challenges and barriers in an open constructive format. Instead of negative conversation going underground, it is now legitimate to talk about it in the meeting.

## Construction

1. Define the desired change and list at the top of the page.

2. Brainstorm the driving forces (resources, attitudes, experiences that will support the change.) List on the left-hand column.

3. Brainstorm the restraining forces (resources, attitudes, experiences that will resist the change.) List on the right-hand column.

4. Prioritize forces on both sides to determine what are the strongest drivers and restrainers.

5. Match and use drivers wherever possible to reduce and eliminate restrainers. Allow for conversation about how to approach the change.

6. Write an Action Plan at the bottom of the diagram. You may use consensus assist tools such as NGT or Multivoting to generate the final plan.

7. You may also plot your plan on a Systematic/Tree Diagram or a WWW Chart.

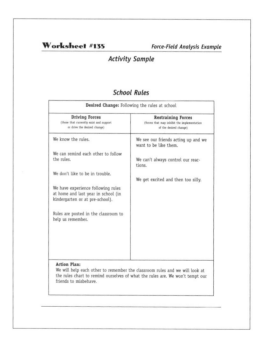

# Gallery Walk

## Definition

A communication/consensus tool to allow everyone in the group/team to provide input in a structured manner, creating a written record of all ideas.

## Utility

A Gallery Walk is used when asking a group (less than ten members) to respond to several issues or questions. By breaking the large group into smaller conversation clusters, all participants are allowed a voice.

## Construction

1. Generate a list of questions or issues you wish to have the group address.

2. Write each question or issue on a flip chart paper or board.

3. Place the paper or board at stations around the room on tables or walls. Allow plenty of space for the cluster to move about and write at the station.

4. Break the large group into the same number of clusters as you have stations by counting off, or by any other method that makes sense to you. (A cluster should have at least three, and no more than 10 people.)

5. Assign each cluster to a station. If you have fewer clusters than you have stations, space the clusters throughout the stations, leaving no more than one consecutive station without a cluster.

6. Give the group some time to get acquainted if you have just put them together. Then give work time to answer the question or address the issue at the station. (Usually 10 to 15 minutes).

7. Ask the cluster to rotate clockwise to the next station and decrease the time at the station by 20 percent (8 to 12 minutes).

8. Continue the station rotation until each cluster has had a chance to respond to each question/issue.

9. Ask the last group at each station to prepare a debrief of that station for the group.

# Lotus Diagram

## Definition

A tool to expand thinking around a single topic. The expansion may include types, categories, details, or questions around a theme. It is a simple, effective way to organize the output around Brainstorming.

## Utility

The Lotus is a good choice to organize the output of our Brainstorming around any central theme. An example might be: Theme—State Reports; Brainstorming—"What questions should we answer as part of our state reports?"

## Construction

1. Identify the central topic or theme the group is to deal with.

2. Ask for the type of expansion you would like the group to make. (Example: Egypt—What do you know about the land? . . . the history? . . . the people/culture? . . . the economy?) (Example: Red—What things in your home or our classroom are red?)

3. Record or ask the group to record the responses in the blocks around the Lotus. You may use a Lotus form, or simply fold a piece or paper into thirds both length-wise and width-wise.

4. If you wish, expand your nine-block Lotus to an 81-block Lotus.

5. Discuss the Lotus and use it for its intended purpose.

**Worksheet #18**  *Lotus Diagram Example*
*Activity Sample*

| | | |
|---|---|---|
| square | sphere | circle |
| cube | *Geometric Figures* | triangle |
| rectangular prism | rectangle | pyramid |

# Multivoting/Light Voting

## Definition

A tool to assist groups in reaching consensus by narrowing a list through conducting one or more straw polls.

## Utility

Multivoting reduces the time spent on discussions and the difficulty some groups encounter because of strong personalities by narrowing the issues a group can pursue through a series of votes.

After a Brainstorming session, Multivoting can be used to focus on several ideas concerning topics for improvement, root causes, solutions, and so on.

## Construction

1. Generate a list of items (through Brainstorming).

2. Combine ideas that are similar, with the permission of the group.

3. Letter the final list of ideas. (A, B, C, and so on)

4. Ask each team member to choose about one third of the ideas (total 30 ideas, choose 8–10), and write the numbers on a slip of paper. Giving team members a number of dots and asking them to place a dot by their choices can also accomplish this.

5. Have the facilitator tally the votes, silently if the group needs to feel safe, aloud if not.

6. Have the facilitator reduce the list with the group's permission by eliminating the ideas with the fewest votes (group agrees to remove anything with two or fewer votes).

7. Repeat these steps until you have a manageable list for the group to work toward consensus.

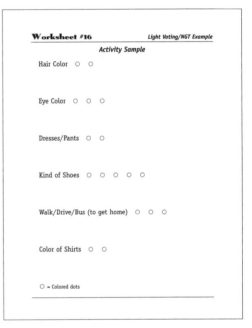

# Nominal Group Technique (NGT)/Light Voting

## Definition

A structured group process used to help teams make decisions without falling into voting or other decision-making modes that can divide the team.

## Utility

It gives everyone on the team an equal voice in the decision and reduces the pressure of traditional decision-making model to conform (political pressure, the loudest, the most persistent, and so on). It is used anytime a team needs to generate and choose a course of action for improvement (may be used several times during the course of the improvement process).

## Construction

1. Leader writes the defined area of opportunity or problem to be addressed.

2. The group silently generates action items.

3. Ideas are stated and recorded. Ideas may also be recorded and collected silently to preserve anonymity.

4. Each item on the list is discussed to clarify understanding, not to promote or "sell" ideas.

5. Leader will establish criteria for the voting. (What factors are important to consider?)

6. Leader conducts the preliminary vote. (Facilitator determines how many votes each person will have and explains voting—assigning highest value of vote to first choice, and so on.)

   • Team members choose the items most important to them.

   • Rank order the card or items on the list.

   • Votes are recorded.

   • Results are discussed. (Note—numbers should not be tallied for ideas to get a score, rather teams should look at any idea that received many votes or top choice votes.)

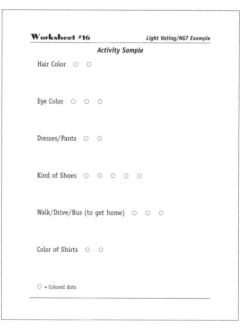

Worksheet #16 — Light Voting/NGT Example
*Activity Sample*

Hair Color ○ ○

Eye Color ○ ○ ○

Dresses/Pants ○ ○

Kind of Shoes ○ ○ ○ ○ ○

Walk/Drive/Bus (to get home) ○ ○ ○

Color of Shirts ○ ○

○ = Colored dots

# Operational Definition

## Definition

A standard process for measuring our critical quality characteristics. The Operational Definition is consistently applied, is understandable by everyone, and makes getting valid data easier.

## Utility

Operational Definitions create a common understanding and way to measure between everyone in the system, and help assure that data are collected consistently between people and over time. Because we base our decision making on our data, Operational Definitions should be used with every improvement project or whenever data are to be collected. It is important that the data collection plan be thought out and an Operational Definition is part of that plan prior to the start of data collection.

## Construction

1. Identify the measures that matter to you, that you seek to improve.

2. Select the measuring instrument that you will use to evaluate the data collected. Examples—visual inspection against a standard, a rubric, a clock, a calendar, a survey, and so on.

3. Describe the test method listing specifically how the test is to be applied and defining all factors within the test.

4. State the judgment criteria. How will you know if the data pass or fail, or where they fit on the scale you are using to measure?

5. Document the Operational Definition and make it readily available to all who will need to use it.

**Worksheet #89**  *Operational Definition Template*

*Activity Worksheet*

Name: _____

Date: _____

Students can fill this out in small groups or one could be filled out on chart paper for the whole class.

1. Characteristics to be measured:

2. Instrument used to measure:

3. Method used to measure:

4. Judgement criteria:

# Pareto Diagram

## Definition

Ranks data in categories from largest to smallest in terms of frequency of occurrence, cost, or time. Evaluates related measures of a problem or categories.

## Utility

A Pareto Diagram is useful because it graphically represents the categories and their value, and helps an improvement team separate the "significant few" categories from the "trivial many" in order to focus their efforts on an area that will yield the most significant results. Any time data can be stratified (separated by type or category), a Pareto is useful. This includes project selection, cause analysis, and location identification.

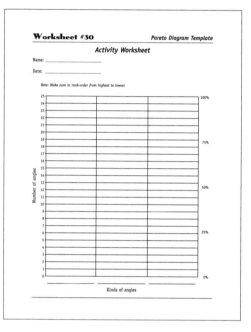

## Construction

1. Choose logical categories to stratify your data.

2. Specify the time period you will collect data.

3. Collect the data on to a frequency table.

4. Draw and scale the horizontal and vertical axes.

5. Draw and label the bars for each category.

6. Review the chart, using these data to focus the team's efforts.

# Plus/Delta Chart

## Definition

A tool to record feedback about the current state or a recent experience concerning what is currently working well, and what needs to change in the future.

## Utility

The Plus/Delta Chart is very useful in providing a forum for feedback for change. Many people are reluctant to give feedback, feeling it is often unwelcome, and the Plus/Delta asks and records all feedback from participants.

## Construction

1. Name the change or situation/event for which you are seeking feedback.

2. Record the statement on the Plus/Delta Chart.

3. Solicit input on pluses (things that we should make sure we keep) and deltas (things that we would want to change).

4. Ask participants to give feedback, either in writing on Post-Its or aloud.

5. Write or post feedback.

6. Evaluate the feedback and move to Action Plan.

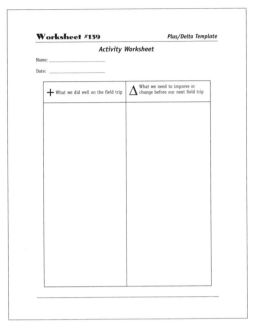

# Radar Chart

## Definition

A graph with multiple scales to report self-assessed knowledge or competence, often several points in time.

## Utility

A Radar Chart is used to identify current level of self-assessed knowledge or competence, and then monitor change or growth across several factors.

## Construction

1. Determine the critical factors, competencies, skills, or bits of knowledge you need to assess.

2. Draw the radar and identify the various spikes by characteristic you are assessing.

3. Determine the scale (numbers often from 0 to 5) and definitions of what each number means, and mark both on the chart.

4. Duplicate the chart, one per person.

5. Ask the group to self-report and mark on the Radar Chart with a date or symbol indicating first measurement.

6. Determine the next measurement point and repeat #5.

7. Analyze data and compare results, if appropriate. You can choose to do a cumulative average of the group by adding and averaging the entire group's scores.

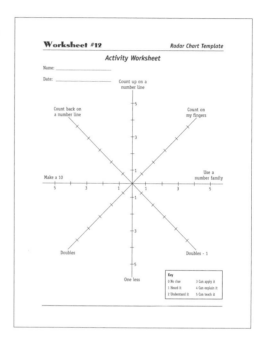

# Relations Diagram

## Definition

A picture of the cause-and-effect relationships between elements of a problem.

## Utility

A Relations Diagram helps teams distinguish between causes and effects and get to root cause(s) and effect(s) of a problem when the group cannot reach consensus on its own. It is particularly useful when the group or team is struggling to get to root cause of a problem because of either the problem's complexity or the symptoms being more visible than the causes.

## Construction

1. The leader clearly defines (writes) the issue or problem (may be taken directly from the Cause-and-Effect Diagram).

2. Construct the diagram layout with the effect (issue or problem) in the center of the diagram and all suspected causes, one per block, around the center.

3. Analyze as a team the relationship between each two factors, asking "Does this affect/influence/exacerbate the other?" Draw arrows from those that influence to those that feel the effect.

4. Count and list the arrows in and the arrows out for each cause category.

5. Identify the root causes (many arrows out, few arrows in) and the root effects (many arrows in, few arrows out). Understand that most root effects will disappear without direct action if root causes are addressed.

6. As a team, study the final diagram to determine root cause and next action steps.

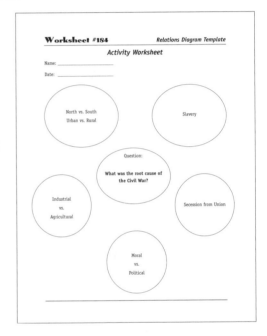

# Run/Control Charts

## Definition

A graphic representation of system performance over time. A Control Chart helps us to determine if a system is stable and predictable over time (no special cause) and gives a team baseline data against which to mark future changes. Both variable and attribute data can be placed on Control Charts.

## Utility

A Run/Control Chart can tell you what kind of variation is at work on your system (special or common cause), and give you an assessment of your systems performance over time. It can help you avoid undercontrolling or overcontrolling your system by understanding what is normal, predictable variation and what is not. At the beginning of every improvement project, a team should evaluate the system performance to help gather baseline of results data against which all changes can be evaluated.

## Construction

1. Begin by planning how and where you will get your data (write an Operational Definition).
2. Complete the chart identifier information (what is being measured, dates, location, collector, and other relevant information) and record the data on the sheet.
3. Calculate the process average (for Control Chart only).
4. Calculate the upper and lower control limits (for Control Chart only).
5. Determine the scaling for the chart on the paper form, draw the center and control lines (for Control Chart), and plot the points.
6. Interpret the chart.

## RULES FOR CONTROL CHART INTERPRETATION

Any of the following indicate an unstable or "out-of-control" system:

1. A point outside the limits (99.7 percent should fall within the limits).

2. A run of seven points:
   - Above the center line
   - Below the center line
   - Going in one direction up
   - Going in one direction down

3. Nonrandom patterns
   - Cycles (may indicate too many data are combined—shift, equipment, and so on)
   - Too close to the average (center line)
   - Too far from the average (center line)

# Scatter Diagram

## Definition

A tool to evaluate the relationship between to factors to help identify causes.

## Utility

A Scatter Diagram is useful when you want to test whether the performance of one factor is influenced by another (look at correlation) to see if potentially a cause and effect relationship exists.

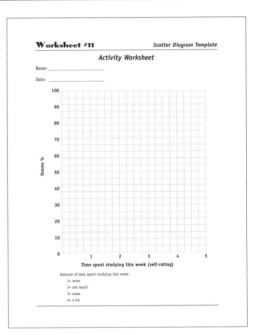

## Construction

1. Draw, scale, and label the horizontal and vertical axes. Remember to put the independent variable (the one you suspect causes the other variable) on the horizontal axis, and the independent (the one you suspect is influenced by the other) on the vertical axis.

2. Gather your data and plot the points. Mark the intersect of the two measures on the chart with a dot.

3. Interpret the chart by looking for patterns. Does one increase as the other decreases? (negative correlation) Does one increase as the other increases? (positive correlation) Is there no distinct pattern? (no correlation) Other shapes are possible, and if you see them ask why these occur.

# Systematic Diagram/Tree Diagram

## Definition

A tool to guide a group in planning for a broad goal or large event.

## Utility

The Systematic or Tree Diagram considers the different levels of action needed to accomplish any large goal or plan a complex event. It helps a group assure that all actions necessary are planned and assigned to individuals with due dates. It is useful any time a complex plan needs to be put into place.

## Construction

1. Identify the large goal or event to be planned for.

2. Ask, "What means will it take to accomplish this end?"

3. Continue asking the "means to the ends" until you have a list of accomplishable tasks that can be assigned and given due dates.

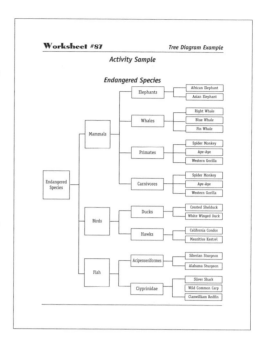

# WWW Chart/Action Plan

## Definition

A description of the actions necessary to make a desired change. In addition to the actions (What), the person responsible (Who) is identified with a deadline for completion of the action (When).

## Utility

The WWW Chart/Action Plan is used whenever a change is desired and a detailed plan will help with both communication and execution of the plan.

## Construction

1. Brainstorm the critical activities that need to take place (using a Force Field Analysis or Systematic/Tree Diagram if desired) and list.

2. Use the group's input to identify who should be involved and when the activity should be completed.

3. Record the "Who" and "When" by the related "What" on the chart.

4. If desired, transfer the WWW's onto a timeline to show how the plan rolls out over time.

**Worksheet #178**  *Action Plan Template*

*Activity Worksheet*

Name: _____

Date: _____

Actions to be taken based on the restraining forces

| Who | What | When | How |
|-----|------|------|-----|
|     |      |      |     |
|     |      |      |     |
|     |      |      |     |
|     |      |      |     |
|     |      |      |     |
|     |      |      |     |